The Political Science Student Writer's Manual and Reader's Guide

Eighth Edition

Gregory M. Scott

University of Central Oklahoma Emeritus

Stephen M. Garrison

University of Central Oklahoma

D0219301

ROWMAN & LITTLEFIELD

Lanham • Boulder • New York • London

Executive Editor: *Nancy Roberts*
Associate Editor: *Molly White*
Senior Marketing Manager: *Deborah Hudson*
Interior Designer: *Ilze Lemesis*
Cover Designer: *Sally Rinehart*

Credits and acknowledgments for material borrowed from other sources, and reproduced with permission, appear on the appropriate page within the text.

Published by Rowman & Littlefield
A wholly owned subsidiary of The Rowman & Littlefield Publishing Group, Inc.
4501 Forbes Boulevard, Suite 200, Lanham, Maryland 20706
www.rowman.com

Unit A, Whitacre Mews, 26-34 Stannary Street, London SE11 4AB, United Kingdom

Copyright © 2017 by Rowman & Littlefield
This book was previously published by Pearson Education, Inc.

All rights reserved. No part of this book may be reproduced in any form or by any electronic or mechanical means, including information storage and retrieval systems, without written permission from the publisher, except by a reviewer who may quote passages in a review.

British Library Cataloguing in Publication Information Available

Library of Congress Cataloging-in-Publication Data
Names: Scott, Gregory M. | Garrison, Stephen M.
Title: The political science student writer's manual and reader's guide / Gregory M. Scott, University of Central Oklahoma Emeritus, Stephen M. Garrison, University of Central Oklahoma.
Other titles: Political science student writer's manual
Description: Eighth Edition. | Lanham : ROWMAN & LITTLEFIELD, [2016] | Series: The Student Writer's Manual: A guide to reading and writing | Previous edition: 2012. | "This book was previously published by Pearson Education, Inc."—T.p. verso. | Includes bibliographical references and index.
Identifiers: LCCN 2016033680 (print) | LCCN 2016034494 (ebook) | ISBN 9781442267091 (hardcover : alk. paper) | ISBN 9781442267107 (paperback : alk. paper) | ISBN 9781442267114 (electronic)
Subjects: LCSH: Political science—Authorship—Style manuals. | Political science—Research—Handbooks, manuals, etc. | Academic writing—Handbooks, manuals, etc. | Report writing—Handbooks, manuals, etc.
Classification: LCC JA86 .S39 2016 (print) | LCC JA86 (ebook) | DDC 808.06/632—dc23
LC record available at https://lccn.loc.gov/2016033680

∞™ The paper used in this publication meets the minimum requirements of American National Standard for Information Sciences—Permanence of Paper for Printed Library Materials, ANSI/NISO Z39.48-1992.

Printed in the United States of America

BRIEF CONTENTS

CONTENTS

WELCOME TO A COMMUNITY OF SKILLED OBSERVERS

One of the most successful books on counseling psychology is *The Skilled Helper,* by Gerard Egan (10th Edition, 2013). The title's elegant simplicity immediately directs students' attention to the essence of what they, if successful, are to become. We have written this book to help you become a particular sort of skilled *observer.* Practitioners of all the social and physical sciences are, most essentially, skilled observers. They carefully and systematically observe behavior, accurately record their observations, and then describe how they have conducted their research and the implications of what they have discovered. Underlying all these activities, most fundamentally, is the skill of writing. Much in the way a funnel directs liquid to its intended container, writing refines and directs your thoughts into clear, capable, professional literary "vessels" through which you communicate with the community of scholars. This book invites and empowers you to join the particular community of skilled *observers* known as political scientists.

The political science community is now, in 2016, officially 2,351 years old. That is because the foundational work of this discipline, Aristotle's (384–322 BCE) *Politics,* was written in 350 BCE. Yes, people before Aristotle had astutely observed and discussed politics. We cannot read Pericles' (425–429 BCE) *Funeral Oration* or Aristophanes' (450–388 BCE) satirical play *Ecclesiazusae* (392 BCE, "Women in the Assembly"), for example, without knowing that much acutely insightful discussion about politics was well under way, and Plato's (428–348 BCE) political thought was both systematic and substantial. But Plato's preeminent political work, the *Republic* (360 BCE), is an account of Socrates's (470–399) discussions with citizens in Athens, which chronicle the "gadfly's" application of deductive logic to the task of deriving a model of the perfect society.

But political science as known today was born with the very first words of Aristotle's *Politics,* his analysis of political behavior: ***Observation shows us . . .*** With these three profound words political science, and indeed all science, was definitively born. Aristotle then proceeded to observe the politics of his own time, chronicle the politics of previous times, and recommend political cultures for the future. It should be noted that through the centuries, whenever political analysis has been based upon skilled observation of human behavior, political science has taken a step forward.

Political science as an academic discipline was launched in 1903 with the founding of *The American Political Science Association* (APSA). Today, political scientists study a wide variety of topics, perhaps best illustrated by APSA's list of organized sections of the discipline:

APSA Organized Sections:

African Politics Conference Group
Canadian Politics
Class and Inequality
Comparative Democratization
Comparative Politics
Conflict Processes

Elections, Public Opinion, and Voting
   Behavior
European Politics and Society
Experimental Research
Federalism & Intergovernmental
   Relations

Foreign Policy
Foundations of Political Theory
Health Politics and Policy
Human Rights
Ideas, Knowledge and Politics
Information Technology and Politics
International History and Politics
International Security and Arms Control
Law and Courts
Legislative Studies
Migration and Citizenship
New Political Science
Political Communication
Political Economy
Political Methodology
Political Networks
Political Organizations and Parties

Political Psychology
Political Science Education
Politics and History
Politics, Literature, and Film
Presidents and Executive Politics
Public Administration
Public Policy
Qualitative and Multi-Method Research
Race, Ethnicity, and Politics
Religion and Politics
Representation and Electoral Systems
Science, Technology, & Environmental
    Politics
Sexuality and Politics
State Politics and Policy
Urban and Local Politics
Women and Politics Research

As you peruse this list, you will see that the breadth of the discipline offers a wide variety of opportunities to study human behavior.

We shall make two final notes about this ancient and new discipline. First, its accomplishments within and without academia are generally little appreciated and understood. Everyone understands what a historian does, but many people confuse political scientists with historians. One reason for this is that, in general, these scientists of politics eschew publicly marketing their work or their discipline. But sometimes, political scientists break into public view. Here are a few who have done so:

Zbigniew Brzezinski, United States
    National Security Advisor to
    President Jimmy Carter
Ralph Bunche, Nobel Peace Prize winner
Condoleezza Rice, Secretary of State

Donna Shalala, United States Secretary of
    Health and Human Services
Herbert A. Simon, Nobel Prize winner
Woodrow Wilson, President of the
    United States

And this is the final note. Americans are little aware of the enormous influence political scientists continue to have on the practices of American politics, which are in some ways foundationally different from what they were a century ago. The best example of the influence of political science is in the conduct of campaigns and elections. Today's contests are increasingly won by candidates who employ highly sophisticated techniques for identifying, locating, organizing, and mobilizing potential voters. Where did these techniques come from? Political science. Starting in the 1950s, political scientists began conducting studies to understand voting behavior, and now, decades later, their continuing efforts and insights are employed in highly sophisticated ways for practical effect. Much of the credit for President Obama's electoral victories, for example, is often given to the superior electoral organization he founded, an organization empowered by political science.

TO THE TEACHER

WHAT'S NEW IN THE EIGHTH EDITION?

While at times today's world appears to be an uninterrupted stream of reinvention, some things change slowly, if at all. That is why this book's primary value to you, the teacher, has remained the same for more than two decades. This book helps in dealing with three problems commonly faced by teachers of political science:

1. Students increasingly need specific directions to produce a good paper.
2. Political scientists, as always, want to teach political science, not English.
3. Students do not yet understand how and why to avoid plagiarism.

How many times have you assigned papers in your political science classes and found yourself teaching the basics of writing—not only in terms of content but form and grammar as well? This text, which may either accompany the primary text you assign in any class or stand on its own, allows you to assign any of the types of papers described in Parts 2 and 3, with the knowledge that virtually everything the student must know, from grammar to sources of information to reference style, is in Part 1 of this one volume.

What's New in *The Political Science Student Writer's Manual and Reader's Guide, Eighth Edition*

Every chapter and chapter section has been updated and revised, many substantially.

Twelve new chapter sections have been added to the 8th edition:

Reading Politics Analytically
Reading News as Political Power
Skillful Reading Techniques: How to Read the News Like a Political Scientist
Analytical Reading Techniques: How to Read Editorials and Op-Ed Essays
Welcome to the National Archives
Welcome to the Library of Congress
How to Read the *Congressional Record*
How to Read the *Federal Register*
The Presidential Decision-Making Process
The Law-Making Process
How to Read Political Science Scholarship
Discover the Network of International Relations Agencies

Twenty-two new reading and writing exercises have been added to the eighth edition:

Read & Write: Analyze a Presidential Address
Read & Write: Compare the Slants of Front Pages
Read & Write: Critique a Lead News Article
Read & Write: What to Say? Explain or Persuade?
Read & Write: Freewriting
Read & Write: Write an Outline for a Paper Inspired by a Published Article
Read & Write: Jargon and Descriptive Writing
Read & Write: Identify the Sentence Fragment

Read & Write: Identify Errors In This Speech

Read & Write: Explain the Data in This Table

Read & Write: Create an Actually Usable Bibliography

Read & Write: Properly Summarize an Article from *The Economist* or *Mother Jones*

Read & Write: Describe Five Images from the Digital Vaults

Read & Write: Recall Some Actual American Slave Narratives

Classroom Project: Create Your Own Campaign Commercial

Read & Write: Report on a Local Government Agency Meeting

Listen and Write: Styles of Presidential Decision-Making

Read & Write: Analyze a Bill Currently Before Congress

Read & Write: Explain the Content of a Recent Article from a Political Science Journal

Read & Write: Critique a Recent Article from a Political Science Journal

Read & Write: Locate a Dozen High Quality Sources

Read & Write: Write a Political Philosophy Paper

We hope you find *The Political Science Student Writer's Manual and Reader's Guide, Eighth Edition* to be helpful to your students and you and we wish you all success.

1

READ AND WRITE TO

UNDERSTAND POLITICS

1.1 READING POLITICS ANALYTICALLY

Getting Started

It doesn't matter how good a reader you are right now, how much you enjoy reading, how often you read, what sorts of texts you like or avoid, how fast you read, or how effective your level of retention is. The fact is that the remainder of your academic career—the remainder, in fact, of your life—would be made richer if you were better at reading than you are now. This book attempts to make you a better reader—first, by offering you tips for improvement and suggestions aimed at enhancing your enjoyment and understanding of any text, and second, by supplying you with exercises to improve your reading in the specific discipline of political science.

But why do we need improvement in writing? It's such a basic skill, something we all learned to do in grade school. Right?

Well, sort of. Our grade school teachers taught us the basics: how to distinguish words in the characters on a page and how to pace ourselves through a sentence or a paragraph to arrive at a coherent meaning. Without these fundamental skills, we couldn't read at all. That's what secondary school focuses on: giving us the basics.

The problem is that there is more to reading than just those first few steps. If there weren't, then we would all be able to read any text pretty much as well as anybody else. It goes without saying, however, that all of us read at different levels of comprehension and with varying degrees of enjoyment, depending on what we're reading. We are all different people, each with our own preferences, a unique set of experiences that resonate with certain stimuli and less so with others.

Think of all the different worlds you inhabit, your favorite pastimes, hobbies, sports, and school subjects. Each is its own world, with its own set of rules and traditions, modes of behavior and thought, and its own language. Do you remember the first time you watched a professional basketball game on television? The action on the court was no doubt dizzying, but so was the conversation by which the sportscasters and commentators explained each play as it happened. What's a "pick and roll"? A "double double"—or, for that matter, a "triple double"? Why do some penalties allow for a free throw or two, while some don't? Basketball is a world with its own rules, its own ways of thinking and speaking. How long did it take you to become comfortable in this world—to become an *insider*?

Okay, so what about politics? If you are a politics junkie, you will understand every word of the following paragraph that a blogger might write to criticize Ted Cruz and some of his followers:

> Critics of Ted Cruz decry his pandering to the Tea Party, also known as Baggers—a bunch of disgruntled Kool-Aid drinkers, mostly RINOs and former blue dogs. Recent studies show they are mostly unaware of the greenwashing that sanitizes their Frankenfood. Looking forward to be rid of the lame duck in the White House, they cling to Cruz, a birther whose own lineage is finally helping him grow in office.

If some of this paragraph is not quite intelligible to you, you have yet to become a *political insider*.

To read well in virtually any subject, particularly in any school subject or profession, it is essential that you acknowledge to yourself, as you begin to read, that you are entering a new world, one inhabited by insiders and one that can be difficult to understand for people who aren't insiders.

Difficult, but not impossible.

It is possible for us to learn how to tailor our reading skills to texts in different disciplines, including those for which we do not have a natural affinity or a set of closely related personal experiences. It requires energy and imagination and, above all, a shift in attitude.

Whether you are reading a textbook chapter, a newspaper or magazine article, an essay in a journal, a book, or a blog, here are some tips to help you master the text.

Read with Patience

Different texts require varying degrees of patience from the reader. When you read a text written in an unfamiliar discipline, be sure you are reading carefully to allow the material—and the world from which it comes—to sink in. Reading with patience means performing certain prereading activities that can help you in mastering the text. Some of these activities are discussed below.

Reading with patience requires making sure to give yourself plenty of time to read the text. If it's a homework assignment, don't start reading the night before it's due. The sense of urgency—if not panic—that attends a rushed reading assignment can drive the material right out of your head before you can master it. Reading with patience also means eliminating distractions—the television blaring in the next room or the MP3 player driving songs through those earbuds you're wearing. Too many people in the apartment? Go find a coffee house with only a few customers or hit the library and find a comfortable chair in the reading room. Would a snack help or hurt your ability to immerse yourself in the text?

To read with patience means arranging your environment to enhance the clarity of your reading experience. The optimal environment is different for each person. What if you actually find television noise or earphone music helpful to your reading? If so, use it, but be honest with yourself about the effect of external stimuli on your reading. The point is to do whatever you can to *reduce your resistance to reading*.

Clarify Your Goals Before You Begin to Read

What is it *exactly* that you hope reading this text will do for you? Are you merely looking for a few facts to shore up a point you are making in a paper? Are you cramming for a test? Are you working to establish a general understanding of a particular topic, or the contours and details of a many-sided argument? Or are you simply reading to amuse yourself? Whatever the reasons that sent you to the text, remind yourself of them from time to time as you read, comparing what you are finding in the text to whatever you are hoping to find. Be ready to revise your goals depending on what you learn from the text. If, for example, you begin reading an article in the *New Republic* examining Republican Congressional opposition to funding gun violence studies, would you become interested in examining the National Rifle Association's (NRA's) campaign contributions to members of Congress?

Explore the Text's Format

Reconnoiter before diving in. You need to remember that the writer, whoever it is, wants you to understand his or her writing and has used a variety of devices to help you. If the text has headings and subheadings, read through them first to see if they give you a sense of the author's direction and purpose. Note any distinctions among the headings, some of which might use larger type or bold print to underscore their organizational importance. Understanding the relationship among headings can help you determine the shape of the text's argument.

Are there illustrations? Graphs? Charts? Photographs or drawings? If so, a quick study of them will enhance your understanding of the text's goals and its potential usefulness to you.

Keep in Mind the Writer's Goals

Read carefully the first paragraph or the first page of the text looking for the writer's main idea and strategy for presenting it. Even if you don't find a specific thesis statement—a sentence or two explaining clearly the purpose of the text—most writers will find a way to signal what it is they hope their text accomplishes. Often the thesis is in the title, as it was for a December 30, 2015, *New York Times* article by Noam Scheiber and Patricia Cohen with the following, rather long-winded title: "For the Wealthiest, a Private Tax System That Saves Them Billions: The Very Richest Are Able to Quietly Shape Tax Policy That Will Allow Them to Shield Billions in Income." Note how the first paragraph of this article neatly answers the question implied in the title, namely, "*How do these billionaires shape tax policy to suit them?*"

> WASHINGTON—The hedge fund magnates Daniel S. Loeb, Louis Moore Bacon and Steven A. Cohen have much in common. They have managed billions of dollars in capital, earning vast fortunes. They have invested large sums in art—and millions more in political candidates. Moreover, each has exploited an esoteric tax loophole that saved them millions in taxes. The trick? Route the money to Bermuda and back.[1]

[1] Noam Scheiber and Patricia Cohen. 2015. "For the Wealthiest, a Private Tax System That Saves Them Billions: The Very Richest Are Able to Quietly Shape Tax Policy that will Allow Them to Shield Billions in Income." *New York Times*, 29 December. http://www.nytimes.com/2015/12/30/business/economy/for-the-wealthiest-private-tax-system-saves-them-billions.html (February 23, 2016).

Remember, too, that there is always another goal the writer hopes to achieve: *he or she is writing to change you* by inviting you to step a little further, and at a slightly different angle than before, into the world of the text, whatever that might be: politics, cuisine, sports, fashion design, music, animal physiology, higher mathematics, or film history. The text is the writer's way of asking you to pass through a doorway into an environment with which you may not be familiar but which, the writer is convinced, offers you a worthwhile experience. As you read and understand the text, you are becoming more of an insider in that particular environment, broadening the way you look at the world.

Take Notes

Jot down notes based on your early explorations of text features. Your assessment of critical features—headings, illustrations, the introduction—has no doubt set up expectations in your mind about the direction and content of the text. Quickly listing down those expectations and then comparing them with what you find as you actually read the text can help in setting the text material in high relief in your mind.

Note-Taking Strategies   Your goal in taking down notes is to help you remember those elements in the text that will be useful to you, known during your reading. Two prominent strategies for effective note-taking are:

(1) restating the material from the text in your own language and (2) phrasing notes in a way that establishes a dialogue with the text's writer.

Translate noteworthy material into your language. Any method of note-taking that requires rewriting the text in your own words requires you to engage the text at its most basic level, that of its language. To restate the text, you must understand it. Merely recopying the text's words doesn't require the level of engagement that restating does.

Similarly, underlining or highlighting text is usually not a very effective way to "own" what it is saying. It's just too easy. You often find yourself highlighting so many lines that the marking loses its effectiveness. Also, by highlighting the text, you do not run the material through your own language-making processes, which means you don't participate in the making of meaning as significantly as you must.

Engage in a give-and-take with the author. Besides recasting the wording of the text into your own language in your notes, you can also enhance your understanding by adopting a note format that actually establishes a dialogue with the author.

Ask questions. Rather than simply finding equivalents for key words or phrases in the text, consider phrasing your note in the form of a question or a criticism aimed at the writer's argument. This sort of give-and-take helps you in clarifying and controlling the range of expectations that occur to you as you read. This is a good way to sharpen your thinking about the text. For example, after reading the *New York Times* article quoted above, you might write:

Why do the wealthiest citizens enjoy special tax privileges that most U.S. citizens don't? Why can't ordinary citizens do what the wealthy do? Why does the general public let the wealthy get away with not paying their fair share of taxes?

It takes very little time to formulate useful questions about the material in almost any text. Never forget the six basic questions: *who, what, when, where, how,* and *why.* Practice using these questions in the exploratory stages of your reading until asking them becomes almost a reflex as you read.

Once you have examined the obvious features of a text and formulated some basic questions, you're ready to read.

Observe How Sentence Structure Aids Understanding

Pay attention to the little words. As we thread our way through the pages of any text, our movement is actually directed by little words, mostly prepositions and conjunctions. These little words don't actually add facts or narrative information but act as traffic signals, preparing us for a shift in emphasis or direction. Phrases such as "furthermore," "however," "on the contrary," and "nevertheless" reinforce our interpretation of a preceding passage and prepare us to understand how the next passage will fit along with it. There are words that *add* the meaning of the coming passage to the last one: "also," "and," "furthermore," "not only . . . but also," "too." And there are phrases that *contrast* the preceding passage with the coming one: "but," "despite," "nevertheless," "instead of," "rather than," "yet." The phrase "of course" indicates that the next fact follows obviously from the last one, as does the word "obviously." Phrases such as "if," "provided," and "unless" indicate that the truth contained in the passage you've just read may be changed by what the next passage adds to the argument.

You know such little words so well that it's easy to overlook their usefulness as markers. Don't. They are extremely important to your reading, shoring up your confidence line-by-line and preparing your mind for the next passage.

Pay attention to the rhythms of the sentences. Often, writers invite you to anticipate the way a sentence moves, perhaps by repeating a word, a phrase, or a syntactical structure, setting up a rhythmic expectation in your mind that, when satisfied, adds greatly to your grasp of the passage's meaning.

In his brief address commemorating the establishment of a military cemetery at the Gettysburg Battlefield, Abraham Lincoln uses the repetition of a syntactical pattern to stop the forward motion of his speech and to shift its focus from the audience's participation in the ceremony to the sacrifice that has occasioned the need for the graveyard:

> But, in a larger sense, we cannot dedicate—we cannot consecrate—we cannot hallow—this ground. The brave men, living and dead, who struggled here, have consecrated it, far above our poor power to add or detract.

As You Read, Be Aware of Other Language Tools

Your writer will employ a range of devices designed to make you feel comfortable in the world of text. Look for them and allow them to do their work.

- An *analogy* is a comparison between two things that are similar in some important way. Expect to find your writer composing analogies in which some element of the world of the text—unfamiliar to a noninsider—is compared with some element more common in everyday life. Here's an example. On a campaign stop during the 2012 presidential election, President Obama said:

  > This notion that somehow we [Democrats] caused the [budget] deficits is just wrong. . . . It's like somebody goes to a restaurant, orders a big steak dinner, martini, all that stuff and then just as you're sitting down, they leave and accuse you of running up the tab.[2]

  Analogies can be helpful in clarifying policies and issues. To what extent, for example, is President Obama's steak dinner analogy a valid characterization of the Republican Party's role in driving up government deficits?

---

[2] "Obama: Republicans Left Me with the Check for a Steak Dinner." 2016. *Real Clear Politics*, 12 June. http://www.realclearpolitics.com/video/2012/06/12/obama_republicans_left_me_with_the_check_for_a_steak_dinner.html (July 3, 2016).

- *Concrete details*—those that evoke and engage the senses—can often do more to communicate meaning and intent than the most elaborate abstract description. A powerful example is the campaign ad that Lyndon Johnson ran, just once, on television in his 1964 presidential race against Republican Senator Barry Goldwater. Instead of offering a spoken appeal for voters to reject what Johnson's campaign was painting as Goldwater's dangerously warlike attitude toward the Soviet Union, the ad simply shows a little girl standing in a field pulling petals off a flower and counting them as they fall, until the girl's soft voice is suddenly replaced by a man's echoing harshly the countdown to a rocket launch and the image of the girl's face is replaced by that of an exploding nuclear bomb.[3]

Test Your Recollection

It is easy to forget material right after you've learned it, so as you read you must stop occasionally and recollect to yourself the material you have just acquired. Recite it *in your own language* to ensure that you have truly assimilated the content. This recollection is an important part of the reading process but can be dangerous, in that if you stop to recollect too often, you can lose your sense of forward motion through the text. So, no matter how often you find yourself stopping to recollect material, and it may happen frequently in a difficult text, try not to stop for long. Remember that the very next sentence may unravel the difficulty that has induced you to make a momentary stop. *Keep going.*

Reread

The single most effective strategy for mastering a text is to reread it. The first time through you are finding your way, and the text's concepts, facts, and lines of argument are forming themselves in your mind as you read, which means you have difficulty anticipating the text's direction. To use an analogy, reading a challenging text for the first time is like driving down a twisting country road at night, one you have never traveled before, with only your car's headlights to guide you. But once you've experienced that road, you will be able to navigate it again more confidently, anticipating its tricky turns. The same thing happens when you reread a text. Having been there before, you now know where the argument is going and can see more clearly not only what the writer is trying to say but also his or her motives for saying it.

Rereading as an aid to understanding a text is most effective once you have gotten through the *entire* text. Only then will you have experienced the entire shape of the writer's argument and can commit your full attention to clarifying passages that were difficult during your first run-through.

Pacing Is Vital

How can you possibly pay attention to all the reading tips just discussed and get any sense at all out of the text they are trying to help you understand? Practice. Learning

---

[3] Drew Babb. 2014. "LBJ's 1964 Attack Ad 'Daisy' Leaves a Legacy for Modern Campaigns." *Washington Post*, 5 September.https://www.washingtonpost.com/opinions/lbjs-1964-attack-ad-daisy-leaves-a-legacy-for-modern-campaigns/2014/09/05/d00e66b0-33b4-11e4-9e92-0899b306bbea_story.html (February 23, 2016).

how to improve your reading effectiveness takes time. Try one or two of the suggestions often enough to incorporate them into your reading routine, and then move on to others. The more reading you do, the better you'll get at it, and the wider and more interesting your world will become.

Read&Write 1.1   Analyze a Presidential Address

Here is a brief address from Barack Obama made during the last year of his presidency. Read through it and then read it again, looking for the strategies discussed above for enhancing reader involvement.

Remarks of President Barack Obama
Weekly Address
The White House
January 1, 2016

Happy New Year, everybody. I am fired up for the year that stretches out before us. That's because of what we've accomplished together over the past seven.

Seven years ago, our businesses were losing 800,000 jobs a month. They've now created jobs for 69 straight months, driving the unemployment rate from a high of 10% down to 5%.

Seven years ago, too many Americans went without health insurance. We've now covered more than 17 million people, dropping the rate of the uninsured below 10% for the very first time.

Seven years ago, we were addicted to foreign oil. Now our oil imports have plummeted, our clean energy industry is booming, and America is a global leader in the fight against climate change.

Seven years ago, there were only two states in America with marriage equality. And now there are 50.

All of this progress is because of you. And we've got so much more to do. So my New Year's resolution is to move forward on our unfinished business as much as I can. And I'll be more frequently asking for your help. That's what this American project is all about.

That's especially true for one piece of unfinished business, that's our epidemic of gun violence.

Last month, we remembered the third anniversary of Newtown. This Friday, I'll be thinking about my friend Gabby Giffords, five years into her recovery from the shooting in Tucson. And all across America, survivors of gun violence and those who lost a child, a parent, a spouse to gun violence are forced to mark such awful anniversaries every single day.

And yet Congress still hasn't done anything to prevent what happened to them from happening to other families. Three years ago, a bipartisan, commonsense bill would have required background checks for virtually everyone who buys a gun. Keep in mind, this policy was supported by some 90% of the American people. It was supported by a majority of NRA households. But the gun lobby mobilized against it. And the Senate blocked it.

Since then, tens of thousands of our fellow Americans have been mowed down by gun violence. Tens of thousands. Each time, we're told that commonsense reforms like background checks might not have stopped the last massacre, or the one before that, so we shouldn't do anything.

We know that we can't stop every act of violence. But what if we tried to stop even one? What if Congress did something—anything—to protect our kids from gun violence?

A few months ago, I directed my team at the White House to look into any new actions I can take to help reduce gun violence. And on Monday, I'll meet with our Attorney General, Loretta Lynch, to discuss our options. Because I get too many letters from parents, and teachers, and kids, to sit around and do nothing. I get letters from responsible gun owners who grieve with us every time these tragedies happen; who share my belief that the Second Amendment guarantees a right to bear arms; and who share my belief we can protect that right while keeping an irresponsible, dangerous few from inflicting harm on a massive scale.[4]

1.2   READING NEWS AS POLITICAL POWER

Political Science: Helping You Perceive and Consciously Respond to Power

A central focus of political science is the study of the mechanisms of power: political, economic, cultural, and social. One of the most important mechanisms of power on the planet is what we commonly call the news. Without a free-flowing supply of news in a country, freedom, democracy, and security are unavailable, and personal vitality and fulfillment for most people are severely impaired. Even with a free flow of news, those who control that flow have enormous influence.

Power Is Deciding Who Shows up on the Radar Screen and the Size of Their Blip   Control of the news means controlling what people know and what they don't know. It means controlling who makes the local, national, and international radar screen and who does not. A local news story about a child dying of cancer

---

[4] Barack Obama. 2016. "Weekly Address: Making America Safer for Our Children." The White House, 1 January. https://www.whitehouse.gov/the-press-office/2016/01/01/weekly-address-making-america -safer-our-children (February 23, 2016).

can produce an immediate inflow of assistance that many other families in similar situations must go without. In some areas of the world, making the radar screen is a matter of life and death for millions of people. At any particular time, tens of thousands of people worldwide face war, disease, famine, and natural disasters. Some get a lot of help, some get moderate assistance, and some get virtually none at all. What determines who gets what?

Politics always plays a role, but publicity can be equally important. "The pen is mightier than the sword," wrote Edward Bulwer-Lytton in his play *Richelieu; Or the Conspiracy* in 1839.[5] Here are three historical examples of the power of the press . . .

. . . to save lives:

One of the most notable and successful efforts to save lives by exploiting the media radar screen was conducted by Mohandas Gandhi (1869–1948). Having developed techniques of nonviolent resistance to racial oppression in South Africa in the 1890s, Gandhi went to India during World War I and began organizing peaceful demonstrations against the British occupation there. His first task was to liberate India from the British without a violent Civil War. Through several prison terms, large-scale protest marches, and well-orchestrated trips to London to see top officials, Gandhi attracted press attention wherever he went. When Civil War between Hindus and Muslims began to threaten India after World War II, Gandhi walked hundreds of miles through villages of both religions. In so doing, Gandhi not only succeeded in averting a war of independence, saving hundreds of thousands of lives but also averted a Civil War saving hundreds of thousands more. His deep commitment to justice and nonviolence, and his superior management of publicity, helped him save more lives than anyone else in history.

. . . to defeat racism:

Sometimes lives are saved when the words and actions of certain people are denied making the media radar screen. Atop Magnetic Mountain, overlooking the rolling verdant hills of Eureka Springs, Arkansas, stands a 65.5-foot-tall statue of Jesus, beckoning visitors to *The Great Passion Play*, a dramatic depiction of the last week of Jesus's life. The play and statue are monuments to the energies of evangelist and political organizer Gerald L. K. Smith (1898–1976). A powerful speaker who attracted sizeable crowds, Smith was a Christian nationalist and white supremacist. Virulently anti-Semitic, Smith founded the America First Party in 1946. A firm believer that the Jews killed Jesus and that they have been a primary source of evil ever since, after World War II, Smith preached against Jews at every opportunity while defending Nazis. The Holocaust, in which several million Jews were killed in Nazi death camps, was a fresh memory in the late 1940s and early 1950s. The world over, Jews knew they had to energetically combat anti-Semitism wherever they encountered it, so Smith naturally became a prime concern for the Jewish Anti-Defamation League (ADL) and the American Jewish Committee (AJC). Jewish leaders adopted a tactic of "dynamic silence." They asked newspaper editors to first consider the extent to which their coverage was helping Smith draw so much attention. Then they asked the editors to consider whether Smith's hatred-filled rants deserved the free publicity they were getting. They proposed that if the papers stopped covering Smith's rallies,

---

[5] Edward Bulwer-Lytton. 1839. *Richelieu: Or, the Conspiracy, a Plan in Five Acts.* II, ii, p. 39. New York: Samuel French, [186–?]. *Making of America.* Ann Arbor, University of Michigan Library, 2005. http://name.umdl.umich.edu/AAX3994.0001.001 (February 23, 2016).

his movement would dry up along with his publicity. The editors agreed and stopped coverage, and Smith's momentum declined. Although Smith continued work on his statue and passion play, his movement never recovered.

... *to make policy, not always for the better:*

Finally, sometimes the radar screen is purposely distorted in the interest of particular news media. By the late 1880s, Cuba was a prosperous Spanish colony whose sugar plantations sweetened American muffins, piña coladas, and Coca-Colas. But American-owned Hawaiian plantations became sufficiently powerful to gain import-tax advantages from Congress. Its main market for its primary product gone, Cuba's economy collapsed. Penniless and hungry, the plantation workers revolted. Spain responded by sending troops who rounded up thousands of protestors and herded them into *concentrado* camps, a name borrowed by the Nazis for use in the Holocaust. A decade of unrest followed, which, unfortunately, was useful to newspaper czar William Randolph Hearst, who wanted to create news to outsell his competition, and to Assistant Secretary of the Navy (later President) Theodore Roosevelt, who wanted to increase America's image as a world power. Pumping up false charges against Spain of cruelty (in what became known as *yellow journalism*), and blaming the sinking of the American battleship USS *Maine* in Havana Harbor, America declared war on Spain in 1898 and wrested control of Spanish territories in the Caribbean and the Pacific.

Read&Write 1.2 Compare the Slants of Front Pages

A "slant" is a repeated emphasis of one viewpoint as opposed to another or of one type of content as opposed to another. This writing exercise is relatively simple. The online versions of major newspapers contain much more content than printed versions because web pages provide more space for links to many more articles than appear on printed front pages.

When you visit the home pages of the online versions of the *New York Times* (nytimes.com) and the *Wall Street Journal* (wsj.com), you will find a "Today's Paper" link immediately under the masthead.

Start by visiting the home pages of both of these papers, and select the "Today's Paper" link on both of them. Here you will find the most recent news that is featured in their print editions. Copy into a Word file the titles of the half dozen or so bold-print articles you find on each page. In a page or two, describe what you infer about the character and aims of each paper from the article titles in each newspaper. How do the priorities of the two papers differ? What are the political implications of that difference? Is there an obvious political slant to the articles selected? To what do you attribute the slant(s) you find, if any?

1.3 SKILLFUL READING TECHNIQUES: HOW TO READ NEWSPAPERS AS A POLITICAL SCIENTIST

Because political scientists spend a lot of their time reading newspapers, it is vital for them to know how to read skillfully—how to understand and evaluate newspaper material accurately and quickly. Learning how to do so requires the mastery of certain reading techniques that people may not typically apply to the reading of their local paper. This chapter offers tips that can help you read a newspaper like a political scientist.

Understand the Task

Besides entertainment and advertising, the content of any newspaper includes news and opinions, and because these two categories can be easily and even intentionally confused, and because accurately differentiating them is essential, let's take a quick look at them.

News is composed of two types of data: information and analysis.

- *Information* is composed of facts, specifically, accounts of events and background. The title of an account of an event could be "Conservative Christians Hold 'City on a Hill' Conference." A background statement could be "This is the third time this year that Conservative Christians have met in Washington, DC."

- *Analysis* comprises interpretations of the information rendered in the news story. After observing the goings-on at the "City on a Hill" conference, the reporter interprets what he or she has witnessed there: "A primary purpose of the conference seems to have been to encourage Conservative Christians to develop a new strategy to restrict abortions."

Opinions are evaluations of the information reported in newspapers and are composed of editorials, op-ed pieces (opinion pieces written by named authors who are not on the newspaper's staff), opinion columns, blogs, and other contributions such as transcripts of interviews. An opinion concerning the "City on a Hill" conference, published in one of the newspaper's editorials, might read, "Once again conservatives seek to consolidate their weakening power by angering a variety of social constituencies." Clearly, the line between analysis and opinion is a thin one.

A Conundrum   On a daily basis, renowned newspapers such as the *New York Times* and the *Wall Street Journal* attempt to clearly identify and separate news from opinion. Their integrity and credibility depend on their success. Their articles are clearly identifiable as news or opinion, and usually their news articles have a high degree of objectivity. Opinion is opinion and is persuasive to the extent it seems reasonable or appeals to a certain prejudice. Intelligent readers rarely confuse opinion with news.

But "news" suffers from a congenital defect. No matter how objective a reporter tries to be, perfection is intrinsically beyond reach. Philosopher Karl Popper (1902–1994) was fond of starting courses with a simple command to his students: "Observe." He would stand quietly and wait until a student broke the tension with the question "Observe what?" "Precisely," was Popper's retort. His point was that no observation is purely objective and value-free. The moment we try to observe, we necessarily choose what to observe, and that choice is always full of values.

When editors assign stories, their selections are affected by not only their experienced sense of importance but also their perceptions of the prospective author and their estimate of what sells as well. Therefore, although "objective reporting" is the hallmark of a good newspaper, good reporters understand and exploit the tension between "news" and "opinion," allowing, at least to some extent, their quest for relevance to temper their thirst for facts.

Read the Front Page

Daily newspapers are much like highway maps, providing thousands of bits of information, which together form a coherent web that can be imagined as a compact image of life on this planet, or on part of it, on any particular day. The newspaper's front page is the symbol key to that map. Start reading your newspaper by noting both what is included on the front page and what is not. Here is your front-page analytical checklist:

Content What gets premium front-page coverage tells you what the newspaper's priorities and biases are. Here are the front-page stories of the *New York Times* on December 15, 2015:

- Top News: All Los Angeles Public Schools Closed After Bomb Threat
- Jurors in Freddie Gray Case Say They Are Deadlocked
- U.S. Prosecutors Expected to Charge Two Venezuelans
- Experts Were Wrong About Where Health Care Costs Less
- Do Areas that Spend Less on Medicare Also Spend Less on Health Care Overall?
- Curing Hepatitis C, in an Experiment the Size of Egypt
- Where the Candidates Stand on 2016's Biggest Issues
- How Trump Could Win, and Why He Probably Won't
- Setting Sights on Cruz, and Pondering a Tricky Target in Trump
- Trump to Meet Donor Sheldon Adelson Before Debate
- A Refugee Crisis, a Greek Debt Showdown, Russian Aggression and Terrorism in the Streets: How 2015 Has Threatened the E.U.
- Towers of Secrecy A "Starship" and a Shell Company Stir Resentment
- In the Booming, High-end Market of Los Angeles, One House Stands Out
- New Scrutiny of New York Prison Diversion Programs: Some Aid to Afghans Ends Up Helping Taliban, United States Says
- International Atomic Agency Ends Iran Inquiry
- Fabled Nazi Gold Train Looks Like a Fable
- New York City Homelessness Chief Is Leaving
- "Shamed and Victimized for Life": Rape in India

By contrast, here are the articles on the cover of *New York Post* for December 15, 2015:

- Catching Fish: Brilliant Beckham Lifts Giants
- Sleazy Riders: Subway Sex Crimes Skyrocket
- Cosby Sues Seven Accusers

And here are the front-page stories of the *Wall Street Journal* on December 15, 2015:

- Fed Poised to Mark The End of an Era
- Stocks Rise Ahead of Fed Decision
- L.A. Officials Defend Decision to Close Schools After Threat
- E.U. Officials Settle on Privacy Law
- Second-Tier Hopefuls Face Off in GOP Debate

- Republican Presidential Candidates Are Gathering in Las Vegas on Tuesday Night for the Fifth Night of Presidential Debates. Here Is Our Live Blog of the Event
- Analysis: Seven Insights About the Republican Field
- The Inevitable Cruz–Rubio Collision
- Trump Supporters in Nevada Struggle With Caucus Process
- Poll Finds National Security Now a Top Concern
- U.N. Experts Say Iran Missile Firing Violated Sanctions
- Iran's Firing of a Medium-Range Ballistic Missile in October Violated U.N. Sanctions Banning the Islamic Republic from Launches Capable of Delivering Nuclear Weapons, U.N. Experts Said in a New Report
- IAEA Board Agrees to Close File on Iran's Past Nuclear Activities
- Jurors in Baltimore Police Officer Trial Say They Are Deadlocked
- Jurors in the First Baltimore Police Officer Trial in Connection with the Death of Freddie Gray Last April Told the Judge Tuesday Afternoon They Were Deadlocked. The Judge Told Them to Continue Deliberations
- U.S. Boosts Online Scrutiny
- U.S. Graduation Rate Rises
- Meet Your Child's New Partner
- Ousted Cheniere Energy CEO in Line for Big Payout

What assumptions about the character of each newspaper's can you make by comparing the contents of their front pages?

Layout   The position on the front page indicates the editor's estimate of the importance of the article. A banner headline is big-time news. Traditionally, newspapers are in the habit of placing the lead article in the upper-right corner of the front page because when they are displayed on old-style newsstands, the papers are folded in the middle and arrayed so that the upper-right part of the paper is visible. The second most important story appears on the upper left. The bigger the title font, the more important the article.

Everything about the front page of a newspaper is done on purpose. Did you ever notice that when you enter Walgreens to pick up a prescription, the pharmacy is in the rear of the store? Try getting to the pharmacy without getting distracted, if ever so slightly, by the candies, cosmetics, cuticle clippers, coffee cups, crayons, and birthday cards. The front page of a typical newspaper is organized a bit like the aisles in Walgreen, offering something for everyone.

Structure of an Article   Every article in a newspaper has three jobs to do:

1. Get your attention.
2. Tell you the story's bottom line.
3. Tell a convincing story in a very short time.

To meet these goals, the news articles must follow a standard format known as the *inverted pyramid*. While literary stories start with small details and build to a climax at the end, news articles do the opposite. The article title is the "bottom line." It tells you the punch line of the story right up front. Details follow in descending order with the most important ones appearing first. Background and incidentals come last.

Read & Write 1.3 Critique a Lead News Article

Read the following article from the *Washington Post*, a highly reputed newspaper, and examine, in a response of approximately 500 words, the hierarchy of flow within it. Is it an inverted pyramid? Explain.

Actor Sean Penn Secretly Interviewed Mexico's 'El Chapo' in Hideout
The Washington Post
By Joshua Partlow, January 10 at 12:15 AM

CULIACAN, Mexico—The Joaquín "El Chapo" Guzmán story could hardly have seemed more unbelievable, with its multiple prison breaks, endless sewers and tunnels, outlandish sums of money, and feverish manhunts. And then Sean Penn entered the story.

While Guzmán was the world's most wanted fugitive, dodging Mexican military operations and U.S. Drug Enforcement Administration surveillance, he was secretly meeting with the Hollywood movie star in an undisclosed Mexican hideout and has now provided what appears to be the first public interview of his drug-running career, published Saturday by Rolling Stone.

Among the revelations in the article, Guzmán, who was captured Friday morning in his home state of Sinaloa, bragged to Penn about his prowess in the drug trade.

"I supply more heroin, methamphetamine, cocaine and marijuana than anybody else in the world," Guzmán said. "I have a fleet of submarines, airplanes, trucks and boats."

The Associated Press reported that a Mexican law enforcement official said the Penn meeting helped authorities locate Guzmán in Durango state in October.

Escaped Mexican drug lord 'El Chapo' recaptured

The leader of the Sinaloa cartel, who had been locked up in what has been described as the country's most impenetrable prison, was recaptured in western Mexico after a shootout that left five dead.

Penn provides a lengthy account of how he met the elusive criminal. Penn tried to protect his communications using burner phones and encryption and anonymous email addresses. The meeting was brokered by the Mexican actress Kate del Castillo and took place at an undisclosed location in the Mexican mountains.

Penn reportedly spent seven hours with Guzmán and then did follow-up interviews by phone and video, including one posted on the Rolling Stone website of Guzmán in a paisley blue shirt speaking in front of a chain-link fence.

Guzmán, who in the past has denied participation in the drug trade and portrayed himself as a peasant farmer, spoke unapologetically and serenely about his lucrative trade.

Where he grew up, in the mountains of Sinaloa state, "the only way to have money to buy food, to survive, is to grow poppy, marijuana," he said, and he began at a young age.

"It's a reality that drugs destroy. Unfortunately, as I said, where I grew up there was no other way and there still isn't a way to survive, no way to work in our economy to be able to make a living."

Despite the deadly wars his Sinaloa cartel has fought with other gangs and authorities, Guzmán described himself as not a violent person.

"Look, all I do is defend myself, nothing more," he said. "But do I start trouble? Never."

The interview with Penn may have helped authorities finally recapture Guzmán, who was arrested Friday after a military raid on a house in the coastal city of Los Mochis. Guzmán fled in a sewer and carjacked a getaway vehicle but was stopped on the highway.

Mexico's attorney general, Arely Gómez González said on Friday night that authorities zeroed in on Guzmán after movie producers and actresses made contact with him.

Penn met with Guzmán in early October, just before a military operation targeting Guzman in a ranch in the town of Pueblo Nuevo in Durango. Mexican authorities said Guzmán got away because a helicopter didn't want to fire at him because he was fleeing with two women and a girl.

Guzmán wrote to Penn that eight helicopters pursued him and the "marines dispersed throughout the farms. The families had to escape and abandon their homes with the fear of being killed. We still don't know how many dead in total."

Guzmán said his injuries were "not like they said. I only hurt my leg a little bit."

A senior Mexican official, who could not confirm whether Penn's interview contributed to Guzmán's arrest, described the interview with Penn as "an act of propaganda" that contributed to Guzmán's outsized myth.

"Nothing that appears in the interview changes that he is a criminal who has assassinated many people and trafficked in drugs that resulted in the deaths of many people," the official said.

The Penn interview was the latest twist in the wild "El Chapo" saga that included his dramatic arrest on Friday.

In the pre-dawn darkness, Mexican marines quietly surrounded a little white house in Los Mochis where the druglord was staying.

But the elusive Guzmán—who had escaped twice from federal prison—did it again. He vanished down an escape hatch and into the sewer. It wasn't until he popped up four blocks away, stole a car, and sped out of town that Mexican authorities finally captured him on the highway and ended six months of national humiliation for letting the world's top drug lord escape.

Guzmán was later flown to Mexico City and returned to Altiplano prison, the facility he escaped from in July.

Guzmán's capture was celebrated by law enforcement officials in Washington because Guzmán runs a drug-trafficking network with vast international reach that has been dumping tons of cocaine and heroin into U.S. cities for years. But more than that, it represented a massive vindication, at least symbolically, for a Mexican government that has often seemed incapable of alleviating the brutal drug war violence that has left some 100,000 dead in the past decade.

After two prison escapes, many expect the Mexican government to extradite Guzmán to the United States. The Mexican attorney general's office said in a statement Saturday that extradition procedures would begin. But that could take weeks or months, as the accusations against Guzmán must be reviewed and a judge needs to recommend a course of action.

"There are a series of things that could take months," one official said.

Joshua Partlow is the *Post*'s bureau chief in Mexico. He has served previously as the bureau chief in Kabul and as a correspondent in Brazil and Iraq.[6]

---

[6] Joshua Partlow. 2016. "Actor Sean Penn Secretly Interviewed Mexico's 'El Chapo' in Hideout." *Washington Post*, 10 January. https://www.washingtonpost.com/world/actor-sean-penn-secretly-interviewed-el-chapo-in-hideout-before-capture/2016/01/09/4cce48db-1dc5-40b2-9b21-aa412c87e7bc_story.html (February 23, 2016).

Reading News Reports To accurately read a news article, you have a lot of work to do. Happily, as time goes on, you become familiar with the publications, the journalists, their sources, and other matters, but it takes practice. Here is a news article appraisal checklist:

- *Reputation.* What does the reading public think of the newspaper? What does the quality of the front page tell you? Earlier in this chapter you were invited to compare front pages of the *New York Times* and *New York Post*. Which of these two newspapers would you rather cite as a source for information in your own term paper?

- *Author.* What are the credentials and reputation of the author of the news story? Does he or she have the background to accurately report the news? A newspaper's website normally provides the credentials of its reporters.

- *Information sources.* What sources of information does the author use? Are they credible? Are they recognized individuals or institutions? Is the information source appropriate for the article's topic? Is the topic timely, and is the information it provides up to date? Does the author include multiple sources to support his or her statements?

- *Writing quality.* Is the article well written? Is it clear and cogent? Does it use a lot of jargon? Can you understand it? Does it employ many adverbs? In general, adjectives and adverbs tend to be "opinion-words" rather than "news-words." For example, is the adverb in the following sentence questionable? "Morgan *willfully* ran over my bicycle in the driveway."

- *Quantity of information.* Is the article sufficiently comprehensive to substantiate its thesis? Does it answer the proverbial questions who? what? when? where? and why?

- *Unsupported assumptions.* Beware of statements like this: "Statistics prove that children in traditional two-parent households are happier than children in other households." What statistics? Does the article identify them?

- *Balance.* If you are reading a *news* article about a controversial subject, the article should include information from more than one side of an argument. Also, a well-written *opinion* article normally identifies the content of opposing views, even if only to discredit them.

1.4 ANALYTICAL READING TECHNIQUES: HOW TO READ EDITORIALS AND OP-ED ESSAYS

Reading Opinion Articles: A Tale of Two Journalists

Conservative author and commentator David Brooks and liberal economist Paul Krugman have both been op-ed columnists for the *New York Times* for more than a decade. In July 2015, each wrote a *Times* column on recent proposals to raise the minimum wage.

In his article "The Minimum Wage Muddle" (July 24, 2015), David Brooks, in a typical conservative manner, reveals once again his distrust in government intervention in the economy in general and proposals to raise the minimum wage in particular. Brooks states, "Some economists have reported that there is no longer any evidence that raising wages will cost jobs."[7] Brooks may well have had in mind a *New York Times* article by Paul Krugman, titled "Liberals and Wages" (July 17, 2012), which states, "There's just no evidence that raising the minimum wage costs jobs, at least when the starting point is as low as it is in modern America."[8] Both Brooks and Krugman cite multiple studies as evidence for their arguments opposing (Brooks) and supporting (Krugman) minimum wages.

If you open the *New York Times* website and read both articles (select the "Columnists" link in the "Opinion Pages" section), you will find that each columnist focuses on different, if overlapping, slices of the effects of raising the minimum wage. Each article provides an interesting, well-supported education in certain aspects of the issue, one that will inspire many studies before the political debate subsides.

But here we can learn an important lesson: What is the central point, the *thesis* of each article? From Brooks, we have a bold and unsupported further assertion: "Raising the minimum wage will produce winners among job holders from all backgrounds, but it will disproportionately punish those with the lowest skills, who are least likely to be able to justify higher employment costs."

We have already quoted Krugman's thesis that there is no evidence suggesting that raising the minimum wage will cost jobs, "at least when the starting point is as low as it is in modern America." Krugman continues his argument with an unsupported conclusion, asserting that the market for labor isn't like the market for, say, wheat, because workers are people. And because they're people, there are important benefits, even to the employer, from paying them more, such as better morale, lower turnover, and increased productivity. These benefits, says Krugman, largely offset the direct effect of higher labor costs, so that raising the minimum wage needn't cost jobs after all.

At this point, it is evident that if you want to adequately examine the arguments of each columnist, you must read their articles and examine the evidence they provide. But the important lesson here is the relative authority of the authors on the subjects they are discussing. Consider the two columnists' credentials.

According to his biography on the *New York Times* website, David Brooks also appears on *PBS NewsHour*, NPR's *All Things Considered*, and NBC's *Meet the Press*. He has authored three books: *Bobos in Paradise: The New Upper Class and How They Got There* (New York: Simon & Schuster, 2000), *On Paradise Drive: How We Live Now (And Always Have) in the Future Tense* (New York: Simon & Schuster, 2004), and *The Social Animal: The Hidden Sources of Love, Character, and Achievement* (New York: Random House, 2011), a "No. 1 *New York Times* best seller." He also teaches at Yale University.

Paul Krugman is Professor of Economics and International Affairs at Princeton University. He has taught at Yale, Stanford, and MIT, and has authored or edited 27 books and 200 academic and professional papers. A founder of "new trade theory," a substantial revision of international trade theory, he has received the American Economic Association's John Bates Clark Medal (1991) and the Nobel Prize in Economics (2008).

---

[7] David Brooks. 2015. "The Minimum-Wage Muddle." *New York Times*, July 24. http://www.nytimes.com/2015/07/24/opinion/david-brooks-the-minimum-wage-muddle.html?_r=0 (March 7, 2016).

[8] Paul Krugman. 2015. "Liberals and Wages." *New York Times*, July 17. http://www.nytimes.com/2015/07/17/opinion/paul-krugman-liberals-and-wages.html (March 7, 2016).

Which author is better qualified to draw general conclusions about effects of the minimum wage from his research? Paul Krugman, the economist, is far better qualified to draw conclusions, and owing to the enormous amount of research he has done in economics, he is far more credible *on this topic*. If you read numerous columns by David Brooks, you may well conclude that they are well written, entertaining, and contain much well-documented support for his theses. But if you read closely, you will find that he often oversteps the bounds of his professional credibility. This does not mean that Krugman is obviously correct on this particular issue. But it strongly suggests that if you want to test Krugman's assertions, you must find an equivalent authority: a solid conservative economist.

Political scientists are predisposed to be suspicious of journalism, rolling their eyes at factual errors and inaccuracies. A healthy skepticism is part of their job. But they understand that, while they have the luxury of digging deep over a substantial period of time, a journalist must often get a story and get it straight within a matter of hours. And when all is said and done, the academicians do not hesitate to affirm that nothing is as essential to the vitality of democracy as a vigorous, capable, and dedicated news media.

Read&Write 1.4 Respond to an Editorial

Perhaps at this point you are ready to launch into the real world of public discussion of national issues. One way to do so is to respond to an editorial. It is probably best to start with the newspaper in your hometown. Most newspapers, if not all, provide detailed information on submitting such a letter. To write a letter to the editor of the *Washington Post*, for example, click the "How to Contact the Newsroom" link in the "Opinion" section:
http://help.washingtonpost.com/link/portal/15067/15080/ArticleFolder/80/ How-to-Contact-the-Newsroom

Be sure to ask your instructor before submitting your letter. Newspapers can be very selective about the letters they accept for publication, and you may be up against a lot of competition. You instructor will be able to provide some suggestions that will increase your chances of success. Follow the paper's directions exactly.

Good luck!

2

WRITE EFFECTIVELY

Writing is a way of ordering your experience. Think about it. No matter what you are writing—a paper for your American government class, a short story, a limerick, a grocery list—you are putting pieces of your world together in new ways and making yourself freshly conscious of those pieces. This is one of the reasons why writing is so hard. From the infinite welter of data that your mind continually processes and locks in your memory, you are selecting only certain items significant to the task at hand, relating them to other items, and phrasing them with a new coherence. You are mapping a part of your universe that has hitherto been unknown territory. You are gaining a little more control over the processes by which you interact with the world around you.

This is why the act of writing, no matter what its result, is never insignificant. It is always *communication*—if not with another human being, then with yourself. It is a way of making a fresh connection with your world.

Writing, therefore, is also one of the best ways to learn. This statement may sound odd at first. If you are an unpracticed writer, you may share a common notion that the only purpose of writing is to express what you already know or think. According to this view, any learning that you as a writer might have experienced has already occurred by the time your pen meets the paper; your task is thus to inform and even surprise the reader. But, if you are a practiced writer, you know that at any moment as you write, you are capable of surprising yourself. And it is that surprise that you look for: the shock of seeing what happens in your own mind when you drop an old, established opinion into a batch of new facts or bump into a cherished belief from a different angle. Writing synthesizes new understanding for the writer. E. M. Forster's famous question "How can I tell what I think till I see what I say?" is one that all of us could ask.[1] We make meaning as we write, jolting ourselves by little, surprising discoveries into a larger and more interesting universe.

[1] E. M. Forster. [1927] 1956. *Aspects of the Novel*, 101. New York: Harvest.

A SIMULTANEOUS TANGLE
OF ACTIVITIES

One reason that writing is difficult is that it is not actually a single activity at all but a process consisting of several activities that can overlap, with two or more sometimes operating simultaneously as you labor to organize and phrase your thoughts. (We will discuss these activities later in this chapter.) The writing process tends to be sloppy for everyone, an often-frustrating search for meaning and for the best way to articulate that meaning.

Frustrating though that search may sometimes be, it need not be futile. Remember this: the writing process uses skills that we all have. The ability to write, in other words, is not some magical competence bestowed on the rare, fortunate individual. We are all capable of phrasing thoughts clearly and in a well-organized fashion. But learning how to do so takes practice.

One sure way to improve your writing is to write.

One of the toughest but most important jobs in writing is to maintain enthusiasm for your writing project. Such commitment may sometimes be hard to achieve, given the difficulties that are inherent in the writing process and that can be made worse when the project is unappealing at first glance. How, for example, can you be enthusiastic about writing a paper analyzing campaign financing for the 1998 Congressional elections, when you have never once thought about campaign finances and can see no use in doing so now?

Sometimes unpracticed student writers fail to assume responsibility for keeping themselves interested in their writing. No matter how hard it may seem at first to drum up interest in your topic, you have to do it—that is, if you want to write a paper you can be proud of, one that contributes useful material and a fresh point of view to the topic. One thing is guaranteed: if you are bored with your writing, your reader will be, too. So what can you do to keep your interest and energy level high?

Challenge yourself. Think of the paper not as an assignment but as a piece of writing that has a point to make. To get this point across persuasively is the real reason you are writing, and not because a teacher has assigned you a project. If someone were to ask you why you are writing your paper and your immediate, unthinking response is, "Because I've been given a writing assignment," or "Because I want a good grade," or some other non-answer along these lines, your paper may be in trouble.

If, on the other hand, your first impulse is to explain the challenge of your main point—"I'm writing to show how campaign finance reform will benefit every taxpayer in America"—then you are thinking usefully about your topic.

Maintain Self-Confidence

Having confidence in your ability to write well about your topic is essential for good writing. This does not mean that you will always know what the result of a particular writing activity will be. In fact, you have to cultivate your ability to tolerate a high degree of uncertainty while weighing evidence, testing hypotheses, and experimenting with organizational strategies and wording. Be ready for temporary confusion and for seeming dead ends, and remember that every writer faces these obstacles. It is out of your struggle to combine fact with fact, to buttress conjecture with evidence, that order will arise.

Do not be intimidated by the amount and quality of work that others have already done in your field of inquiry. The array of opinion and evidence that confronts you in the literature can be confusing. But remember that no important topic is ever exhausted. There are always gaps—questions that have not been satisfactorily explored in either the published research or the prevailing popular opinion. It is in these gaps that you establish your own authority and your own sense of control.

Remember that the various stages of the writing process reinforce each other. Establishing a solid motivation strengthens your sense of confidence about the project, which in turn influences how successfully you organize and write. If you start out well, use good work habits, and allow ample time for the various activities to coalesce, you should produce a paper that reflects your best work, one that your audience will find both readable and useful.

2.1   GET INTO THE FLOW OF WRITING

The Nature of the Process

As you engage in the writing process, you are doing many things at once. While planning, you are, no doubt, defining the audience for your paper at the same time that you are thinking about its purpose. As you draft the paper, you may organize your next sentence while revising the one you have just written. Different parts of the writing process overlap, and much of the difficulty of writing occurs because so many things happen at once. Through practice—in other words, through *writing*—it is possible to learn to control those parts of the process that can in fact be controlled and to encourage those mysterious, less controllable activities.

No two people write exactly the same way. It is important to recognize the routines—modes of thought as well as individual exercises—that help you negotiate the process successfully. It is also important to give yourself as much time as possible to complete the process. Procrastination is one of the greatest enemies of writers. It saps confidence, undermines energy, and destroys concentration. Writing regularly and following a well-planned schedule as closely as possible often make the difference between a successful paper and an embarrassment.

Although the various parts of the writing process are interwoven, there is naturally a general order in the work of writing. You have to start somewhere! What follows is a description of the various stages of the writing process—planning, drafting, revising, editing, and proofreading—along with suggestions on how to approach each most successfully.

Plan   Planning includes all activities that lead to the writing of the first draft of a paper. The particular activities in this stage differ from person to person. Some writers, for instance, prefer to compile a formal outline before writing the draft. Others perform brief writing exercises to jump-start their imaginations. Some draw diagrams; some doodle. Later, we will look at a few starting strategies, and you can determine which may help you.

Now, however, let us discuss certain early choices that all writers must make during the planning stage. These choices concern *topic, purpose, and audience* elements that make up the writing context, or the terms under which we all write. Every time you write, even if you are only writing a diary entry or a note to the milkman, these elements are present. You may not give conscious consideration to all of them in each piece of your writing, but it is extremely important to think carefully about them when you are writing a political science paper. Some or all of these defining elements may be dictated by your assignment, yet you will always have a degree of control over them.

Select a Topic   No matter how restrictive an assignment may seem, there is no reason to feel trapped by it. Within any assigned subject, you can find a range of topics to explore. What you are looking for is a topic that engages your own interest. Let your curiosity be your guide. If, for example, you are assigned the subject of campaign finances, then find some issues concerning the topic that interests you. (For example, how influential are campaign finances in the average state senate race? What would be the repercussions of limiting financial contributions from special interest groups?) Any good topic comes with a set of questions; you may well find that your interest increases if you simply begin asking questions. One strong recommendation: ask your questions *on paper*. Like most mental activities, the process of exploring your way through a topic is transformed when you write down your thoughts as they arise, instead of letting them fly through your mind unrecorded. Remember the words of Louis Agassiz: "A pen is often the best of eyes."[2]

Although it is vital to be interested in your topic, you do not have to know much about it at the outset of your investigation. In fact, having too heartfelt a commitment to a topic can be an impediment to writing about it; emotions can get in the way of objectivity. It is often better to choose a topic that has piqued your interest, yet remained something of a mystery to you—a topic discussed in one of your classes, perhaps, or mentioned on television or in a conversation with friends.

Narrow the Topic   The task of narrowing your topic offers you a tremendous opportunity to establish a measure of control over the writing project. It is up to you to hone your topic to just the right shape and size to suit both your own interests and the requirements of the assignment. Do a good job of it, and you will go a long way toward guaranteeing yourself sufficient motivation and confidence for the tasks ahead. However, if you do not do it well, somewhere along the way you may find yourself directionless and out of energy.

Generally, the first topics that come to your mind will be too large for you to handle in your research paper. For example, the subject of a national income security policy has recently generated a tremendous number of news reports. Yet despite all the attention, there is still plenty of room for you to investigate the topic on a level that has real meaning for you and that does not merely recapitulate the published research. What about an analysis of how one of the proposed income security policies might affect insurance costs in a locally owned company?

The problem with most topics is not that they are too narrow or have been completely explored, but rather that they are so rich that it is often difficult to choose the most useful way to address them. Take some time to narrow your topic. Think through the possibilities that occur to you and, as always, jot down your thoughts.

Students in an undergraduate course on political theory were told to write an essay of 2,500 words on one of the following issues. Next to each general topic is an example of how students narrowed it into a manageable paper topic.

---

[2] Catherine Owens Pearce. 1958. *A Scientist of Two Worlds: Louis Agassiz*, 106. Philadelphia: Lippincott.

General Topic	Narrowed Topic
Barack Obama	Obama's view of the role of religion in politics
Freedom	A comparison of Jean Jacques Rousseau's concept of freedom with that of John Locke
Interest Groups	The political power of the National Rifle Association
Bart Simpson	Bart Simpson's political ideology

Read & Write 2.1   Narrowing Topics

Without doing research, see how you can narrow the following general topics:

Example

General topic	The United Nations
Narrowed Topics	The United Nations' intervention in civil wars
	The United Nations' attempts to end starvation
	The role of the United Nations in stopping nuclear proliferation

General Topics

War in Iraq	Gun control	Freedom of marriage
International terrorism	Political corruption	Abortion rights
Education	Military spending	
Freedom of speech	The budget deficit	

Find a Thesis   As you plan your writing, be on the lookout for an idea that can serve as your thesis. A *thesis* is not a fact, which can be immediately verified by data, but an assertion worth discussing, and an argument with more than one possible conclusion. Your thesis sentence reveals not only the argument you have chosen but also your orientation toward it and the conclusion that your paper will attempt to prove.

In looking for a thesis, you are doing many jobs at once:

1. You are limiting the amount and kind of material that you must cover, thus making them manageable.
2. You are increasing your own interest in the narrowing field of study.
3. You are working to establish your paper's purpose, the reason you are writing about your topic. (If the only reason you can see for writing is to earn a good grade, then you probably won't!)
4. You are establishing your notion of who your audience is and what sort of approach to the subject might best catch its interest.

In short, you are gaining control over your writing context. Therefore, it is good to come up with a thesis early on, a *working thesis* which will probably change as your thinking deepens but will allow you to establish a measure of order in the planning stage.

The Thesis Sentence The introduction of your paper will contain a sentence that expresses the task that you intend to accomplish. This *thesis sentence* communicates your main idea, the one you are going to prove, defend, or illustrate. It sets up an expectation in the reader's mind that it is your job to satisfy. But, in the planning stage, a thesis sentence is more than just the statement that informs your reader of your goal: it is a valuable tool to help you narrow your focus and confirm in your own mind your paper's purpose.

Developing a Thesis Students in a class on public policy analysis were assigned a 20-page paper on a problem currently being faced by the municipal authorities in their own city. The choice of the problem was left to the students. One, Richard Cory, decided to investigate the problem posed by the large number of abandoned buildings in a downtown neighborhood through which he drove on his way to the university. His first working thesis was as follows:

Abandoned houses result in negative social effects to the city.

The problem with this thesis, as Richard found out, was that it was not an idea that could be argued, but rather a fact that could be easily corroborated by the sources he began to consult. As he read reports from such groups as the Urban Land Institute and the City Planning Commission, and talked with representatives from the Community Planning Department, he began to get interested in the dilemma his city faced in responding to the problem of abandoned buildings. Richard's second working thesis was as follows:

Removal of abandoned buildings is a major problem facing the city.

While his second thesis narrowed the topic somewhat and gave Richard an opportunity to use material from his research, there was still no real comment attached to it. It still stated a bare fact, easily proved. At this point, Richard became interested in the even narrower topic of how building removal should best be handled. He found that the major issue was funding and that different civic groups favored different methods of accomplishing this. As Richard explored the arguments for and against the various funding plans, he began to feel that one of them might be best for the city. As a result, Richard developed his third working thesis:

Assessing a demolition fee on each property offers a viable solution to the city's building removal problem.

Note how this thesis narrows the focus of Richard's paper even further than the other two had, while also presenting an arguable hypothesis. It tells Richard what he has to do in his paper, just as it tells his readers what to expect.

At some time during your preliminary thinking on a topic, you should consult a library to see how much published work on your issue exists. This search has at least two benefits:

1. It acquaints you with a body of writing that will become very important in the research phase of your paper.
2. It gives you a sense of how your topic is generally addressed by the community of scholars you are joining. Is the topic as important as you think it is? Has there been so much research done on the subject as to make your inquiry, in its present formulation, irrelevant?

While determining your topic, remember that one goal of your political science writing in college is always to enhance your own understanding of the political process, to build an accurate model of the way politics works. Let this goal help you to direct your research into areas that you know are important to your knowledge of the discipline.

Define a Purpose   There are many ways to classify the purposes of writing, but in general most writing is undertaken either to inform or to persuade an audience. The goal of informative, or expository, writing is simply to impart information about a particular subject, whereas the aim of persuasive writing is to convince your reader of your point of view on an issue. The distinction between expository and persuasive writing is not hard and fast, and most writing in political science has elements of both types. Most effective writing, however, is clearly focused on either exposition or persuasion. Position papers (arguments for adopting particular policies), for example, are designed to persuade, whereas policy analysis papers (Chapter 9) are meant to inform. When you begin writing, consciously select a primary approach of exposition or persuasion, and then set out to achieve that goal.

EXERCISE   To Explain or Persuade

Can you tell from the titles of these two papers, both on the same topic, which is an expository paper and which is a persuasive paper?

1. Social Services Funding in the Second Obama Administration
2. How the Second Obama Administration Increased Social Services Funding

Again taking up the subject of campaign finances, let us assume that you must write a paper explaining how finances were managed in the 2016 Republican presidential campaign. If you are writing an expository paper, your task could be to describe as coherently and as impartially as possible the methods by which the Republicans administered their campaign funds. If, however, you are attempting to convince your readers that the 2016 Republican campaign finances were criminally mismanaged by an elected official, you are writing to persuade, and your strategy will be radically different. Persuasive writing seeks to influence the opinions of its audience toward its subject.

Learn what you want to say   By the time you write your final draft, you must have a very sound notion of the point you wish to argue. If, as you write that final draft, someone were to ask you to state your thesis, you should be able to give a satisfactory answer with a minimum of delay and no prompting. If, on the other hand, you have to hedge your answer because you cannot easily express your thesis, you may not yet be ready to write a final draft. You may have to write a draft or two or engage in various prewriting activities to form a secure understanding of your task.

EXERCISE   Knowing What You Want to Say

Two writers have been asked to state the thesis of their papers. Which one better understands the writing task?

Writer 1: "My paper is about tax reform for the middle class."

Writer 2: "My paper argues that tax reform for the middle class would be unfair to the upper and lower classes, who would then have to share more responsibility for the cost of government."

Watch out for bias! There is no such thing as pure objectivity. You are not a machine. No matter how hard you may try to produce an objective paper, the fact is that every choice you make as you write is influenced to some extent by your personal beliefs and opinions. What you tell your readers is truth, in other words, is influenced, sometimes without your knowledge, by a multitude of factors: your environment, upbringing, and education; your attitude toward your audience; your political affiliation; your race and gender; your career goals; and your ambitions for the paper you are writing. The influence of such factors can be very subtle, and it is something you must work to identify in your own writing and in the writing of others in order not to mislead or to be misled. Remember that one of the reasons for writing is *self-discovery*. The writing you will do in political science classes—and for the rest of your life—will give you a chance to discover and confront honestly your own views on your subjects. Responsible writers keep an eye on their own biases and are honest about them with their readers.

Define Your Audience In any class that requires you to write, you may sometimes find it difficult to remember that the point of your writing is not simply to jump-through the technical hoops imposed by the assignment. The point is *communication*—the transmission of your knowledge and your conclusions to readers in a way that suits you. Your task is to pass on to your readers the spark of your own enthusiasm for your topic. Readers who were indifferent to your topic before reading your paper should look at it in a new way after finishing it. This is the great challenge of writing: to enter a reader's mind and leave behind both new knowledge and new questions.

It is tempting to think that most writing problems would be solved if the writer could view the writing as if it were produced by another person. The discrepancy between the understanding of the writer and that of the audience is the single greatest impediment to accurate communication. To overcome this barrier you must consider your audience's needs. By the time you begin drafting, most, if not all, of your ideas would be attaining coherent shape in your mind, so that virtually any words with which you try to express those ideas will reflect your thoughts accurately—to you. Your readers, however, do not already hold the conclusions that you have so painstakingly achieved. If you omit from your writing the material that is necessary to complete your readers' understanding of your argument, they may well be unable to supply that information themselves.

The potential for misunderstanding is present for any audience, whether it is made up of general readers, experts in the field, or your professor, who is reading in part to see how well you have mastered the constraints that govern the relationship between writer and reader. Make your presentation as complete as possible, bearing in mind your audience's knowledge of your topic.

2.2 THINK CREATIVELY

We have discussed various methods of selecting and narrowing the topic of a paper. As your focus on a specific topic sharpens, you will naturally begin to think about the kinds of information that will go into the paper. In the case of papers that do not require formal research, this material will come largely from your own recollections. Indeed, one of the reasons instructors assign such papers is to convince you of the incredible richness of your memory, the vastness and variety of the "database" that you have accumulated and that, moment by moment, you continue to build.

Your hoard of information is so vast that it can sometimes be difficult to find within it the material that would best suit your paper. In other words, finding out what you already know about a topic is not always easy. *Invention* a term borrowed from classical rhetoric, refers to the task of discovering, or recovering from memory, such information. As we write, we go through an invention procedure that helps us explore our topic. Some writers seem to have little problem coming up with material; others need more help. Over the centuries, writers have devised different exercises that can help locate useful material housed in memory. We will look at a few of these briefly.

Freewriting *Freewriting* is an activity that forces you to get something down on paper. There is no waiting around for inspiration. Instead, you set a time limit—perhaps 3–5 minutes—and write for that length of time without stopping, not even to lift the pen from the paper or your hands from the keyboard. Focus on the topic, and do not let the difficulty of finding relevant material stop you from writing. If necessary, you may begin by writing, over and over, some seemingly useless phrase, such as, "I cannot think of anything to write," or perhaps the name of your topic. Eventually, something else will occur to you. (It is surprising how long a 3-minute period of freewriting can seem to last!) At the end of the freewriting, look over what you have produced for anything you might be able to use. Much of the writing will be unusable, but there might be an insight or two that you did not know you had.

In addition to its ability to help you recover usable material from your memory for your paper, freewriting has certain other benefits. First, it takes little time, which means that you may repeat the exercise as often as you like. Second, it breaks down some of the resistance that stands between you and the act of writing. There is no initial struggle to find something to say; you just write.

For his introductory American government class, Bill Alexander had to write a paper on some aspects of local government. Bill, who felt his understanding of local government was slight, began the job of finding a topic that interested him with 2 minutes of freewriting. Thinking about local government, Bill wrote steadily for this period without lifting his pen from the paper. Here is the result of his freewriting:

Okay okay local government. Local, what does that mean? Like police? the mayor—whoever that is? judges? I got that parking ticket last year, went to court, had to pay it anyway, bummer. Maybe trace what happens to a single parking ticket—and my money. Find out the public officials who deal with it, from the traffic cop who gives it out to wherever it ends up. Point would be, what? Point point point. To find out how much the local government spends to give out and process a $35 parking ticket—how much do they really make after expenses, and where does that money go? Have to include cop's salary? judge's? Printing costs for ticket? Salary for clerk or whoever deals only with ticket. Is there somebody who lives whole life only processing traffic tickets? Are traffic tickets and *parking tickets handled differently? Assuming the guy fights it. Maybe find out the difference in revenue between a contested and an uncontested ticket? Lots of phone calls to make. Who? Where to start?*

Brainstorming *Brainstorming* is the process of making a list of ideas about a topic. It can be done quickly and at first without any need to order items in a coherent pattern. The point is to write down everything that occurs to you as quickly and briefly as possible, using individual words or short phrases. Once you have a good-sized list of items, you can then group them according to relationships that you see among them. Brainstorming thus allows you to uncover both ideas stored in your memory and useful associations among those ideas.

A professor in constitutional law asked his students to write a 700-word paper, in the form of a letter to be translated and published in a Warsaw newspaper, giving Polish readers useful advice about living in a democracy. One student, Melissa Jessup, started thinking about the assignment by brainstorming. First, she simply wrote down anything about life in a democracy that occurred to her:

voting rights	welfare	freedom of press
protest movements	everybody equal	minorities
racial prejudice	American Dream	injustice
the individual	no job security	lobbyists and PACs
justice takes time	psychological factors	aristocracy of wealth
size of bureaucracy		

Thinking through her list, Melissa decided to divide it into two separate lists: one devoted to positive aspects of life in a democracy; the other, to negative aspects. At this point, she decided to discard some items that were redundant or did not seem to have much potential. As you can see, Melissa had some questions about where some of her items would fit:

Positive	Negative
voting rights	aristocracy of wealth
freedom of the press	justice takes time
everybody equal	racial prejudice
American Dream	welfare
psychological factors	lobbyists and PACs
protest movements (positive?)	size of bureaucracy

At this point, Melissa decided that her topic would be about the ways in which money and special interests affect a democratically elected government. Which items on her lists would be relevant to her paper?

Asking Questions It is always possible to ask most or all of the following questions about any topic: *Who? What? When? Where? Why? How?* They force you to approach the topic as a journalist does, setting it within different perspectives that can then be compared.

A professor asked her class on the judicial process to write a paper describing the impact of Supreme Court clerks on the decision-making process. One student developed the following questions as he began to think about a thesis:

Who are the Supreme Court's clerks? (How old? What is their racial and gender mix? What are their politics?)

What are their qualifications for the job?

What exactly is their job?

When during the court term are they most influential?

Where do they come from? (Is there any geographical or religious pattern in the way they are chosen? Do certain law schools contribute a significantly greater number of clerks than others?)

How are they chosen? (Are they appointed? elected?)

When in their careers do they serve?

Why are they chosen as they are?

Who have been some influential court clerks? (Have any gone on to sit on the bench themselves?)

Can you think of other questions that would make for useful inquiry?

Maintaining Flexibility   As you engage in invention strategies, you are also performing other writing tasks. You are still narrowing your topic, for example, as well as making decisions that will affect your choice of tone or audience. You are moving forward on all fronts with each decision you make affecting the others. This means that you must be flexible enough to allow for slight adjustments in understanding your paper's development and your goal. Never be so determined to prove a particular theory that you fail to notice when your own understanding of it changes. Stay objective.

Read&Write 2.2 Freewriting to Engage Your Creativity

Political scientists are, at heart, problem solvers. The problems of society intrigue them intensely. The foremost agent for solving societal problems is government. This is not to say, by any means, that all problems should be solved by government, and perhaps the primary difference between conservatives and liberals is precisely the question of what role, if any, government should take in solving a particular problem. By default, however, problem solvers normally look first, when seeking a solution to any societal problem (crime, poverty, terrorism, and climate change), to government to determine what government can and should do. This is because government presents an open gateway that private institutions do not. People have a relatively open access (letters, visits, protest demonstrations) to mayors, governors, senators, and representatives that private corporations simply do not provide. Furthermore, the allegiance of corporations is to their stockholders, while elected officials are responsible to their voting constituencies.

Access to government, therefore, presents many opportunities. In this case, you have an opportunity to do some freewriting on a topic of your choice. First, find a newspaper, online or in print. Then select an article that identifies or comments on a societal problem. Following the sample in this chapter, do some freewriting. The objective of your freewriting is to establish an initial approach to find a solution to the societal problem you have selected.

2.3 ORGANIZE YOUR WRITING

A paper that contains all the necessary facts but presents them in an ineffective order will confuse rather than inform or persuade. Although there are various methods of grouping ideas, none is potentially more effective than outlining. Unfortunately, no organizing process is more often misunderstood.

The Importance of Outlining

Outline for Yourself Outlining can do two jobs. First, it can force you, the writer, to gain a better understanding of your ideas by arranging them according to their interrelationships. There is one primary rule of outlining: ideas of equal weight are placed on the same level within the outline. This rule requires you to determine the relative importance of your ideas. You must decide which ideas are of the same type or order, and into which subtopic each idea best fits.

In the planning stage, if you carefully arrange your ideas in a coherent outline, your grasp of your topic will be greatly enhanced. You will have linked your ideas logically together and given a basic structure to the body of the paper. This sort of subordinating and coordinating activity is difficult, however, and as a result, inexperienced writers sometimes begin to write their first draft without an effective outline, hoping for the best. This hope is usually unfulfilled, especially in complex papers involving research.

EXERCISE Organizing Thoughts

Rodrigo, a student in a second-year class in government management, researched the impact of a worker-retraining program in his state and came up with the following facts and theories. Number them in logical order:

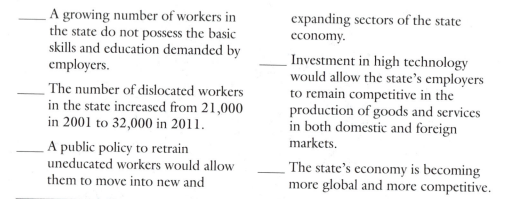

_____ A growing number of workers in the state do not possess the basic skills and education demanded by employers.

_____ The number of dislocated workers in the state increased from 21,000 in 2001 to 32,000 in 2011.

_____ A public policy to retrain uneducated workers would allow them to move into new and expanding sectors of the state economy.

_____ Investment in high technology would allow the state's employers to remain competitive in the production of goods and services in both domestic and foreign markets.

_____ The state's economy is becoming more global and more competitive.

Outline for Your Reader The second job of an outline is to serve as a reader's blueprint to the paper, summarizing its points and their interrelationships. By consulting your outline, a busy policymaker can quickly get a sense of your paper's goal and the argument you have used to promote it. The clarity and coherence of the outline help determine how much attention your audience will give to your ideas.

As political science students, you will be given a great deal of help with the arrangement of your material into an outline to accompany your paper. The formats presented in Chapter 3 of this manual show you how strictly these formal outlines are structured. But, although you must pay close attention to these requirements, do not forget how powerful a tool an outline can be in the early planning stages of your paper.

The Formal Outline Pattern   By following this pattern accurately during the planning stage of your paper, you can place your ideas logically:

Thesis sentence (precedes the formal outline)

I. First main idea

    A. First subordinate idea

        1. Reason, example, or illustration

            a. Supporting detail

            b. Supporting detail

            c. Supporting detail

        2. Reason, example, or illustration

            a. Supporting detail

            b. Supporting detail

            c. Supporting detail

    B. Second subordinate idea

II. Second main idea

Notice that each level of the paper must have more than one entry; for every A there must be at least a B (and, if required, a C, a D, and so on), and for every 1 there must be a 2. This arrangement forces you to *compare ideas* looking carefully at each one to determine its place among the others. The insistence on assigning relative values to your ideas is what makes an outline an effective organizing tool.

Read & Write 2.3   Write an Outline for a Paper Inspired by a Newspaper Article

This is a relatively simple exercise, but it does require some thought. Start by perusing today's newspaper (local or national). When you come to an article that "gets under your skin," stop. Suppose the article is one like this, from the *New York Times*:

> HEMPSTEAD, N.Y.—A man accused of firing the bullet that fatally struck a 12-year-old girl as she sat in her Long Island home in October was retaliating after his younger brother's hoverboard was stolen, the police said on Monday.
>
> The man, Jakwan Keller, 20, wearing a bulletproof vest declined to comment as detectives led him out of Nassau County Police Headquarters. He later pleaded not guilty to murder, weapons possession, and other charges in connection with the death of the girl, Dejah Joyner.[3]

[3] "Stray Bullet That Killed Long Island Girl Was Fired in Retaliation for Hoverboard Theft, Police Say." 2016. *New York Times,* January 11. http://www.nytimes.com/2016/01/12/ nyregion/stray-bullet-that-killed-long-island-girl-was-fired-in-retaliation-for-theft-police-say.html?_r=0 (March 7, 2016).

Think. What is it about the article that irritates you? Is it the waste of a person's life? Is it the availability of guns? Is it a lack of law enforcement?

Now, following the outline format described in this chapter section, write an outline of a paper you might write because you read this article. Your outline will not *summarize* the article, although a short summary might be included in your paper. Your paper outline might look something like this:

How to Reduce Accidental Gun Deaths

I. The history of accidental deaths is a long one.

  A. Most deaths on nineteenth century wagon trains were accidental shootings.

    1. Loaded guns were always at hand.

    2. Bumpy trails led to frequent discharges.

  B. Loaded guns at home are a danger to children.

    1. Children play with guns.

    2. Adults are not required to store guns securely.

    3. Adults want loaded guns easily available.

II. The number of accidental gun deaths is alarming.

  A. The number of accidental gun deaths has risen from 1860 to 2016.

    1. There were few early efforts to reduce the death rate.

    2. Gun deaths were accepted as a way of life.

  B. The prevalence of guns is increasing in the twenty-first century.

  1. Gun sales rise with each new mass shooting.

  2. The NRA presses for open carry laws.

  3. Open carry on campus and in bars becomes controversial.

III. The number of options for reducing gun deaths is growing.

  A. There are criminal penalties for negligent parents.

    1. Some parents have received long prison sentences.

    2. Capital punishment is an alternative under discussion.

  B. The outlawing of semi-automatic weapons is a controversial possibility.

    1. Critics complain about financial costs.

    2. Political costs may prevent meaningful legislation.

  C. Advocates see public education on gun safety as essential.

    1. Courses in elementary and secondary schools are becoming feasible.

    2. Enrollments in online seminars for adults are increasing.

The Patterns of Political Science Papers

The structure of any particular type of political science paper is governed by a formal pattern. When rigid external controls are placed on their writing, some writers feel that their creativity is hampered by a kind of "paint-by-numbers" approach to structure. It is vital to the success of your paper that you are never overwhelmed by the pattern rules for any type of paper. Remember that such controls exist not to limit your creativity but to make the paper immediately and easily useful to its intended audience. It is as necessary to write clearly and confidently in a position paper or a policy analysis paper as in a term paper for English literature, a résumé, a short story, or a job application letter.

2.4 DRAFT, REVISE, EDIT, AND PROOFREAD

Write the Rough Draft

After planning comes the writing of the first draft. Using your thesis and outline as direction markers, you must now weave your amalgam of ideas, data, and persuasion strategies into logically ordered sentences and paragraphs. Although adequate prewriting may facilitate drafting, it still will not be easy. Writers establish their own individual methods of encouraging themselves to forge ahead with the draft, but here are some tips:

1. Remember that this is a rough draft, not the final paper. At this stage, it is not necessary that every word be the best possible choice. Do not put that sort of pressure on yourself. You must not allow anything to slow you down now. Writing is not like sculpting in stone, where every chip is permanent; you can always go back to your draft and add, delete, reword, and rearrange. *No matter how much effort you have put into planning, you cannot be sure how much of this first draft you will eventually keep.* It may take several drafts to get one that you find satisfactory.

2. Give yourself sufficient time to write. Do not delay the first draft by telling yourself there is still more research to do. You cannot uncover all the material there is to know on a particular subject, so do not fool yourself into trying. Remember that writing is a process of discovery. You may have to begin writing before you can see exactly what sort of research you need to do. Remember that there are other tasks waiting for you after the first draft is finished, so allow for them as you determine your writing schedule.

   More importantly, give yourself time to write, because the more time that passes after you have written a draft, the better your ability to view it with objectivity. It is very difficult to evaluate your writing accurately soon after you complete it. You need to cool down, to recover from the effort of putting all those words together. The "colder" you get on your writing, the better you are able to read it as if it were written by someone else and thus acknowledge the changes needed to strengthen the paper.

3. Stay sharp. Keep in mind the plan you created as you narrowed your topic, composed a thesis sentence, and outlined the material. But, if you begin to feel a strong need to change the plan a bit, do not be afraid to do so. Be ready for surprises dealt you by your own growing understanding of your topic. Your goal is to record your best thinking on the subject as accurately as possible.

Paragraph development There is no absolute requirement for the structure of any paragraph in your paper except that all its sentences must be clearly related to each other and each must carry the job of saying what you want to say about your thesis *one step farther.* In other words, simply restating what is already said elsewhere in the paper is a waste of your time and the reader's. It isn't unusual for a paragraph to have, somewhere in it, a *topic* sentence that serves as the key to the paragraph's organization and announces the paragraph's connection to the paper's thesis. But not all paragraphs need topic sentences.

What all paragraphs in the paper *do* need is an organizational strategy. Here are four typical organizational models, any one of which, if you keep it in mind, can help you build a coherent paragraph:

- *Chronological organization*: The sentences of the paragraph describe a series of events, steps, or observations as they occur over time: this happens, then that, and then that.
- *Spatial organization*: The sentences of the paragraph record details of its subject in some logical order: top to bottom, up to down, outside to inside.
- *General-to-specific organization*: The paragraph starts with a statement of its main idea and then goes into detail as it discusses that idea.
- *Specific-to-general organization*: The paragraph begins with smaller, nuts-and-bolts details, arranging them in a larger pattern that, by the end of the paragraph, leads to the conclusion that is the paragraph's main idea.

These aren't the only organizational strategies available to you, and, of course, different paragraphs in a paper can use different strategies; however, a paragraph that employs more than one organizational plan is risking incoherence. It is important that each sentence in the paragraph must bear a logical relationship to the one before it and the one after it. It is this notion of *interconnectedness* that can prevent you from getting off track and stuffing extraneous material in your paragraphs.

Like all other aspects of the writing process, paragraph development is a challenge. But remember, one of the helpful facts about paragraphs is that they are relatively small, especially compared to the overall scope of your paper. Each paragraph can basically do only one job—handle or help to handle a single idea, which is itself only a part of the overall development of the larger thesis idea. That paragraphs are small and aimed at a single task means that it is relatively easy to revise them. By focusing clearly on the single job a paragraph does and filtering out all the paper's other claims for your attention, you should gain enough clarity of vision during the revision process to understand what you need to do to make that paragraph work better.

Authority To be convincing, your writing has to be authoritative; that is, you have to sound as if you have complete confidence in your ability to convey your ideas in words. Sentences that sound stilted, or that suffer from weak phrasing or the use of clichés, are not going to win supporters for the positions that you express in your paper. So a major question becomes, "How can I sound confident?"

Consider these points to convey to your reader that necessary sense of authority:

Level of Formality Tone is one of the primary methods by which you signal to the readers who you are and what your attitude is toward them and toward your topic. Your major decision is which level of language formality is most appropriate to your audience. The informal tone you would use in a letter to a friend may be out of place in a paper on "Waste in Military Spending" written for your government professor. Remember that tone is only part of the overall decision you make about presenting your information. Formality is, to some extent, a function of individual word choices and phrasing. For example, is it appropriate to use contractions such as *isn't* or *they'll*? Would the strategic use of a sentence fragment for effect be out of place? The use of informal language, the personal *I* and the second-person *you* is traditionally forbidden—for better or worse—in certain kinds of writing. Often, part of the challenge of writing a formal paper is simply how to give your prose impact while staying within the conventions.

Jargon   One way to lose readers quickly is to overwhelm them with *jargon*—phrases that have a special, usually technical meaning within your discipline but that are unfamiliar to the average reader. An occasional use of jargon may add an effective touch of atmosphere, but anything more than that will severely dampen a reader's enthusiasm for the paper. Often the writer uses jargon in an effort to impress the reader by sounding lofty or knowledgeable. Unfortunately, jargon usually causes confusion. In fact, the use of jargon indicates a writer's lack of connection to the audience.

Political science writing is a haven for jargon. Perhaps writers of policy analyses and position papers believe their readers are all completely attuned to their terminology. Or some may hope to obscure damaging information or potentially unpopular ideas in confusing language. In other cases, the problem could simply be unclear thinking by the writer. Whatever the reason, the fact is that political science papers too often sound like prose made by machines to be read by machines.

Some students may feel that, to be accepted as political scientists, their papers should conform to the practices of their published peers. This is a mistake. Remember that it is never better to write a cluttered or confusing sentence than a clear one, and burying your ideas in jargon defeats the effort that you went through to form them.

EXERCISE   Revising Jargon

What words in the following sentence, from an article in a political science journal, are jargon? Can you rewrite it to clarify its meaning?
The implementation of statute-mandated regulated inputs exceeds the conceptualization of the administrative technicians.

Clichés   In the heat of composition, as you are looking for words to help you form your ideas, it is sometimes easy to plug in a *cliché*—a phrase that has attained universal recognition by overuse. (*Note:* Clichés differ from jargon in that clichés are part of the general public's everyday language, whereas jargon is specific to the language of experts in a field.) Our vocabularies are brimming with clichés:

It's raining cats and dogs.

That issue is as dead as a doornail.

It's time for the governor to face the music.

Angry voters made a beeline for the ballot box.

The problem with clichés is that they are virtually meaningless. Once a colorful means of expression, they have lost their color through overuse, and they tend to bleed energy and color from the surrounding words. When revising, replace clichés with fresh wording that more accurately conveys your point.

Descriptive Language Language that appeals to readers' senses will always engage their interest more fully than language that is abstract. This is especially important for writing in disciplines that tend to deal in abstracts, such as political science. A typical political science paper, with its discussions of principles, demographics, or points of law, is usually in danger of floating off into abstraction, with each paragraph drifting further away from the felt life of the readers. Whenever appropriate, appeal to your readers' sense of sight, hearing, taste, touch, or smell.

EXERCISE Using Descriptive Language

Which of these two sentences is more effective?

1. The housing project had deteriorated badly since the last inspection.
2. The housing project had deteriorated badly since the last inspection; stench rose from the plumbing, grime coated the walls and floors, and rats scurried through the hallways.

Bias-free and Gender-Neutral Writing Language can be a very powerful method of either reinforcing or destroying cultural stereotypes. By treating the sexes in subtly different ways in your language, you may unknowingly be committing an act of discrimination. A common example is the use of the pronoun *he* to refer to a person whose gender has not been identified.

Some writers, faced with this dilemma, alternate the use of male and female personal pronouns; others use the plural to avoid the need to use a pronoun of either gender:

Sexist: A lawyer should always treat his client with respect.

Corrected: A lawyer should always treat his or her client with respect.

Or: Lawyers should always treat their clients with respect.

Sexist: Man is a political animal.

Corrected: People are political animals.

Remember that language is more than the mere vehicle of your thoughts. Your words shape perceptions for your readers. How well you say something will profoundly affect your readers' response to what you say. Sexist language denies to a large number of your readers the basic right to fair and equal treatment. Make sure your writing is not guilty of this form of discrimination.

Revise

After all the work you have gone through writing it, you may feel "married" to the first draft of your paper. However, revision is one of the most important steps in ensuring your paper's success. Although unpracticed writers often think of revision as little more than making sure all the *i*'s are dotted and *t*'s are crossed, it is much more than that. Revising is *reseeing* the essay, looking at it from other perspectives, trying always to align your view with the one that will be held by your audience. Research indicates that we are actually revising all the time, in every phase of the writing process, as we reread phrases, rethink the placement of an item in an outline, or test a new topic sentence for a paragraph. Subjecting your entire hard-fought draft to cold, objective scrutiny is one of the toughest activities to master, but it is absolutely necessary. You have to ensure that you have said everything that needs to be said clearly and logically. One confusing passage will deflect the reader's attention from where you want it to be. Suddenly the reader has to become a detective, trying to figure out why you wrote what you did and what you meant by it. You do not want to throw such obstacles in the path of understanding.

Here are some tips to help you with revision:

1. Give yourself adequate time for revision. As discussed above, you need time to become "cold" on your paper to analyze it objectively. After you have written your draft, spend some time away from it. Then try to reread it as if someone else had written it.

2. Read the paper carefully. This is tougher than it sounds. One good strategy is to read it aloud yourself or to have a friend read it aloud while you listen. (Note, however, that friends are usually not the best critics. They are rarely trained in revision techniques and are often unwilling to risk disappointing you by giving your paper a really thorough examination.)

3. Have a list of specific items to check. It is important to revise in an orderly fashion, in stages, first looking at large concerns, such as the overall organization, and then at smaller elements, such as paragraph or sentence structure.

4. Check for unity—the clear and logical relation of all parts of the essay to its thesis. Make sure that every paragraph relates well to the whole of the paper and is in the right place.

5. Check for coherence. Make sure there are no gaps between the various parts of the argument. Look to see that you have adequate transitions everywhere they are needed. Transitional elements are markers indicating places where the paper's focus or attitude changes. Such elements can take the form of one word—*however, although, unfortunately, luckily*—or an entire sentence or a paragraph: *In order to fully appreciate the importance of democracy as a shaping presence in post-Cold War Polish politics, it is necessary to examine briefly the Poles' last historical attempt to implement democratic government.*

   Transitional elements rarely introduce new material. Instead, they are direction pointers, either indicating a shift to new subject matter or signaling how the writer wishes certain material to be interpreted by the reader. Because you, the writer, already know where and why your paper changes direction and how you want particular passages to be received, it can be very difficult for you to catch those places where transition is needed.

6. Avoid unnecessary repetition. Two types of repetition can annoy a reader: repetition of content and repetition of wording.

   Repetition of content occurs when you return to a subject you have already discussed. Ideally, you should deal with a topic once, memorably, and then move on to your next subject. Organizing a paper is a difficult task, however, which usually occurs through a process of enlightenment in terms of purposes and strategies, and repetition of content can happen even if you have used prewriting strategies. What is worse, it can be difficult for you to be aware of the repetition in your own writing. As you write and revise, remember that any unnecessary repetition of content in your final draft is potentially annoying to your readers, who are working to make sense of the argument they are reading and do not want to be distracted by a passage repeating material they have already encountered. You must train yourself, through practice, to look for material that you have repeated unnecessarily.

Repetition of wording occurs when you overuse certain phrases or words. This can make your prose sound choppy and uninspired, as the following examples demonstrate:

The subcommittee's report on education reform will surprise a number of people. A number of people will want copies of the report.

The chairman said at a press conference that he is happy with the report. He will circulate it to the local news agencies in the morning. He will also make sure that the city council has copies.

I became upset when I heard how the committee had voted. I called the chairman and expressed my reservations about the committee's decision. I told him I felt that he had let the teachers and students of the state down. I also issued a press statement.

The last passage illustrates a condition known by composition teachers as the *I-syndrome*. Can you hear how such duplicated phrasing can hurt a paper? Your language should sound fresh and energetic. Make sure, before you submit your final draft, to read through your paper carefully, looking for such repetition. However, not all repetition is bad. You may wish to repeat a phrase for rhetorical effect or special emphasis: "I came. I saw. I conquered." Just make sure that any repetition in your paper is intentional, placed there to produce a specific effect.

Edit

Editing is sometimes confused with the more involved process of revising. But editing is done later in the writing process, after you have wrestled through your first draft—and maybe your second and third—and arrived at the final draft. Even though your draft now contains all the information you want to impart and has the information arranged to your satisfaction, there are still many factors to check, such as sentence structure, spelling, and punctuation.

It is at this point that an unpracticed writer might be less than vigilant. After all, most of the work on the paper is finished, as the "big jobs" of discovering, organizing, and drafting information have been completed. But watch out! Editing is as important as any other part of the writing process. Any error that you allow in the final draft will count against you in the mind of the reader. This may not seem fair, but even a minor error—a misspelling or confusing placement of a comma—will make a much greater impression on your reader than perhaps it should. Remember that everything about your paper is your responsibility, including performing even the supposedly little jobs correctly. Careless editing undermines the effectiveness of your paper. It would be a shame if all the hard work you put into prewriting, drafting, and revising were to be damaged because you carelessly allowed a comma splice!

Most of the tips given above for revising hold for editing as well. It is best to edit in stages, looking for only one or two kinds of errors each time you reread the paper. Focus especially on errors that you remember committing in the past. If, for instance, you know that you have a tendency to misplace commas, go through your paper looking at each comma carefully. If you have a weakness for writing unintentional sentence fragments, read each sentence aloud to make sure that it is indeed a complete sentence. Have you accidentally shifted verb tenses anywhere, moving from past to present tense for no reason? Do all the subjects in your sentences agree in number with their verbs? *Now is the time to find out.*

Watch out for *miscues*—problems with a sentence that the writer simply does not see. Remember that your search for errors is hampered in two ways:

1. As a writer, you hope not to find any errors in your work. This desire can cause you to miss mistakes when they do occur.
2. Because you know your material so well, it is easy, as you read, to unconsciously supply missing material—a word, a piece of punctuation—as if it were present.

How difficult is it to see that something is missing in the following sentence?

Unfortunately, legislators often have too little regard their constituents.

We can guess that the missing word is probably *for* which should be inserted after *regard*. It is quite possible, however, that the writer of the sentence would automatically supply the missing *for* as if it were on the page. This is a miscue, which can be hard for writers to spot because they are so close to their material.

One tactic for catching mistakes in sentence structure is to read the sentences aloud, starting with the last one in the paper and then moving to the next-to-last, then to the previous sentence, and thus going backward through the paper (reading each sentence in the normal, left-to-right manner, of course) until you reach the first sentence of the introduction. This backward progression strips each sentence of its rhetorical context and helps you focus on its internal structure.

Editing is the stage in which you finally answer those minor-questions that you had put off when you were wrestling with wording and organization. Any ambiguities regarding the use of abbreviations, italics, numerals, capital letters, titles (When do you capitalize the title *president*, for example?), hyphens, dashes (usually created on a typewriter or computer by striking the hyphen key twice), apostrophes, and quotation marks have to be cleared up now. You must also check to see that you have used the required formats for footnotes, endnotes, margins, page numbers, and the like.

Guessing is not allowed. Sometimes unpracticed writers who realize that they do not quite understand a particular rule of grammar, punctuation, or format do nothing to fill that knowledge gap. Instead, they rely on guesswork and their own logic—which is not always up to the task of dealing with so contrary a language as English—to get them through problems that they could solve if they referred to a writing manual. Remember that it does not matter to the reader why or how an error shows up in your writing. It only matters that you have dropped your guard. You must not allow a careless error to undo all the good work that you have done.

Proofread

Before you hand in the final version of your paper, it is vital that you check it one more time to ensure that there are no errors of any sort. This job is called *proofreading* or *proofing*. In essence, you are looking for many of the same things you had checked for during editing, but now you are doing it on the last draft, which is about to be submitted to your audience. Proofreading is as important as editing; you may have missed an error that you still have time to find, or an error may have been introduced when the draft was recopied or typed for the last time. Like every other stage of the writing process, proofreading is your responsibility.

At this point, you must check for typing mistakes: transposed or deleted letters, words, phrases, or punctuation. If you have had the paper professionally typed, you still must check it carefully. Do not rely solely on the typist's proofreading. If you are creating your paper on a computer or a word processor, it is possible for you to unintentionally insert a command that alters your document drastically by slicing out a word, line, or sentence at the touch of a key. Make sure such accidental deletions have not occurred.

Above all else, remember that your paper represents you. It is a product of your best thinking, your most energetic and imaginative response to a writing challenge. If you have maintained your enthusiasm for the project and worked through the stages of the writing process honestly and carefully, you should produce a paper you can be proud of, one that will serve its readers well.

Read & Write 2.4 Discover Your Own Identity and Style

Here is another opportunity to do some freewriting. The wisdom of the Oracle of Delphi was noted by Socrates, who affirmed the Oracle's belief that the key to wisdom itself was to "Know Yourself." Fulfilling this admonition can become a life-long occupation. As psychologists may tell you, helping others to know themselves offers a potentially fulfilling career. Let's start our writing project by accepting, though with apologies for an ancient philosopher's gender bias, Aristotle's observation that "Man is by nature a political animal."[4] If you are a political animal, what does this mean about you personally? In this case, think about politics in the broadest sense, not just running for office, but as a mode of conduct in which you exert influence on other people, most specifically to get your needs and desires met. Have fun! When you are done freewriting, write one solid paper in which you describe who you are as a "political animal."

---

[4] Aristotle. *Politics.* 1.1253a. http://data.perseus.org/citations/urn:cts:greekLit:tlg0086.tlg035. perseus-eng1:1.1253a (March 7, 2016).

3

PRACTICE THE CRAFT
OF SCHOLARSHIP

3.1   THE COMPETENT WRITER

Good writing places your thoughts in your readers' minds in exactly the way you want them to be there. Good writing tells your readers just what you want them to know without telling them anything you do not want them to know. This may sound odd, but the fact is that writers have to be careful not to let unwanted messages slip into their writing. Look, for example, at the passage below, taken from a paper analyzing the impact of a worker-retraining program. Hidden within the prose is a message that jeopardizes the paper's success. Can you detect the message?

> Recent articles written on the subject of dislocated workers have had little to say about the particular problems dealt within this paper. Because few of these articles focus on the problem at the state level.

Chances are, when you reached the end of the second "sentence," you felt that something was missing and perceived a gap in logic or coherence, so you went back through both sentences to find the place where things had gone wrong. The second sentence is actually not a sentence at all. It does have certain features of a sentence—for example, a subject (*few*) and a verb (*focus*)—but its first word (*Because*) subordinates the entire clause that follows, taking away its ability to stand on its own as a complete idea. The second "sentence," which is properly called a *subordinate clause*, merely fills in some information about the first sentence, telling us why recent articles about dislocated workers fail to deal with problems discussed in the present paper.

The sort of error represented by the second "sentence" is commonly called a *sentence fragment*, and it conveys to the reader a message that no writer wants to send: that the writer either is careless or, worse, has not mastered the language. Language errors such as fragments, misplaced commas, or shifts in verb tense send out warnings to the readers' minds. As a result, readers lose some of their concentration on the issue being discussed; they become distracted and begin to wonder about the language competency of the writer. The writing loses its effectiveness.

> **Note:** Whatever goal you set for your paper—whether to persuade, describe, analyze, or speculate—you must also set one other goal: to display your language competence. If your paper does not meet this goal, it will not completely achieve its other aims. Language errors spread doubt like a virus; they jeopardize all the hard work you have done in your paper.

Language competence is especially important in political science, for credibility in politics depends on such skill. Anyone who doubts this should remember the beating that Vice President Dan Quayle took in the press for misspelling the word *potato* at a 1992 spelling bee. His error caused a storm of humiliating publicity for the hapless Quayle, adding to an impression of his general incompetence.

Correctness Is Relative

Although they may seem minor, the sort of language errors we are discussing—often called *surface errors*—can be extremely damaging in certain kinds of writing. Surface errors come in various types, including misspellings, punctuation problems, grammar errors, and the inconsistent use of abbreviations, capitalization, and numerals. These errors are an affront to your readers' notion of correctness, and therein lies one of the biggest problems with surface errors. Different audiences tolerate different levels of correctness. You know that you can get away with surface errors in, say, a letter to a friend, who will probably not judge you harshly for them, whereas those same errors in a job application letter might eliminate you from being considered for the position. Correctness depends to an extent on the context.

Another problem is that the rules governing correctness shift over a period of time. What would have been an error to your grandmother's generation—the splitting of an infinitive, for example, or the ending of a sentence with a preposition—is taken in stride by most readers today.

So how do you write correctly when the rules shift from person to person and over a period of time? Here are some tips:

Consider Your Audience   One of the great risks of writing is that even the simplest of choices regarding wording or punctuation can sometimes prejudice your audience against you in ways that may seem unfair. For example, look again at the old grammar rule forbidding the splitting of infinitives. After decades of telling students to never split an infinitive (something just done in this sentence), most composition experts now concede that a split infinitive is *not* a grammar crime. Suppose you have written a position paper trying to convince your city council of the need to hire security personnel for the library, and half of the council members—the people you wish to convince—remember their eighth-grade grammar teacher's warning about splitting infinitives. How will they respond when you tell them, in your introduction, that librarians are compelled "to always accompany" visitors to the rare book room because of the threat of vandalism? How much of their attention have you suddenly lost because of their automatic recollection of what is now a nonrule? It is possible, in other words, to write correctly and still offend your readers' notions of language competence.

Make sure that you tailor the surface features and the degree of formality in your writing to the level of competency that your readers require. When in doubt, take a conservative approach. Your audience might be just as distracted by a contraction as by a split infinitive.

Aim for Consistency   When you are dealing with a language question for which there are different answers—such as whether to use a comma before the conjunction in a series of three ("The mayor's speech addressed taxes, housing for the poor, and the job situation.")—always use the same strategy throughout your paper. If, for example, you avoid splitting one infinitive, avoid splitting *all* infinitives.

Have Confidence in What You Know About Writing!

It is easy for unpracticed writers to allow their occasional mistakes to shake their confidence in their writing ability. The fact is, however, that most of what we know about writing is correct. We are all capable, for example, of writing grammatically sound phrases, even if we cannot list the rules by which we achieve coherence. Most writers who worry about their chronic errors make fewer mistakes than they think. Becoming distressed about errors makes writing even more difficult.

Read & Write 3.1   Rephrase to Eliminate a Sentence Fragment

See how many ways you can rewrite this two "sentence" passage to eliminate the fragment and make the passage syntactically correct.

The presidential primary in New Hampshire predicts political party nominees only about half of the time. Except when the incumbent is running for reelection.

3.2   AVOID ERRORS IN GRAMMAR AND PUNCTUATION

As various composition theorists have pointed out, the word *grammar* has several definitions. One meaning is "the formal patterns in which words must be arranged in order to convey meaning." We learn these patterns very early in life and use them spontaneously, without even thinking. Our understanding of grammatical patterns is extremely sophisticated, despite the fact that few of us can actually cite the rules by which the patterns work. Patrick Hartwell tested grammar learning by asking native English speakers of different ages and levels of education, including high school teachers, to arrange these words in natural order:

French   the   young   girls   four

Everyone could produce the natural order for this phrase: "the four young French girls." Yet none of Hartwell's respondents said they knew the rule that governs the order of the words.[1]

---

[1] Patrick Hartwell. 1985. "Grammar, Grammars, and the Teaching of Grammar." *College English* 47 (Feb.): 105–27.

Eliminate Chronic Errors If just thinking about our errors has a negative effect on our writing, then how do we learn to write more correctly? Perhaps the best answer is simply to write as often as possible. Give yourself lots of practice in putting your thoughts into written shape—and then in revising and proofing your work. As you write and revise, be honest with yourself—and patient. Chronic errors are like bad habits; getting rid of them takes time.

You probably know of one or two problem areas in your writing that you could have eliminated but have not. Instead, you may have "fudged" your writing at the critical points, relying on half-remembered formulas from past English classes or trying to come up with logical solutions to your writing problems. (*Warning:* The English language does not always work in a way that seems logical.) You may have simply decided that comma rules are unlearnable or that you will never understand the difference between the verbs *lay* and *lie*. And so you guess, and you come up with the wrong answer a good part of the time. What a shame, when just a little extra work would give you mastery over those few gaps in your understanding and boost your confidence as well.

Instead of continuing with this sort of guesswork and living with the holes in your knowledge, why not face the problem areas now and learn the rules that have heretofore escaped you? What follows is a discussion of those surface features of writing in which errors most commonly occur. You will probably be familiar with most, if not all, of the rules discussed, but there may well be a few you have not yet mastered. Now is the time to do so.

Apostrophes

An apostrophe is used to show possession. When you wish to say that something belongs to someone or something, you add either an apostrophe and an *s* or an apostrophe alone to the word that represents the owner.

- When the owner is singular (a single person or thing), the apostrophe precedes an added *s:*

    According to Mayor Anderson's secretary, the news broadcast has been canceled.

    The union's lawyers challenged the government's policy in court.

    Somebody's briefcase was left in the auditorium.

- The same rule applies if the word showing possession is a plural that does not end in *s:*

    The women's club sponsored several debates during the last presidential campaign.

    Governor Smith has proven himself a tireless worker for children's rights.

- When the word expressing ownership is a plural ending in *s,* the apostrophe follows the *s:*

    The new legislation was discussed at the secretaries' conference.

    There are two ways to form the possessive for two or more nouns:

1. To show joint possession (both nouns owning the same thing or things), the last noun in the series is possessive:

    The president and first lady's invitations were sent out yesterday.

2. To indicate that each noun owns an item or items individually, each noun must show possession:

> Mayor Scott's and Mayor MacKay's speeches took different approaches to the same problem.

The importance of the apostrophe is obvious when you consider the difference in meaning between the following two sentences:

Be sure to pick up the senator's bags on your way to the airport.

Be sure to pick up the senators' bags on your way to the airport.

In the first sentence, you have only one senator to worry about, whereas in the second, you have at least two!

A Prepostrophe?

James Swanson, political commentator and editor of the *Gesundheit Gazette*, occasionally encounters political statements that he finds to be preposterous. He believes that journalists should warn us when they print one of these statements by placing a "prepostrophe" (^) at the end of a preposterous sentence.[2] Consider, for example, how a prepostrophe might assist the reader in the following statement: "We can cut taxes without reducing services ^" For even more preposterous statements, we add more prepostrophes: "Iraq has weapons of mass destruction ^ ^"

Capitalization

Here is a brief summary of some hard-to-remember capitalization rules:

1. You may, if you choose, capitalize the first letter of the first word in a sentence that follows a colon. However, make sure you use one pattern consistently throughout your paper:

> Our instructions are explicit: *Do not* allow anyone into the conference without an identification badge.

> Our instructions are explicit: *do not* allow anyone into the conference without an identification badge.

2. Capitalize *proper nouns* (names of specific people, places, or things) and *proper adjectives* (adjectives made from proper nouns). A common noun following a proper adjective is usually not capitalized, nor is a common adjective preceding a proper adjective (such as *a*, *an*, or *the*):

Proper Nouns	Proper Adjectives
Poland	Polish officials
Iraq	the Iraqi ambassador
Shakespeare	a Shakespearean tragedy

Proper nouns include:

- *Names of monuments and buildings:* the Washington Monument, the Empire State Building, the Library of Congress

---

[2] James Swanson is an uncle of one of this book's authors. The *Gesundheit Gazette* was a private correspondence between uncle and nephew.

- *Historical events, eras, and certain terms concerning calendar dates:* the Civil War, the Dark Ages, Monday, December, Columbus Day
- *Parts of the country:* North, Southwest, Eastern Seaboard, the West Coast, New England.

> **Note:** When words like *north, south, east, west,* and *northwest* are used to designate direction rather than geographical region, they are not capitalized: "We drove east to Boston and then made a tour of the East Coast."

- *Words referring to race, religion, and nationality:* Islam, Muslim, Caucasian, White (or white), Asian, Negro, Black (or black), Slavic, Arab, Jewish, Hebrew, Buddhism, Buddhists, Southern Baptists, the Bible, the Koran, American
- *Names of languages:* English, Chinese, Latin, Sanskrit
- *Titles of corporations, institutions, universities, and organizations:* Dow Chemical, General Motors, the National Endowment for the Humanities, University of Tennessee, Colby College, Kiwanis Club, American Association of Retired Persons, Oklahoma State Senate

> **Note:** Some words once considered proper nouns or adjectives have, over time, become common and are no longer capitalized, such as *french fries, pasteurized milk, arabic numerals, and italics.*

3. Titles of individuals may be capitalized if they precede a proper name; otherwise, titles are usually not capitalized:

The committee honored Senator Jones.

The committee honored the senator from Kansas.

We phoned Doctor Jessup, who arrived shortly afterward.

We phoned the doctor, who arrived shortly afterward.

A story on Queen Elizabeth's health appeared in yesterday's paper.

A story on the queen's health appeared in yesterday's paper.

Pope John Paul's visit to Colorado was a public relations success.

The pope's visit to Colorado was a public relations success.

When Not to Capitalize   In general, you do not capitalize nouns when your reference is nonspecific. For example, you would not capitalize *the senator,* but you would capitalize *Senator Smith.* The second reference is as much a title as it is a term of identification, whereas the first reference is a mere identifier. Likewise, there is a difference in degree of specificity between *the state treasury* and *the Texas State Treasury.*

Note: The meaning of a term may change somewhat depending on its capitalization. What, for example, might be the difference between a *Democrat* and a *democrat?* When capitalized, the word refers to a member of a specific political party; when not capitalized, it refers to someone who believes in the democratic form of government.

Capitalization depends to some extent on the context of your writing. For example, if you are writing a policy analysis for a specific corporation, you may capitalize words and phrases that refer to that corporation—such as *Board of Directors, Chairman of the Board,* and *the Institute*—that would not be capitalized in a paper written for a more general audience. Likewise, in some contexts, it is not unusual to see the titles of certain powerful officials capitalized even when not accompanying a proper noun:

The President took few members of his staff to Camp David with him.

Colons

We all know certain uses for the colon. A colon can, for example, separate the parts of a statement of time (*4:25* a.m.), separate chapter and verse in a biblical quotation *(John 3:16),* and close the salutation of a business letter (*Dear Senator Keaton:*). *But the colon has other, less well-known uses that can add extra flexibility to sentence structure.*

The colon can introduce into a sentence certain kinds of material, such as a list, a quotation, or a restatement or description of material mentioned earlier:

List

The committee's research proposal promised to do three things: (1) establish the extent of the problem, (2) examine several possible solutions, and (3) estimate the cost of each solution.

Quotation

In his speech, the mayor challenged us with these words: "How will your council's work make a difference in the life of our city?"

Restatement or Description

Ahead of us, according to the senator's chief of staff, lay the biggest job of all: convincing our constituents of the plan's benefits.

Commas

The comma is perhaps the most troublesome of all marks of punctuation, no doubt because its use is governed by so many variables, such as sentence length, rhetorical emphasis, and changing notions of style. The most common problems are outlined below.

The Comma Splice   A *comma splice* is the joining of two complete sentences with only a comma:

An impeachment is merely an indictment of a government official, actual removal usually requires a vote by a legislative body.

An unemployed worker who has been effectively retrained is no longer an economic problem for the community, he has become an asset.

It might be possible for the city to assess fees on the sale of real estate, however, such a move would be criticized by the community of real estate developers.

In each of these passages, two complete sentences (also called *independent clauses*) have been spliced together by a comma, which is an inadequate break between the two sentences.

One foolproof way to check your paper for comma splices is to read the structures on both sides of each comma carefully. If you find a complete sentence on each side, and if the sentence following the comma does not begin with a coordinating conjunction (*and, but, for, nor, or, so, yet*), then you have found a comma splice.

Simply reading the draft to try to "hear" the comma splices may not work because the rhetorical features of your prose—its "movement"—may make it hard to detect this kind of error in sentence completeness. There are five commonly used ways to correct comma splices:

1. Place a period between the two independent clauses:

INCORRECT   A political candidate receives many benefits from his or her affiliation with a political party, there are liabilities as well.

CORRECT   A political candidate receives many benefits from his or her affiliation with a political party. There are liabilities as well.

2. Place a comma and a coordinating conjunction (*and, but, for, or, nor, so, yet*) between the independent clauses:

INCORRECT   The councilman's speech described the major differences of opinion over the economic situation, it also suggested a possible course of action.

CORRECT   The councilman's speech described the major differences of opinion over the economic situation, and it also suggested a possible course of action.

3. Place a semicolon between the independent clauses:

INCORRECT   Some people feel that the federal government should play a large role in establishing a housing policy for the homeless, many others disagree.

CORRECT   Some people feel that the federal government should play a large role in establishing a housing policy for the homeless; many others disagree.

4. Rewrite the two clauses as one independent clause:

INCORRECT   Television ads played a big part in the campaign, however they were not the deciding factor in the challenger's victory over the incumbent.

CORRECT   Television ads played a large but not a decisive role in the challenger's victory over the incumbent.

5. Change one of the independent clauses into a dependent clause by beginning it with a subordinating word (*although, after, as, because, before, if, though, unless, when, which, where*), which prevents the clause from being able to stand on its own as a complete sentence.

INCORRECT   The election was held last Tuesday, there was a poor voter turnout.

CORRECT   When the election was held last Tuesday, there was a poor voter turnout.

Commas in a Compound Sentence   A *compound sentence* is composed of two or more independent clauses—two complete sentences. When these two clauses are joined by a coordinating conjunction, the conjunction should be preceded by a comma to signal the reader that another independent clause follows. (This is method number 2 for fixing a comma splice, described above.) When the comma is missing, the reader is not expecting to find the second half of a compound sentence and may be distracted from the text.

As the following examples indicate, the missing comma is especially a problem in longer sentences or in sentences in which other coordinating conjunctions appear. Notice how the comma sorts out the two main parts of the compound sentence, eliminating confusion:

INCORRECT   The senator promised to visit the hospital and investigate the problem and then he called the press conference to a close.

CORRECT   The senator promised to visit the hospital and investigate the problem, and then he called the press conference to a close.

INCORRECT   The water board can neither make policy nor enforce it nor can its members serve on auxiliary water committees.

CORRECT   The water board can neither make policy nor enforce it, nor can its members serve on auxiliary water committees.

An exception to this rule arises in shorter sentences, where the comma may not be necessary to make the meaning clear:

The mayor phoned and we thanked him for his support.

However, it is never wrong to place a comma after the conjunction between independent clauses. If you are the least bit unsure of your audience's notion of "proper" grammar, it is a good idea to take the conservative approach and use the comma:

The mayor phoned, and we thanked him for his support.

Commas with Restrictive and Nonrestrictive Elements   A *nonrestrictive element* is a part of a sentence—a word, phrase, or clause—that adds information about another element in the sentence without restricting or limiting its meaning.

Although this information may be useful, the nonrestrictive element is not needed for the sentence to make sense. To signal its inessential nature, the nonrestrictive element is set off from the rest of the sentence with commas.

The failure to use commas to indicate the nonrestrictive nature of a sentence element can cause confusion. See, for example, how the presence or absence of commas affects our understanding of the following sentence:

The mayor was talking with the policeman, who won the outstanding service award last year.

The mayor was talking with the policeman who won the outstanding service award last year.

Can you see that the comma changes the meaning of the sentence? In the first version of the sentence, the comma makes the information that follows it incidental: *The mayor was talking with the policeman, who happens to have won the service award last year.* In the second version of the sentence, the information following the word *policeman* is vital to the sense of the sentence; it tells us specifically *which* policeman—presumably there are more than one—the mayor was addressing. Here, the lack of a comma has transformed the material following the word *policeman* into a *restrictive element*, which means that it is necessary to our understanding of the sentence.

Be sure that you make a clear distinction in your paper between nonrestrictive and restrictive elements by setting off the nonrestrictive elements with commas.

Commas in a Series   A series is any two or more items of a similar nature that appear consecutively in a sentence. These items may be individual words, phrases, or clauses. In a series of three or more items, the items are separated by commas:

The senator, the mayor, and the police chief all attended the ceremony.

Because of the new zoning regulations, all trailer parks must be moved out of the neighborhood, all small businesses must apply for recertification and tax status, and the two local churches must repave their parking lots.

The final comma in the series, the one before *and*, is sometimes left out, especially in newspaper writing. This practice, however, can make for confusion, especially in longer, complicated sentences like the second example above. Here is the way this sentence would read without the final, or serial, comma:

Because of the new zoning regulations, all trailer parks must be moved out of the neighborhood, all small businesses must apply for recertification and tax status and the two local churches must repave their parking lots.

Notice that, without a comma, the division between the second and third items in the series is not clear. This is the sort of ambiguous structure that can cause a reader to backtrack and lose concentration. You can avoid such confusion by always using that final comma. Remember, however, that if you decide to include it, do so consistently; make sure it appears in every series in your paper.

Misplaced Modifiers

A *modifier* is a word or group of words used to describe, or modify, another word in the sentence. A *misplaced modifier*, sometimes called a dangling modifier, appears at either the beginning or the end of a sentence and seems to be describing some word other than the one the writer obviously intended. The modifier therefore "dangles," disconnected from its correct meaning. It is often hard for the writer to spot a dangling modifier, but readers can—and will—find them, and the result can be disastrous for the sentence, as the following examples demonstrate:

INCORRECT   Flying low over Washington, the White House was seen.

CORRECT   Flying low over Washington, we saw the White House.

INCORRECT   Worried at the cost of the program, sections of the bill were trimmed in committee.

CORRECT   Worried at the cost of the program, the committee trimmed sections of the bill.

INCORRECT   To lobby for prison reform, a lot of effort went into the television ads.

CORRECT   The lobby group put a lot of effort into the television ads advocating prison reform.

INCORRECT   Stunned, the television broadcast the defeated senator's concession speech.

CORRECT   The television broadcast the stunned senator's concession speech.

Note that, in the first two incorrect sentences above, the confusion is largely due to the use of *passive-voice* verbs: "the White House *was seen*," "sections of the bill *were trimmed*." Often, although not always, a dangling modifier results because the actor in the sentence—*we* in the first sentence, *the committee* in the second—is either distanced from the modifier or obliterated by the passive-voice verb. It is a good idea to avoid using the passive voice unless you have a specific reason for doing so.

One way to check for dangling modifiers is to examine all modifiers at the beginning or end of your sentences. Look especially for *to be* phrases or for words ending in *-ing* or *-ed* at the start of the modifier. Then see if the modified word is close enough to the phrase to be properly connected.

Parallelism

Series of two or more words, phrases, or clauses within a sentence should have the same grammatical structure, a situation called *parallelism*. Parallel structures can add power and balance to your writing by creating a strong rhetorical rhythm. Here is a famous example of parallelism from the Preamble to the U.S. Constitution (the capitalization follows that of the original eighteenth-century document; parallel structures have been italicized):

> We the People of the United States, in Order to *form a more perfect Union, Establish justice, insure Domestic Tranquility, provide for the common defense, promote the general Welfare*, and *secure the Blessings of Liberty to ourselves and our Posterity*, do *ordain* and *establish* this Constitution for the United States of America.

There are actually two series in this sentence: the first, composed of six phrases, each of which completes the infinitive phrase beginning with the word to [*to form, (to) Establish, (to) insure, (to) provide, (to) promote*, and *(to) secure*]; the second, consisting of two verbs (*ordain* and *establish*). These parallel series appeal to our love of balance and pattern, and give an authoritative tone to the sentence. The writer, we feel, has thought long and carefully about the matter at hand and has taken firm control of it.

Because we find a special satisfaction in balanced structures, we are more likely to remember ideas phrased in parallelisms than in less highly ordered language. For this reason, as well as for the sense of authority and control that they suggest, parallel structures are common in political utterances:

> *We hold these truths to be self-evident, that all men are created equal, that they are endowed by their Creator with certain unalienable rights, that among these are life, liberty, and the pursuit of happiness.*
>
> —The Declaration of Independence, 1776

> *Ask not what your country can do for you, ask what you can do for your country.*
>
> —John F. Kennedy, Inaugural Address, 1961

Faulty Parallelism   If the parallelism of a passage is not carefully maintained, the writing can seem sloppy and out of balance. Scan your writing to ensure that all series and lists have parallel structures. The following examples show how to correct faulty parallelism:

INCORRECT   The mayor promises not only *to reform* the police department but also *the giving of raises* to all city employees. (Connective structures such as *not only . . . but also* and *both . . . and* introduce elements that should be parallel.)

CORRECT   The mayor promises not only *to reform* the police department but also *to give* raises to all city employees.

INCORRECT   The cost *of doing nothing* is greater than the cost *to renovate* the apartment block.

CORRECT   The cost *of doing nothing* is greater than the cost *of renovating* the apartment block.

INCORRECT   Here are the items on the committee's agenda: (1) *to discuss* the new property tax; (2) *to revise* the wording of the city charter; (3) *a vote* on the city manager's request for an assistant.

CORRECT   Here are the items on the committee's agenda: (1) *to discuss* the new property tax; (2) *to revise* the wording of the city charter; (3) *to vote* on the city manager's request for an assistant.

Fused (Run-on) Sentences

A *fused sentence* is one in which two or more independent clauses (passages that can stand as complete sentences) have been run together without the aid of any suitable connecting word, phrase, or punctuation. There are several ways to correct a fused sentence:

INCORRECT   The council members were exhausted they had debated for two hours.

CORRECT   The council members were exhausted. They had debated for two hours. (The clauses have been separated into two sentences.)

CORRECT   The council members were exhausted; they had debated for two hours. (The clauses have been separated by a semicolon.)

CORRECT   The council members were exhausted, having debated for two hours. (The second clause has been rephrased as a dependent clause.)

INCORRECT   Our policy analysis impressed the committee it also convinced them to reconsider their action.

CORRECT   Our policy analysis impressed the committee and also convinced them to reconsider their action. (The second clause has been rephrased as part of the first clause.)

CORRECT   Our policy analysis impressed the committee, and it also convinced them to reconsider their action. (The clauses have been separated by a comma and a coordinating word.)

Although a fused sentence is easily noticeable to the reader, it can be maddeningly difficult for the writer to catch. Unpracticed writers tend to read through the fused spots, sometimes supplying the break that is usually heard when sentences are spoken. To check for fused sentences, read the independent clauses in your paper carefully, ensuring that there are adequate breaks among all of them.

Pronouns

Its* Versus *It's   Do not make the mistake of trying to form the possessive of *it* in the same way that you form the possessive of most nouns. The pronoun *it* shows possession by simply adding an *s*.

The prosecuting attorney argued the case on its merits.

The word *it's* is a contraction of *it is*:

It's the most expensive program ever launched by the council.

What makes the *its/it's* rule so confusing is that most nouns form the singular possessive by adding an apostrophe and an *s*:

The jury's verdict startled the crowd.

When proofreading, any time you come to the word *it's* substitute the phrase *it is* while you read. If the phrase makes sense, you have used the correct form. If you have used the word *it's*:

The newspaper article was misleading in *it's* analysis of the election.

then read it as *it is*:

The newspaper article was misleading in *it is* analysis of the election.

If the phrase makes no sense, substitute *its* for *it's*:

The newspaper article was misleading in *its* analysis of the election.

Vague Pronoun References   Pronouns are words that take the place of nouns or other pronouns that have already been mentioned in your writing. The most common pronouns include *he, she, it, they, them, those, which,* and *who.* You must make sure there is no confusion about the word to which each pronoun refers:

The mayor said that he would support our bill if the city council would also back it.

The word that the pronoun replaces is called its *antecedent.* To check the accuracy of your pronoun references, ask yourself, "To what does the pronoun refer?" Then answer the question carefully, ensuring that there is not more than one possible antecedent. Consider the following example:

Several special interest groups decided to defeat the new health care bill. This became the turning point of the government's reform campaign.

To what does the word *this* refer? The immediate answer seems to be the word *bill* at the end of the previous sentence. It is more likely that the writer was referring to the attempt of the special interest groups to defeat the bill, but there is no word in the first sentence that refers specifically to this action. The pronoun reference is thus unclear. One way to clarify the reference is to change the beginning of the second sentence:

Several special interest groups decided to defeat the new health care bill. Their attack on the bill became the turning point of the government's reform campaign.

Here is another example:

When John F. Kennedy appointed his brother Robert to the position of U.S. attorney general, he had little idea how widespread the corruption in the Teamsters Union was.

To whom does the word *he* refer? It is unclear whether the writer is referring to John or Robert Kennedy. One way to clarify the reference is simply to repeat the antecedent instead of using a pronoun:

When John F. Kennedy appointed his brother Robert to the position of U.S. attorney general, Robert had little idea how widespread the corruption in the Teamsters Union was.

Pronoun Agreement   A pronoun must agree with its antecedent in both gender and number, as the following examples demonstrate:

Mayor Smith said that he appreciated our club's support in the election.

One reporter asked the senator what she would do if the president offered her a cabinet post.

Having listened to our case, the judge decided to rule on it within the week.

Engineers working on the housing project said they were pleased with the renovation so far.

Certain words, however, can be troublesome antecedents because they may look like plural pronouns but are actually singular:

| anyone | each | either | everybody | everyone |
| nobody | no one | somebody | someone | |

A pronoun referring to one of these words in a sentence must be singular too:

INCORRECT   Each of the women in the support group brought their children.

CORRECT   Each of the women in the support group brought her children.

INCORRECT   Has everybody received their ballot?

CORRECT   Has everybody received his or her ballot? (The two gender-specific pronouns are used to avoid sexist language.)

CORRECT   Have all the delegates received their ballots? (The singular antecedent has been changed to a plural one.)

A Shift in Person

It is important to avoid shifting unnecessarily among first person (*I, we*), second person (*you*), and third person (*she, he, it, one, they*). Such shifts can cause confusion:

INCORRECT   Most people (third person) who run for office find that if you (second person) tell the truth during your campaign, you will gain the voters' respect.

CORRECT   Most people who run for office find that if they tell the truth during their campaigns, they will gain the voters' respect.

INCORRECT   One (first person) cannot tell whether they (third person) are suited for public office until they decide to run.

CORRECT   One cannot tell whether one is suited for public office until one decides to run.

Quotation Marks

It can be difficult to remember when to use quotation marks and where they go in relation to other punctuation. When faced with these questions, unpracticed writers often try to rely on logic rather than on a rule book, but the rules do not always seem to rely on logic. The only way to make sure of your use of quotation marks is to memorize the rules. Luckily, there are not many.

The Use of Quotation Marks   Use quotation marks to enclose direct quotations that are no longer than 100 words or eight typed lines:

In a stinging rebuke to those members of the committee who voted against the measure, Mayor Jenkins, in a press conference hastily called today, said, "In all my years in public office, never have I had to put up with so much shortsightedness, ingratitude, and cowardice. It makes me wonder how our coalition can survive much longer, or even if it should."

Longer quotations, called *block quotations*, are placed in a double-spaced indented block, without quotation marks:

Senator Malorie began her acceptance speech at the evening presentation with a rare moment of autobiographical candor:

> I was born and raised in Central Texas, in a time when nobody ever talked about how tough they were except those who, it turned out, weren't really very tough at all. At a young age I got to equating silence with toughness. My father was a very quiet man, my mother even quieter, and they were the toughest two people I ever knew. Where I got my love of talk I cannot say. But I think it was what led me into politics. I learned pretty fast that you could talk and talk and talk in an election or a debate and yet still be tough as nails.

Use single quotation marks to set off quotations within quotations:

"I intend," said the senator, "to use in my speech a line from Frost's poem, 'The Road Not Taken.'"

Note: When the quote occurs at the end of the sentence, both the single and double quotation marks are placed outside the period.

Use quotation marks to set off titles of the following:
Short poems (those not printed as a separate volume)
Short stories
Articles or essays
Songs
Episodes of television or radio shows

Use quotation marks to set off words or phrases used in special ways:

- To convey irony:

  The "liberal" administration has done nothing but cater to big business.

- To indicate a technical term:

  To "filibuster" is to delay legislation, usually through prolonged speechmaking. The last notable filibuster occurred just last week in the Senate. (Once the term is defined, it is not placed in quotation marks again.)

Quotation Marks in Relation to Other Punctuation Place commas and periods *inside* closing quotation marks:

"My fellow Americans," said the president, "there are tough times ahead of us."

Place colons and semicolons *outside* closing quotation marks:

In his speech on voting, the governor warned against "an encroaching indolence"; he was referring to the middle class.

There are several victims of the government's campaign to "Turn Back the Clock": the homeless, the elderly, the mentally impaired.

Use the context to determine whether to place question marks, exclamation points, and dashes inside or outside closing quotation marks. If the punctuation is part of the quotation, place it inside the quotation mark:

"When will Congress make up its mind?" asked the ambassador.

The demonstrators shouted, "Free the hostages!" and "No more slavery!"

If the punctuation is not part of the quotation, place it outside the quotation mark:

Which president said, "We have nothing to fear but fear itself"?

Note that although the quote is a complete sentence, you do not place a period after it. There can only be one piece of "terminal" punctuation (punctuation that ends a sentence).

Semicolons

The semicolon is a little-used punctuation mark that you should learn to incorporate into your writing strategy because of its many potential applications. For example, a semicolon can be used to correct a comma splice:

INCORRECT   The union representatives left the meeting in good spirits, their demands were met.

CORRECT   The union representatives left the meeting in good spirits; their demands were met.

INCORRECT   Several guests at the fundraiser had lost their invitations, however, we were able to seat them anyway.

CORRECT   Several guests at the fundraiser had lost their invitations; however, we were able to seat them anyway.

It is important to remember that conjunctive adverbs such as *however, therefore,* and *thus* are not coordinating words (such as *and, but, or, for, so, yet*) and cannot be used with a comma to link independent clauses. If the second independent clause begins with *however*, it must be preceded by either a period or a semicolon. As you can see from the second example above, connecting two independent clauses with a semicolon instead of a period preserves the suggestions that there is a strong relationship between the clauses.

Semicolons can also separate items in a series when the series items themselves contain commas:

The newspaper account of the rally stressed the march, which drew the biggest crowd; the mayor's speech, which drew tremendous applause; and the party in the park, which lasted for hours.

Avoid misusing semicolons. For example, use a comma, not a semicolon, to separate an independent clause from a dependent clause:

INCORRECT   Students from the college volunteered to answer phones during the pledge drive; which was set up to generate money for the new arts center.

CORRECT   Students from the college volunteered to answer phones during the pledge drive, which was set up to generate money for the new arts center.

Do not overuse semicolons. Although they are useful, too many semicolons in your writing can distract your readers' attention. Avoid monotony by using semicolons sparingly.

Sentence Fragments

A *fragment* is an incomplete part of a sentence that is punctuated and capitalized as if it were an entire sentence. It is an especially disruptive error because it obscures the connections that the words of a sentence must make to complete the reader's understanding.

Students sometimes write fragments because they are concerned that a sentence needs to be shortened. Remember that cutting the length of a sentence merely by adding a period somewhere often creates a fragment. When checking a writing for fragments, it is essential that you read each sentence carefully to determine whether it has (1) a complete subject and a verb; and (2) a subordinating word before the subject and verb, which makes the construction a subordinate clause rather than a complete sentence.

Some fragments lack a verb:

INCORRECT   The chairperson of our committee, receiving a letter from the mayor. (Watch out for words that look like verbs but are being used in another way.)

CORRECT   The chairperson of our committee received a letter from the mayor.

Some fragments lack a subject:

INCORRECT   Our study shows that there is broad support for improvement in the health-care system. And in the unemployment system.

CORRECT   Our study shows that there is broad support for improvement in the health care system and in the unemployment system.

Some fragments are subordinate clauses:

INCORRECT   After the latest edition of the newspaper came out. [This clause has the two major components of a complete sentence: a subject (*edition*) and a verb (*came*). Indeed, if the first word (*After*) were deleted, the clause would be a complete sentence. But that first word is a *subordinating word*, which prevents the following clause from standing on its own as a complete sentence. Watch out for this kind of construction. It is called a *subordinate clause*, and it is not a sentence.]

CORRECT   After the latest edition of the newspaper came out, the mayor's press secretary was overwhelmed with phone calls. (A common method of correcting a subordinate clause that has been punctuated as a complete sentence is to connect it to the complete sentence to which it is closest in meaning.)

INCORRECT   Several representatives asked for copies of the vice president's position paper. Which called for reform of the Environmental Protection Agency.

CORRECT   Several representatives asked for copies of the vice president's position paper, which called for reform of the Environmental Protection Agency.

Spelling

All of us have problems spelling certain words that we have not yet committed to memory. But most writers are not as bad at spelling as they believe they are. Usually, an individual finds only a handful of words troubling. It is important to be as sensitive as possible to your own particular spelling problems—and to keep a dictionary handy. There is no excuse for failing to check spelling.

What follows are a list of commonly confused words and a list of commonly misspelled words. Read through the lists, looking for those words that tend to give you trouble. If you have any questions, consult your dictionary.

Commonly Confused Words

accept/except
advice/advise
affect/effect
aisle/isle
allusion/illusion
an/and
angel/angle
ascent/assent
bare/bear
brake/break
breath/breathe
buy/by
capital/capitol
choose/chose
cite/sight/site
complement/compliment
conscience/conscious
corps/corpse
council/counsel
dairy/diary
descent/dissent
desert/dessert
device/devise
die/dye
dominant/dominate
elicit/illicit
eminent/immanent/
  imminent

envelop/envelope
every day/everyday
fair/fare
formally/formerly
forth/fourth
hear/here
heard/herd
hole/whole
human/humane
its/it's
know/no
later/latter
lay/lie
lead/led
lessen/lesson
loose/lose
may be/maybe
miner/minor
moral/morale
of/off
passed/past
patience/patients
peace/piece
personal/personnel
plain/plane
precede/proceed
presence/presents

principal/principle
quiet/quite
rain/reign/rein
raise/raze
reality/realty
respectfully/respectively
reverend/reverent
right/rite/write
road/rode
scene/seen
sense/since
stationary/stationery
straight/strait
taught/taut
than/then
their/there/they're
threw/through
too/to/two
track/tract
waist/waste
waive/wave
weak/week
weather/whether
were/where
which/witch
whose/who's
your/you're

Commonly Misspelled Words

acceptable
accessible
accommodate
accompany
accustomed
acquire
against
annihilate
apparent

arguing
argument
authentic
before
begin
beginning
believe
benefited
bulletin

business
cannot
category
committee
condemn
courteous
definitely
dependent
desperate

develop	mischievous	representative
different	missile	rhythm
disappear	necessary	ridiculous
disappoint	nevertheless	roommate
easily	no one	satellite
efficient	noticeable	scarcity
environment	noticing	scenery
equipped	nuisance	science
exceed	occasion	secede
exercise	occasionally	secession
existence	occurred	secretary
experience	occurrences	senseless
fascinate	omission	separate
finally	omit	sergeant
foresee	opinion	shining
forty	opponent	significant
fulfill	parallel	sincerely
gauge	parole	skiing
guaranteed	peaceable	stubbornness
guard	performance	studying
harass	pertain	succeed
hero	practical	success
heroes	preparation	successfully
humorous	probably	susceptible
hurried	process	suspicious
hurriedly	professor	technical
hypocrite	prominent	temporary
ideally	pronunciation	tendency
immediately	psychology	therefore
immense	publicly	tragedy
incredible	pursue	truly
innocuous	pursuing	tyranny
intercede	questionnaire	unanimous
interrupt	realize	unconscious
irrelevant	receipt	undoubtedly
irresistible	received	until
irritate	recession	vacuum
knowledge	recommend	valuable
license	referring	various
likelihood	religious	vegetable
maintenance	remembrance	visible
manageable	reminisce	without
meanness	repetition	women

Read & Write 3.2   Proofread for the President

It's January 1941, and you're on the staff of the thirty-second President of the United States. Franklin Roosevelt is about to make one of the most important speeches of his presidency, and it's your job to proofread the text before it can be printed for the world to read. There are 15 errors embedded in the copy of the speech that appears below this paragraph. As you locate the errors, circle them with a pencil. When you have finished, check the error key on the following page. Below the error key you'll find a copy of this selection from Roosevelt's speech as it was originally published without the embedded errors.

A Selection from "Franklin D. Roosevelts' 'Four Freedoms Speech' Annual Message to Congress on the State of the Union," January 6, 1941.

In the future days, which we seek to make secure, we look forward to a world founded upon four essential human freedoms.

The first is freedom of speach and expression—everywhere in the world.

The second is freedom of every person to worship God in their own way—everywhere in the world.

The third is freedom from want—which translated into world terms, means economic understandings which will secure to every nation a healthy peacetime life for it's inhabitants everywhere in the world.

The fourth is freedom from fear—which, translated into world terms, means a world-wide reduction of armaments to such a point and in such a thorough fashion that no nation will be in a position to commit an act of physical aggression against any neighbor—anywhere in the world.

That is no vision of a distant milennium, it is a definite basis for a kind of world attainable in our own time and generation. That kind of world is the very antithesis of the so-called new order of tyranny which the dictator's seek to create with the crash of a bomb.

To that new order we oppose the greater conception—the moral order, a good society is able to face schemes of world domination and foreign revolutions alike without fear.

Since the beginning of our American history; we have been engaged in change—in a perpetual peaceful revolution—a revolution which goes on steady, quietly adjusting itself to changing conditions—without the concentration camp or the quick-lime in the ditch. The world order which we seek is the cooperation of free countries. Working together in a friendly, civilized society.

This nation has placed it's destiny in the hands and heads and hearts of its millions of free men and women; and its faith in freedom under the guidance of God. Freedom means the supremacy of human rights everywhere, our support goes to those who struggle to gain those rights or keep them. Our strength is our unity of purpose. To that high concept there can be no end save victory.

Key to "Find the Errors"

The letters, words, and punctuation in **bold font** and underlined below indicate locations of grammar, spelling, and other errors. You can also check the original, error-free copy to find the correct forms of grammar and usage.

A Selection from "Franklin D. Roosevelt**s'** 'Four Freedoms Speech' Annual Message to Congress on the State of the Union**"**, January 6, 1941.

In the future days, which we seek to make secure, we look forward to a world founded upon four essential human freedoms.

The first is freedom of spe**a**ch and expression—everywhere in the world.

The second is freedom of every person to worship God in **their** own way—everywhere in the world. **[Note: Nowadays, it is becoming acceptable, in certain types of writing, to allow the plural "their" to stand in place of "his," which is considered sexist. Another acceptable alternative is "his or her." Think about what pronoun to use, when you come to such a circumstance.]**

The third is freedom from want—whic**h** translated into world terms, means economic understandings which will secure to every nation a healthy peacetime life for **it's** inhabitants everywhere in the world.

The fourth is freedom from fear—which, translated into world terms, means a worldwide reduction of armaments to such a point and in such a thorough fashion that no nation will be in a position to commit an act of physical aggression against any neighbor—anywhere in the world.

That is no vision of a distant mi**le**nnium**, it** is a definite basis for a kind of world attainable in our own time and generation. That kind of world is the very antithesis of the so-called new order of tyranny which the dictator**'s** seek to create with the crash of a bomb.

To that new order we oppose the greater conception—the moral order**, a** good society is able to face schemes of world domination and foreign revolutions alike without fear.

Since the beginning of our American history**;** we have been engaged in change—in a perpetual peaceful revolution—a revolution which goes on stead**y**, quietly adjusting itself to changing conditions—without the concentration camp or the quick-lime in the ditch. The world order which we seek is the cooperation of free countries**. W**orking together in a friendly, civilized society.

This nation has placed **it's** destiny in the hands and heads and hearts of its millions of free men and women; and its faith in freedom under the guidance of God. Freedom means the supremacy of human rights everywhere**, o**ur support goes to those who struggle to gain those rights or keep them. Our strength is our unity of purpose. To that high concept there can be no end save victory.

Original Four Freedoms Speech

A Selection from "Franklin D. Roosevelt's 'Four Freedoms Speech' Annual Message to Congress on the State of the Union," January 6, 1941.

In the future days, which we seek to make secure, we look forward to a world founded upon four essential human freedoms.

The first is freedom of speech and expression—everywhere in the world.

The second is freedom of every person to worship God in his own way—everywhere in the world.

The third is freedom from want—which, translated into world terms, means economic understandings which will secure to every nation a healthy peacetime life for its inhabitants everywhere in the world.

The fourth is freedom from fear—which, translated into world terms, means a world-wide reduction of armaments to such a point and in such a thorough fashion that no nation will be in a position to commit an act of physical aggression against any neighbor—anywhere in the world.

That is no vision of a distant millennium. It is a definite basis for a kind of world attainable in our own time and generation. That kind of world is the very antithesis of the so-called new order of tyranny which the dictators seek to create with the crash of a bomb.

To that new order we oppose the greater conception—the moral order. A good society is able to face schemes of world domination and foreign revolutions alike without fear.

Since the beginning of our American history, we have been engaged in change—in a perpetual peaceful revolution—a revolution which goes on steadily, quietly adjusting itself to changing conditions—without the concentration camp or the quick-lime in the ditch. The world order which we seek is the cooperation of free countries, working together in a friendly, civilized society.

This nation has placed its destiny in the hands and heads and hearts of its millions of free men and women; and its faith in freedom under the guidance of God. Freedom means the supremacy of human rights everywhere. Our support goes to those who struggle to gain those rights or keep them. Our strength is our unity of purpose. To that high concept there can be no end save victory.[3]

---

[3] Franklin D. Roosevelt. 1941. "'Four Freedoms Speech': Annual Message to Congress on the State of the Union." Franklin D. Roosevelt Presidential Library and Museum. January 6. http://www.fdrlibrary .marist.edu/pdfs/fftext.pd (March 8, 2016).

3.3 FORMAT YOUR PAPER AND ITS CONTENTS PROFESSIONALLY

Your format makes your paper's first impression. Justly or not, accurately or not, it announces your professional competence—or the lack of it. A well-executed format implies that your paper is worth reading. More importantly, however, a proper format brings information to your readers in a familiar form that has the effect of setting their minds at ease. Your paper's format should therefore impress your readers with your academic competence as a political scientist by following accepted professional standards. Like the style and clarity of your writing, your format communicates messages that are often more readily and profoundly received than the content of the document itself.

The formats described in this chapter are in conformance with generally accepted standards in the discipline of political science, including instructions for the following elements:

General page formats	Table of contents
Title page	Reference page
Abstract	List of tables and figures
Executive summary	Text
Outline page	Appendices

Except for special instructions from your instructor, follow the directions in this manual exactly.

General Page Formats

Political science assignments should be printed on 8-by-11-inch premium white bond paper, 20 pound or heavier. Do not use any other size or color except to comply with special instructions from your instructor, and do not use off-white or poor-quality (draft) paper. Political science that is worth the time to write and read is worth good paper.

Always submit to your instructor an original typed or computer-printed manuscript. Do not submit a photocopy! Always make a second paper copy and back up your electronic copy for your own files in case the original is lost.

Margins except in theses and dissertations, should be one inch on all sides of the paper. Unless otherwise instructed, all papers should be double-spaced in a 12-point word-processing font or typewriter pica type. Typewriter elite type may be used if another font is not available. Select a font that is plain and easy to read, such as Helvetica, Courier, Garamond, or Times Roman. Do not use script, stylized, or elaborate fonts.

Page numbers should appear in the upper right-hand corner of each page, starting immediately after the title page. No page number should appear on the title page or on the first page of the text. Page numbers should appear one inch from the right side and one-half inch from the top of the page. They should proceed consecutively beginning with the title page (although the first number is not actually printed on the title page). You may use lowercase roman numerals (i, ii, iii, iv, v, vi, vii, viii, ix, x, and so on) for the pages, such as the title page, table of contents, and table of figures, that precede the first page of text, but if you use them, the numbers must be placed at the center of the bottom of the page.

Ask your instructor about bindings. In the absence of further directions, do not bind your paper or enclose it within a plastic cover sheet. Place one staple in the upper left-hand corner, or use a paper clip at the top of the paper. Note that a paper to be submitted to a journal for publication should not be clipped, stapled, or bound in any form.

Title Page

The following information will be centered on the title page:

Title of the paper

Name of writer

Course name, section number, and instructor

College or university

Date

Accomplishments of the Obama Presidency

by

Nicole Ashley Linscheid

The American Presidency

POL213

Dr. Ebenezer Brown

Bay of Fundy University

January 1, 2017

As the sample title page above shows, the title should clearly describe the problem addressed in the paper. If the paper discusses juvenile recidivism in Albemarle County jails, for example, the title "Recidivism in the Albemarle County Criminal Justice System" is professional, clear, and helpful to the reader. "Albemarle County," "Juvenile Justice," or "County Jails" are all too vague to be effective. Also, the title should not be "cute." A cute title may attract attention for a play on Broadway, but it will detract from the credibility of a paper in political science. "Inadequate Solid Waste Disposal Facilities in Denver" is professional. "Down in the Dumps" is not.

In addition, title pages for position papers and policy analysis papers must include the name, title, and organization of the public official who has the authority and responsibility to implement the recommendation of your paper. The person to whom you address the paper should have the responsibility and the authority to make the necessary decision in your paper. The "address" should include the person's name, title, and organization, as shown in the example of a title page for a position paper that follows. To identify the appropriate official, first carefully define the problem and the best solution. Then ascertain the person, or persons, who have the authority to solve the problem. If you recommend installation of a traffic signal at a particular intersection, for example, find out who makes the decisions regarding such actions in your community. It may be the public safety director, a transportation planning commission, or a town council.

Oak City Police Department Personnel Policy Revisions

submitted to

Farley Z. Simmons

Director of Personnel

Police Department

Oak City, Arkansas

by

Luke Tyler Linscheid

American National Government

GOV 1001

Dr. Hickory Stonecipher

Randolph Scott College

January 21, 2016

Abstract

An abstract is a brief summary of a paper written primarily to allow potential readers to see if the paper contains information of sufficient interest for them to read. People conducting research want specific kinds of information, and they often read dozens of abstracts looking for papers that contain relevant data. Abstracts have the designation "Abstract" centered at the top of the page. Next is the title, also centered, followed by a paragraph that precisely states the paper's topic, research and analysis methods, and results, and conclusions. The abstract should be written in one paragraph of no more than 150 words. Remember, an abstract is not an introduction; instead, it is a summary, as demonstrated in the sample below.

Bertrand Russell's View of Mysticism

This paper reviews Bertrand Russell's writings on religion, mysticism, and science, and defines his perspective of the contribution of mysticism to scientific knowledge. Russell drew a sharp distinction between what he considered to be (1) the essence of religion, and (2) dogma or assertions attached to religion by theologians and religious leaders. Although some of his writings, including *Why I Am Not a Christian* appear hostile to all aspects of religion, Russell actually asserts that religion, freed from doctrinal encumbrances, not only fulfills certain psychological needs but evokes many of the most beneficial human impulses. He believes that religious mysticism generates an intellectual disinterestedness that may be useful to science, but that it is not a source of a special type of knowledge beyond investigation by science.

Executive Summary

An executive summary, like an abstract, summarizes the content of a paper but does so in more detail. A sample executive summary is given below. Although abstracts are read by people doing research, executive summaries are more likely to be read by people who need some or all of the information in the paper to make a decision. Many people, however, will read the executive summary to fix clearly in their minds the organization and results of a paper before reading the paper itself.

Executive Summary

Municipal parks in Springfield are deteriorating because of inadequate maintenance, and one park in particular, Oak Ridge Community Park, needs immediate attention. The problem is that parking, picnic, and restroom facilities at Oak Ridge Community Park have deteriorated because of normal wear, adverse weather, and vandalism, and are inadequate to meet public demand. The park was established as a public recreation "Class B" facility in 1967. Only one major renovation has occurred: in the summer of 1987 general building repair was done, and new swing sets were installed. The Park Department estimates that 10,000 square feet of new parking space, 14 items of playground equipment, 17 new picnic tables, and repairs on current facilities would cost about $43,700.

Three possible solutions have been given extensive consideration in this paper. One option is to do nothing. Area residents will use the area less as deterioration continues, but no immediate outlay of public funds will be necessary. The first alternative solution is to make all repairs immediately. Area residents will enjoy immediate and increased use of facilities. Taxpayers have turned down the last three tax increase requests. Revenue bonds may be acceptable to a total of $20,000, according to the City Manager, but no more than $5,000 per year is available from general city revenues.

A second alternative is to make repairs, according to a priority list, over a five-year period, using a combination of general city revenues and a $20,000 first-year bond issue that will require City Council and voter approval. Residents will enjoy the most needed improvements immediately.

The recommendation of this report is that the second alternative be adopted by the City Council. The City Council should, during its May 15 meeting, (1) adopt a resolution of intent to commit $5,000 per year for five years from the general revenue fund, dedicated to this purpose and (2) approve for submission to public vote in the November 2007 election a $20,000 bond issue.

Outline Page

An outline page is a specific type of executive summary. Most often found in position papers and policy analysis papers, an outline page provides more information about the organization of the paper than does an executive summary. The outline shows clearly the sections in the paper and the information in each. An outline page is an asset because it allows busy decision-makers to understand the entire content of a paper without reading it all or to refer quickly to a specific part for more information. Position papers and policy analysis papers are written for people in positions of authority who normally need to make a variety of decisions in a short period. Outline pages reduce the amount of time these people need to understand a policy problem, the alternative solutions, and the author's preferred solution.

Outline pages sequentially list the complete topic sentences of the major paragraphs of a paper, in outline form. In a position paper, for example, you will be stating a problem, defining possible solutions, and then recommending the best solution. These three steps will be the major headings in your outline. (See Chapter 1 for instructions on writing an outline.) Wait until you have completed the paper before writing the outline page. Take the topic sentences from the leading (most important) paragraph in each section of your paper and place them in the appropriate places in your outline. A sample outline page is given on pages 69–70.

Table of Contents

A table of contents does not provide as much information as an outline, but it does include the titles of the major divisions and subdivisions of a paper. Tables of contents are not normally required in student papers or papers presented at professional meetings but may be included. They are normally required, however, in books, theses, and dissertations. The table of contents should consist of the chapter or main section titles, and the headings used in the text, with one additional level of titles, along with their page numbers, as the sample on page 70 demonstrates.

Text

Ask your instructor for the number of pages required for the paper you are writing. The text should follow the directions explained in Chapter 1 of this manual and should conform to the format shown below.

Sample Passage of Text The problem is that parking, picnic, and restroom facilities at Oak Ridge Community Park have deteriorated because of normal wear, adverse weather, and vandalism, and are of inadequate quantity to meet public demand. The paved parking lot has crumbled and eroded. As many as 200 cars park on the lawn during major holidays. Only one of the five swing sets is in safe operating condition. Each set accommodates four children, but during weekends and holidays many children wait turns for the available sets. Spray paint vandalism has marred the rest room facilities, which are inadequate to meet major holiday demands.

The Department of Parks and Recreation established the park as a public recreation Class B facility in 1993. In the summer of 2015, the department conducted general building repair and installed new steel swing sets. Only minimal annual maintenance has occurred since that time.

The department estimates that 10,000 square feet of new parking lot space, 14 items of playground equipment, 17 new picnic tables, and repairs on current facilities would cost about $43,700 (Department of Parks and Recreation 2005). Parking lot improvements include a new surface of coarse gravel on the old paved lot and expansion of the new paved lot by 10,000 square feet. The State Engineering Office estimates the cost of parking lot improvements to be $16,200.

Chapter Headings

Your paper should include no more than three levels of headings:

1. *Primary,* which should be centered, in boldface, and using headline-style capitalization (each word except articles, prepositions, and conjunctions capitalized)
2. *Secondary* which begins at the left margin, in boldface, and also in headline style capitalization
3. *Tertiary* which also begins at the left margin and uses headline style capitalization but is underlined instead of boldfaced and followed immediately by a period and the first line of the succeeding text.

The following illustration shows the proper use of chapter headings:

The House of Representatives (Primary Heading)

Impeachment Procedures of the House (Secondary Heading)

<u>Rules for debate</u>. The first rule states
that Congress . . . (Tertiary Heading)

Reference Page

The format for references is discussed in detail in the source citation information that is contained in section 3.4 of this chapter.

Tables, Illustrations, Figures, and Appendices

If your paper includes tables, illustrations, or figures, include a page after the Table of Contents listing each of them, under the name for it used in the paper's text. List the items in the order in which they appear in the paper, along with their page numbers. You may list tables, illustrations, and figures together under the title "Figures" (and call them all "Figures" in the text), or if you have more than a half page of entries, you may have separate lists for tables, illustrations, and figures (and title them accordingly in the text). An example of the format for such lists is given on pages 70–71.

Outline of Contents

I. The problem is that parking, picnic, and restroom facilities at Oak Ridge Community Park have deteriorated because of normal wear, adverse weather, and vandalism, and are inadequate to meet public demand.
    A. Only one major renovation has occurred since 1967, when the park was opened.
    B. The Park Department estimates that 10,000 square feet of new parking space, 14 items of playground equipment, 17 new picnic tables, and repairs on current facilities would cost about $43,700.

II. The municipal government has given extensive consideration to three possible solutions.

    A. One option is to do nothing. Area residents will use the area less as deterioration continues, but no immediate outlay of public funds will be necessary.

    B. The first alternative solution is to make all repairs immediately. Area residents will enjoy immediate and increased use of facilities. $43,700 in funds will be needed. Sources include: (1) Community Development Block Grant funds, (2) increased property taxes, (3) revenue bonds, and (4) general city revenues.

    C. A second alternative is to make repairs according to a priority list over a five-year period, using a combination of general city revenues and a $20,000 first-year bond issue. Residents will enjoy the most needed improvements immediately. The bond issue will require City Council and voter approval.

III. The recommendation of this report is that alternative C be adopted by the City Council. The benefit/cost analysis demonstrates that residents will be satisfied if basic improvements are made immediately. The City Council should, during its May 15 meeting, (1) adopt a resolution of intent to commit $5,000 per year for five years from the general revenue fund, dedicated to this purpose; and (2) approve for submission to public vote in the November 2007 election a $20,000 bond issue.

Contents

Figures

Tables

Tables are used in the text to show relationships among data, to help the reader come to a conclusion or understand a certain point. Tables that show simple results or "raw" data should be placed in an appendix. They should not reiterate the content of the text. They should say something new, and they should stand on their own. In other words, the reader should be able to understand the table without reading the text. The columns and rows in the table must be labeled clearly. Each word in the title (except articles, prepositions, and conjunctions) should be capitalized. The source of the information should be shown immediately below the table, not in a footnote or endnote. A sample table is shown below.

TABLE 1

Projections of the Total Population of Selected States, 2015–2035 (in thousands)

State	2015	2025	2030	2035
Alabama	4,451	4,631	4,956	5,224
Illinois	12,051	12,266	12,808	13,440
Maine	1,259	1,285	1,362	1,423
New Mexico	1,860	2,016	2,300	2,612
Oklahoma	3,373	3,491	3,789	4,057
Tennessee	5,657	5,966	6,365	6,665
Virginia	6,997	7,324	7,921	8,466

Source: U.S. Census Bureau.

Illustrations and Figures

Illustrations are not normally inserted in the text of a political science paper, even in an appendix, unless they are necessary to explain the content. If illustrations are necessary, do not paste or tape photocopies of photographs or similar materials to the text or the appendix. Instead, photocopy each one on a separate sheet of paper and center it, along with its typed title, within the normal margins of the paper. The format of illustration titles should be the same as that for tables and figures.

Figures in the form of charts and graphs may be very helpful in presenting certain types of information.

Appendices

Appendices are reference materials provided for the convenience of the reader at the back of the paper, after the text. They provide information that supplements important facts in the text, which may include maps, charts, tables, and selected documents. Do not place materials that are merely interesting or decorative in your appendix.

Use only items that will answer questions raised by the text or are necessary to explain the text. Follow the guidelines for formats of tables, illustrations, and figures when adding material in an appendix. At the top center of the page, label your first appendix as "Appendix A," your second appendix as "Appendix B," and so on. Do not append an entire government report, journal article, or other publication, but only the portions of such documents that are necessary to support your paper. The source of the information should always be evident on the appended pages.

Read & Write 3.3 Explain the Data in This Table

The following table presents an abridged set of data derived from *Statistics Japan*, the Statistics Bureau, Ministry of Internal Affairs and Communications, nation of Japan, through this web portal: http://www.stat.go.jp/english/info/guide/2014guide.htm.[4]

Population of Selected Cities of Japan, 1940–1947

City	Population 1940	Population 1947	Change 1940–1947
Sendai-shi	223,630	293,816	70,186
Yamaguchi-shi	34,579	97,975	63,396
Akita-shi	61,791	116,300	54,509
Niigata-shi	150,903	204,477	53,574
Sapporo-shi	206,103	259,602	53,499
Kumamoto-shi	194,139	245,841	51,702
Saitama-shi	59,671	106,176	46,505
Kanazawa-shi	186,297	231,441	45,144
Kochi-shi	106,644	147,120	40,476
Fukushima-shi	48,287	86,763	38,476
Matsuyama-shi	117,534	147,967	30,433
Chiba-shi	92,061	122,006	29,945
Yamagata-shi	69,184	98,632	29,448
Morioka-shi	79,478	107,096	27,618
Miyazaki-shi	66,497	92,144	25,647
Nara-shi	57,273	82,399	25,126
Fukuoka-shi	306,763	328,548	21,785
Nagano-shi	76,861	94,993	18,132
Saga-shi	50,406	64,978	14,572
Otsu-shi	67,532	81,426	13,894
Toyama-shi	127,859	137,818	9,959
Oita-shi	76,985	86,570	9,585
Utsunomiya-shi	87,868	97,075	9,207
Tottori-shi	49,261	57,218	7,957

[4] The data in the table is a partial compilation of data from "Population of Cities (1920–2005)," in "Historical Statistics of Japan: Chapter 2 Populations and Households." *Statistics Japan.* http://www.stat.go.jp/english/data/chouki/02.htm (March 8, 2016).

Matsue-shi	55,506	62,136	6,630
Maebashi-shi	86,997	90,432	3,435
Kofu-shi	102,419	104,993	2,574
Tsu-shi	68,625	68,662	37
Mito-shi	66,293	61,416	−4,877
Gifu-shi	172,340	166,995	−5,345
Shizuoka-shi	212,198	205,737	−6,461
Aomori-shi	99,065	90,828	−8,237
Takamatsu-shi	111,207	101,403	−9,804
Tokushima-shi	119,581	103,320	−16,261
Fukui-shi	94,595	77,320	−17,275
Kagoshima-shi	190,257	170,416	−19,841
Okayama-shi	163,552	140,631	−22,921
Wakayama-shi	195,203	171,800	−23,403
Kawasaki-shi	300,777	252,923	−47,854
Nagasaki-shi	252,630	198,642	−53,988
Kyoto-shi	1,089,726	999,660	−90,066
Hiroshima-shi	343,968	224,100	−119,868
Yokohama-shi	968,091	814,379	−153,712
Kobe-shi	967,234	607,079	−360,155
Nagoya-shi	1,328,084	853,085	−474,999
Osaka-shi	3,252,340	1,559,310	−1,693,030
Ku-area	6,778,804	4,177,548	−2,601,256
Total Change			**−4,925,902**

Read & Write: Explain the Data in This Table

Write a short essay in which you clearly explain

1) What this table tells you, and
2) Likely reasons for the population changes

3.4 CITE YOUR SOURCES PROPERLY IN APSA STYLE

One of your most important jobs as a research writer is to document your use of source material carefully and clearly. Failure to do so causes confusion in your reader, damages the effectiveness of your paper, and perhaps makes you vulnerable to a charge of plagiarism. Proper documentation is more than just good form. It is a powerful indicator of your own commitment to scholarship and the sense of authority that you bring to your writing. Good documentation demonstrates your expertise as a researcher and increases your reader's trust in you and your work.

Unfortunately, as anybody who has ever written a research paper knows, getting the documentation right can be a frustrating, confusing job, especially for the writer who is not familiar with the documentation system he or she is trying to use. Accurately positioning each element of a single reference citation can require a lot of time, looking through the style manual. Even before you begin to work on the specific citations for your paper, there are important questions of style and format to answer.

What to Document

You must always credit direct quotes, as well as certain kinds of paraphrased material. Information that is basic—important dates, universally acknowledged facts, or commonly held opinions—need not be cited. Information that is not widely known, however, should receive documentation. This type of material includes ideas, evaluations, critiques, and descriptions original to your source.

What if you are unsure whether a certain fact is an academic "given" or sufficiently unique to warrant a citation? You are, after all, probably a newcomer to the field in which you are conducting your research. If in doubt, *supply the documentation*. It is better to overdocument than to fail to do justice to a source.

The Choice of Style   There are several documentation styles available, each designed to meet the needs of researchers in particular fields. The reference systems approved by the *Modern Language Association* (MLA) and the *American Psychological Association* (APA) are often used in the humanities and the social sciences and could serve the needs of the political science writer, but this manual offers the style most likely to be appropriate for political science papers: the APSA Author-Date System.

The American Political Science Association (APSA) has adopted a modification of the style elaborated in the *Chicago Manual of Style* (*CMS*), perhaps the most universally approved of all documentation authorities. One of the advantages of using the APSA style, which is outlined in an APSA pamphlet entitled *Style Manual for Political Science* (1993, revised August 2006), is that it is designed to guide the professional political scientist in preparing a manuscript for submission to the *American Political Science Review* the journal of the American Political Science Association (APSA) and the most influential political science journal in publication. Learning the APSA documentation style, then, offers you as a student another crucial connection to the world of the political scientist. For this reason, there are models below of formats described in the APSA *Style Manual* in addition to other models found only in the *CMS*.

Note: The APSA *Style Manual* for Political Science covers only certain basic reference and bibliographical models. For other models and more detailed suggestions about referencing format, the 2006 revised edition of the APSA *Style Manual* refers readers to the "latest edition" of the *CMS*, which at the time was the fifteenth edition, published in 2003. The formats below are based on APSA guidelines, whenever such guidelines are available. Otherwise, the formats follow models taken from the fifteenth (2003) edition of the *CMS*, and, when necessary, from the more exhaustive fourteenth (1993) edition. Models based on the *CMS* are identified as such, with section numbers for relevant passages in the *CMS* given in parentheses, preceded by the number of the edition. For example, *CMS* 14 (15.367) refers to the 367th section of Chapter 15 in the fourteenth edition of the *Chicago Manual of Style*, a section that shows how to cite source material taken from the U.S. Constitution.

The Importance of Consistency

The most important rule regarding documentation of your work is to *be consistent.* Sloppy referencing undermines your reader's trust and does a disservice to the writers whose work you are incorporating into your own argument. And from a purely practical standpoint, inconsistent referencing can severely damage your grade.

Using the Style Manual

Read through the guidelines in the following pages before trying to use them to structure your notes. Unpracticed student researchers tend to ignore this section of the style manual until the moment the first note has to be worked out, and then they skim through the examples looking for the one that perfectly corresponds to the immediate case in hand. But most style manuals do not include every possible documentation model, so the writer must piece together a coherent reference out of elements from several examples. Reading through all the examples before using them can give you a feel for the placement of information in citations for different kinds of sources—such as magazine articles, book chapters, government documents, and electronic texts—as well as for how the referencing system works in general.

When you use the author-date system of citation, you place a note, in parentheses, within the text, following the passage where your source material appears. In order not to distract the reader from the argument, make the reference as brief as possible, containing just enough information to refer the reader to the full citation in the reference list following the text. Usually, the minimum information necessary is the author's last name, the date of the publication of the source, and if you are referring to a specific passage instead of the entire work, the page number(s) of the passage you are using. As indicated by the models below, this information can be given in a number of ways.

Models of full citations that correspond to these parenthetical text references are given in the subsection that begins on page 80. A sample bibliography appears on page 87.

The Author-Date System: Citations

Author, Date, and Page in Parentheses

Several critics found the senator's remarks to be, in the words of one, "hopelessly off the mark and dangerously incendiary" (Northrup 2015, 28).

Note that, when it appears at the end of a sentence, the parenthetical reference is placed inside the period.

Page and Chapter in Notes   A text citation may refer to an entire article, in which case you need not include page numbers, since they are given in the reference list at the end of the paper. However, you will sometimes need to cite specific page and chapter numbers, which follow the date and are preceded by a comma and, in the case of a chapter, the abbreviation *chap.* Note that you do not use the abbreviation *p.* or *pp.* when referring to page numbers.

Page Numbers

Randalson (2016, 84–86) provides a brief but coherent description of the bill's evolution.

Chapter Numbers

Collins (2014, chaps. 9, 10) discusses at length the structure of the Roman senate.

Author and Date in Text   The following example focuses the reader's attention on Northrup's article:

For a highly critical review of the senator's performance, see Northrup 2015 (28).

Author in the Text, Date and Page in Parentheses   Here the emphasis is on the author, for only Northrup's name appears within the grammar of the sentence:

Northrup (2015, 28) called the senator's remarks "hopelessly off the mark and dangerously incendiary."

Source with Two Authors

The administration's efforts at reforming the education system are drawing more praise than condemnation (Younger and Petty 2016).

Notice that the names are not necessarily arranged alphabetically. Use the order that the authors themselves sanctioned on the title page of the book or article.

Source with Three Authors

Most of the farmers in the region support the cooperative's new pricing plan (Moore, Macrory, and Traylor 2016, 132).

Source with Four or More Authors   Place the Latin phrase *et al.*, meaning "and others," after the name of the first author. Note that the phrase appears in roman type, not italics, and is followed by a period:

According to Herring et al. (2004, 42), five builders backed out of the project due to doubts about the local economy.

More Than One Source   Note that the references are arranged alphabetically:

Several commentators have supported the council's decision to expand the ruling (Barrere 2014; Grady 2014; Payne 2014).

Two Authors with the Same Last Name   Use a first initial to differentiate two authors with the same last name:

Research suggests that few taxpayers will appreciate the new budget cuts (B. Grady 2013; L. Grady 2012).

Two Works by the Same Author   If two references by the same author appear in the same note, place a comma between the publication dates:

George (2014, 2007) argues for sweeping tax reform on the national level.

If the two works were published in the same year, differentiate them by adding lowercase letters to the publication dates. Be sure to add the letters to the reference list, too:

The commission's last five annual reports pointed out the same weaknesses in the structure of the city government (Estrada 2009a, 2009b).

Reprints   It is sometimes significant to note the date when an important text was first published, even if you are using a reprint of that work. In this case, the date of the first printing appears in brackets before the date of the reprint:

During that period, there were three advertising campaign strategies that were deemed potentially useful to political campaigners (Adams [1990] 2010, 12).

Classic Texts   You may use the author-date system to structure notes for classic texts, such as the Bible, standard translations of ancient Greek works, or numbers of *The Federalist Papers* by citing the date and page numbers of the edition you are using. Or you may refer to these texts by using the systems by which they are subdivided. Since all editions of a classic text employ the same standard subdivisions, this reference method has the advantage of allowing your reader to find the citation in any published version of the text. For example, you may cite a biblical passage by referring to the particular book, chapter, and verse, all in roman type, with the translation given after the verse number. Titles of books of the Bible should be abbreviated:

"But the path of the just is as the shining light, that shineth more and more unto the perfect day" (Prov. 4:18 King James Version).

The Federalist Papers may be cited by their standard numbers:

Madison addresses the problem of factions in a republic (*Federalist* 10).

Public Documents   According to the 2006 revised edition of the APSA *Style Manual* you may cite public documents using the standard author-date technique. The *Style Manual* recommends consulting the fifteenth edition of *CMS* (17.290–356) and Chapter 12 of the latest edition of Kate L. Turabian's *Manual for Writers of Term Papers, Theses, and Dissertations* (Univ. of Chicago Press, 2004) for more detailed information. While the 2006 APSA *Style Manual* provides models of reference list entries for a few types of government documents, neither it nor the fifteenth edition of *CMS* (2003) offers corresponding examples of parenthetical text citations. The following models are based, therefore, on information taken from the APSA *Style Manual* and from Chapters 15 and 16 of the fourteenth edition of *CMS* (1993).

Congressional Journals   Parenthetical text references to either the *Senate Journal* or the *House Journal* start with the journal title in place of the author, the session year, and, if applicable, the page:

Senator Jones endorsed the proposal as reworded by Senator Edward's committee (*U.S. Senate Journal* 2006, 24).

Congressional Debates   Congressional debates are printed in the daily issues of the *Congressional Record*, which are bound biweekly and then collected and bound at the end of the session. Whenever possible, you should consult the bound yearly collection instead of the biweekly compilations. Your parenthetical reference should begin with the title *Congressional Record* (or *Cong. Rec.*) in place of the author's name and include the year of the congressional session, the volume and part of the *Congressional Record*, and finally the page:

Rep. Valentine and Rep. Beechnut addressed the question of funding for secondary education (*Cong. Rec.* 1930, 72, pt. 8: 9012).

Congressional Reports and Documents   References to these reports and documents, which are numbered sequentially in one- or two-year periods, include the name of the body generating the material, the year, and the page:

Rep. Slavin promised from the floor to answer the charges against him within the next week (U.S. Congress. House 2006, 12–13).

> **Note:** You may omit the *U.S.*, if it is clear from the context that you are referring to the United States. Whichever form you use, be sure to use it consistently, in both the notes and the reference list.

Bills and Resolutions   Bills and resolutions from either house of Congress are usually cited by title within the text, where the date and resolution number are also sometimes given. Be sure to italicize the title:

The *Visa Formalization Act of 2005* prohibits consular officials from rejecting visa requests out of hand (U.S. Congress. Senate 2005).

Statutes

Citing to the Statutes at Large   Bills or resolutions that have become law in a particular year are published in the annual volume of the *United States* Statutes at Large (in legal abbreviation, *Stat.*) before being added to the *United States Code.* According to *CMS* 15 (17.310), you may cite laws to either the *Statutes* or the *U.S. Code* or both:

But FEMA's authority for carrying out the national flood insurance program was increased the next month (*National Flood Insurance Program Enhanced Borrowing Authority Act of 2006*, 317).

Citing to the U.S. Code   According to *CMS* 14 (16.165), once the law has been incorporated into the *U.S. Code* it should be cited, by title, within the running text:

But the next month FEMA's authority for carrying out the national flood insurance program was increased by the *National Flood Insurance Program Enhanced Borrowing Authority Act of 2006.*

United States Constitution   According to *CMS* 14 (15.367), references to the U.S. Constitution include the number of the article or amendment, the section number, and the clause, if necessary:

The president has the power, in extraordinary circumstances, either to convene or to dismiss Congress (U.S. Constitution, art. 3, sec. 3).

It is not necessary to include the Constitution in the reference list.

Executive Department Documents   A reference to a report, bulletin, circular, or any other type of material issued by the executive department starts with the name of the agency issuing the document, although you may use the name of the author, if known:

Recent demographic projections suggest that city growth will continue to be lateral for several more years, as businesses flee downtown areas for the suburbs (Department of Labor 2004, 334).

Legal References

Supreme Court   As with laws, court decisions are rarely given their own parenthetical text citation and reference list entry, but are instead identified in the text. If you wish to use a formal reference, however, you may place within the parentheses the title of the case, in italics, followed by the source (for cases after 1875 this is the

United States Supreme Court Reports, abbreviated *U.S.*), which is preceded by the volume number and followed by the page number:

The judge ruled that Ms. Warren did have an obligation to offer assistance to the survivors of the wreck, an obligation which she failed to meet (*State of Nevada v. Goldie Warren* 324 U.S. 123).

Before 1875, Supreme Court decisions were published under the names of official court reporters. The reference below is to William Cranch, *Reports of Cases Argued and Adjudged in the Supreme Court of the United States, 1801–1815*, 9 vols. (Washington, DC, 1804–17). The number preceding the clerk's name is the volume number; the last number is the page:

The first case in which the Supreme Court ruled a law of Congress to be void was *Marbury v. Madison*, in 1803 (1 Cranch 137).

For most of these parenthetical references, it is possible to move some or all of the material outside the parentheses simply by incorporating it in the text:

In 1969, in *State of Nevada v. Goldie Warren* (324 U.S. 123), the judge ruled that an observer of a traffic accident has an obligation to offer assistance to survivors.

Lower Courts Decisions of lower federal courts are published in the *Federal Reporter*. The note should give the volume of the *Federal Reporter* (*F.*), the series, if it is other than the first (*2d*, in the model below), the page, and, in brackets, an abbreviated reference to the specific court (the example below is to the Second Circuit Court) and the year:

One ruling takes into account the bias that often exists against the defendant in certain types of personal injury lawsuits (*United States v. Sizemore*, 183 F.2d 201 [2d Cir. 1950]).

Publications of Government Commissions According to *CMS* 14 (15.368), references to bulletins, circulars, reports, and study papers that are issued by various government commissions should include the name of the commission, the date of the document, and the page:

This year saw a sharp reaction among large firms to the new tax law (Securities and Exchange Commission 2004, 57).

Corporate Authors Because government documents are often credited to a corporate author with a lengthy name, you may devise an acronym or a shortened form of the name and indicate in your first reference to the source that this name will be used in later citations:

Government statistics over the last year showed a continuing leveling of the inflation rate (*Bulletin of Labor Statistics* 2006, 1954; *hereafter BLS*).

The practice of using a shortened name in subsequent references to any corporate author, whether a public or private organization, is sanctioned in most journals, including the *American Political Science Review*, and approved in *CMS* 14 (15.252). Thus, if you refer often to the *U.N. Monthly Bulletin of Statistics*, you may, after giving the publication's full name in the first reference, use a shortened form of the title—perhaps an acronym such as *UNMBS*—in all later cites.

Publications of State and Local Governments   According to *CMS* 14 (15.377), references to state and local government documents are similar to those for the corresponding national government sources:

> In arguing for the legality of cockfighting, Senator Lynd actually suggested that the "sport" served as a deterrent to crime among the state's young people (Oklahoma Legislature 2004, 24).

CMS 14 (16.178) restricts bibliographical information concerning state laws or municipal ordinances to the running text.

Electronic Sources   Parenthetical references to electronic sources should present the same sorts of information as references to printed sources, when possible. In other words, include the author's last name, the year of publication, and the relevant page number from the source, if given. However, some types of information that appear in standard text citations, such as the author's name and relevant page numbers, are often missing in electronic sources and so cannot appear in the reference. If the author's name is missing, the parenthetical reference can include the title of the document, in quotation marks. If the online article has numbered paragraphs, you may supply numbers for paragraphs bearing the relevant passages:

> The election results that November may have been what startled Congress into taking such an action ("Effects of Landmark Elections" 2004, para. 12–14).

Interviews   According to *CMS* 15 (17.205), unpublished interviews should be identified within the text or in a note rather than in a parenthetical citation. Include in the text the names of the interviewer and the interviewee, the means of communication (whether by telephone, written correspondence, or a formal, face-to-face interview), the date, and, if relevant, the location. If the interview is published, however, it should be given both a text citation and an entry in the reference list at the end of the paper.

Published Interview

> In an interview last March, Simon criticized the use of private funds to build such city projects as the coliseum (Fox 2015, 58–59).

Unpublished Interview Conducted by the Writer of the Paper   If you are citing material from an interview that you conducted, you should identify yourself as the author and give the date of the interview:

> In an interview with the author conducted by phone on 23 April 2004, Dr. Kennedy expressed her disappointment with the new court ruling.

Personal Materials   Handle such items as personal email messages and texts from bulletin board discussions within the text instead of in a parenthetical reference. There is no need to provide a citation for such material in the reference list.

The Author-Date System: Reference List

In a paper using the author-date bibliographic system, the parenthetical references point the reader to the full citations in the reference list. This list, which always follows the text of the paper, is arranged alphabetically according to the first element in each citation. Usually, this element is the last name of the author or editor, but in the absence of such information, the citation is alphabetized according to the title of the work, which is then the first element in the citation.

The bibliography is double-spaced throughout, even between entries. As with most alphabetically arranged bibliographies, there is a kind of reverse indentation system called a "hanging indent": after the first line of a citation, all subsequent lines are indented five spaces.

Capitalization *Style Manual* uses standard, or "headline style," capitalization rules for titles in the bibliographical citations. In this style, all first and last words in a title, and all other words except articles (*a, an, the*), coordinating words (*and, but, or, for, nor*), and all prepositions, are capitalized.

Books

One Author

Northrup, Alan K. 2015. *Living High Off the Hog: Recent Pork Barrel Legislation in the Senate*. Cleveland: Johnstown.

The author's name appears first, inverted, then the date of publication, followed by the title of the book, the place of publication, and the name of the publishing house. For place of publication, do not identify the state unless the city is not well known. In that case, use postal abbreviations to denote the state (e.g., *OK, AR*).

Periods are used to divide most of the elements in the citation, although a colon is used between the place of publication and publisher. Custom dictates that the main title and subtitle be separated by a colon, even though a colon may not appear in the title as printed on the title page of the book.

Two Authors The name of only the first author is reversed, since it is the one by which the citation is alphabetized:

Spence, Michelle, and Kelly Rudd. 2005. *Education and the Law*. Boston: Tildale.

Three Authors

Moore, J. B., Jeannine Macrory, and Natasha Traylor. 2016. *Down on the Farm: Renovating the Farm Loan*. Norman: Univ. of Oklahoma Press.

According to *CMS* 15 (17.104), you may abbreviate the word *University* if it appears in the name of the press.

Four or More Authors

Herring, Ralph, et al. 2004. *Funding City Projects*. Atlanta: Jessup Institute for Policy Development.

Editor, Compiler, or Translator as Author When no author is listed on the title page, *CMS* 15 (17.41) calls for you to begin the citation with the name of the editor, compiler, or translator, followed by the appropriate phrase—*ed., comp*, or *trans.*:

Trakas, Dylan, comp. 2004. *Making the Road-Ways Safe: Essays on Highway Preservation and Funding*. El Paso: Del Norte Press.

Editor, Compiler, or Translator with Author Place the name of the editor, compiler, or translator after the title, prefaced by the appropriate phrase—*Ed., Comp.,* or *Trans.*:

Pound, Ezra. 1953. *Literary Essays*. Ed. T. S. Eliot. New York: New Directions.

Stomper, Jean. 1973. *Grapes and Rain*. Trans. and ed. John Picard. New York: Baldock.

Two or More Works by the Same Author   When citing more than one work by the same author or authors, replace the author names in all entries after the first one with a 3-em dash (the equivalent of six hyphens). Arrange the works chronologically by publication date rather than alphabetically by title:

Russell, Henry. 1978. *Famous Last Words: Notable Supreme Court Cases of the Last Five Years*. New Orleans: Liberty Publications.

------, ed. 1988. *Court Battles to Remember*. Denver: Axel & Myers.

Chapter in a Multiauthor Collection   Gray, Alexa North. 2005. "Foreign Policy and the Foreign Press." In *Current Media Issues,* ed. Barbara Bonnard. New York: Boulanger.

The parenthetical text reference may include the page reference:

(Gray 2005, 191)

If the author and the editor are the same person, you must repeat the name:

Farmer, Susan A. 2004. "Tax Shelters in the New Dispensation: How to Save Your Income." In *Making Ends Meet: Strategies for the Nineties,* ed. Susan A. Farmer. Nashville: Burkette and Hyde.

Author of a Foreword or Introduction   There is no need, according to *CMS* 15 (17.46, 17.74–75), to cite the author of a foreword or introduction in your bibliography, unless you have used material from that author's contribution to the volume. In that case, the bibliography entry is listed under the name of the author of the foreword or introduction. Place the name of the author of the work itself after the title of the work:

Farris, Carla. 2004. Foreword to *Marital Stress and the Professoriat: A Case Study,* by Basil Givan. New York: Galapagos.

The parenthetical text reference cites the name of the author of the foreword or introduction, not the author of the book:

(Farris 2004)

Subsequent Editions   If you are using an edition of a book other than the first, you must cite the number of the edition or the status, such as *Rev. ed.* for *Revised edition,* if there is no edition number:

Hales, Sarah. 2004. *The Coming Water Wars*. 2d ed. Pittsburgh: Blue Skies.

Multivolume Work   If you are citing a multivolume work in its entirety, use the following format:

Graybosch, Charles. 1988–89. *The Rise of the Unions*. 3 vols. New York: Starkfield.

If you are citing only one of the volumes in a multivolume work, use the following format:

Ronsard, Madeleine. 2005. *Monopolies*. Vol. 2 of *A History of Capitalism*. Ed. Joseph M. Sayles. Boston: Renfrow.

Reprints

Adams, Sterling R. [1964] 1988. *How to Win an Election: Promotional Campaign Strategies*. New York: Starkfield.

Modern Editions of Classics   If the original year of publication is known, include it, in brackets, before the publication date for the edition used:

Burke, Edmond. [1790] 1987. *Reflections on the Revolution in France*. Ed. J. G. A. Pocock. Indianapolis: Hackett.

Remember, if the classic text is divided into short, numbered sections (such as the chapter and verse divisions of the Bible), you do not need to include the work in your bibliography unless you wish to specify a particular edition.

Periodicals

Journal Articles   Journals are periodicals, usually published either monthly or quarterly, that specialize in serious scholarly articles in a particular field. The revised 2006 edition of the APSA *Style Manual* stipulates that a reference for a journal article must include either the month, the season, or the issue number (in that order of preference), placed just after the volume number.

Hunzecker, Joan. 2014. "Teaching the Toadies: Cronyism in Municipal Politics." *Review of Local Politics* 4 (June): 250–62.

Note that the name of the journal, which is italicized, is followed without punctuation by the volume number. A colon separates the name of the month, in parentheses, from the inclusive page numbers. Do not use *p.* or *pp.* to introduce the page numbers.

Magazine Articles   Magazines, which are usually published weekly, bimonthly, or monthly, appeal to the popular audience and generally have a wider circulation than journals. *Newsweek* and *Scientific American* are examples of magazines.

Monthly Magazine   The name of the magazine is separated from the month of publication by a comma:

Stapleton, Bonnie. 1981. "How It Was: On the Campaign Trail with Ike." *Lifetime Magazine*, April, 16–21.

Weekly or Bimonthly Magazine   The day of the issue's publication appears before the month:

Bruck, Connie. 2006. "The World of Business: A Mogul's Farewell." *The New Californian*, 18 October.

Newspaper Articles   While the revised 2006 edition of the APSA *Style Manual* does not discuss reference list entries for newspaper articles, *CMS* 15 (15.234–42, 16.117–18) deals with the topic in some detail. Here are two typical models:

New York Times. 2015. Editorial, 10 August.
Fine, Austin. 2014. "Hoag on Trial." *Carrollton (Texas) Tribune*, 24 November.

Note that *The* is omitted from the newspaper's title. If the name of the city in which an American newspaper is published does not appear in the paper's title, it should be appended, in italics. If the city is not well known, the name of the state is added, in italics, in parentheses, as in the second model above.

Public Documents

Congressional Journals References to either the *Senate Journal* or the *House Journal* begin with the journal's title and include the years of the session, the number of the Congress and session, and the month and day of the entry:

U.S. Senate Journal. 2006. 105th Cong., 1st sess., 10 December.

The ordinal numbers *second* and *third* may be represented as *d* (52d, 103d) or as *nd* and *rd*, respectively.

Congressional Debates

Congressional Record 1930. 72st Cong., 2d sess., vol. 72, pt. 8.

Congressional Reports and Documents Following the designation of Senate or House, include as many of the following items as possible, in this order: committee title, year, title of report or document, Congress, session, and report or document number or committee print number.

U.S. Congress. House.Committee on the Budget. 2006. *Report on Government Efficiency As Perceived by the Public.* 105th Cong., 2d sess. H. Rept. 225.

Bills and Resolutions

U.S. Congress. Senate. 2005. *Visa Formalization Act of 2005.* 105th Cong. 1st sess. S.R. 1437.

The abbreviation *S.R.* in the model above stands for *Senate Resolutions,* and the number following is the bill or resolution number. For references to House bills, the abbreviation is *H.R.*

Statutes

Citing to the Statutes at Large

National Flood Insurance Program Enhanced Borrowing Authority Act. 2006. U.S. Statutes at Large. Vol. 120, p. 317.

Citing to the U.S. Code

National Flood Insurance Program Enhanced Borrowing Authority Act. 2006. U.S. Code. Vol. 42, sec. 4001.

United States Constitution While the revised 2006 edition of the APSA *Style Manual* does not discuss references for the U.S. Constitution, *CMS* 14 (16.172) states that the Constitution is not listed in the bibliography.

Executive Department Documents Include the name of the corporate author, the year, title, city, and publisher:

Department of Labor. 2004. *Report on Urban Growth Potential Projections.* Washington, DC: GPO.

The abbreviation for the publisher in the above model, *GPO,* stands for the *Government Printing Office,* which prints and distributes most government publications. According to *CMS* 15 (15.327), you may use any of the following formats to refer to the GPO:

Washington, DC: U.S. Government Printing Office, 2005

Washington, DC: Government Printing Office, 2005

Washington, DC: GPO, 2005

Washington, DC, 2005

Remember to be consistent in using the form you choose.

Legal References

Supreme Court   Use the same format as for the parenthetical text citation, only add the date after the name of the case:

State of Nevada v. Goldie Warren. 1969. 324 U.S. 123.

For a case prior to 1875, use the following format:

Marbury v. Madison. 1803. 1 Cranch 137.

Lower Courts   Include the volume of the *Federal Reporter* (*F.*), the series, if it is other than the first (*2d,* in the model below), the page, and, in parentheses, an abbreviated reference to the specific district.

United States v. Sizemore. 1950. 183 F.2d 201 (2d Cir.).

Publications of Government Commissions

U.S. Securities and Exchange Commission. 1984. *Annual Report of the Securities and Exchange Commission for the Fiscal Year.* Washington, DC: GPO.

Publications of State and Local Governments   Remember that references for state and local government publications are modeled on those for corresponding national government documents:

Oklahoma Legislature. 2006. Joint Committee on Public Recreation. *Final Report to the Legislature, 2006, Regular Session, on Youth Activities.* Oklahoma City.

Electronic Sources   If a source is available in both print and electronic forms, it is preferable to use the print form. But if you have used the electronic version and it is different from the print version, the general practice is to make your reference to the electronic source as similar as possible to that for the print version, adding the full retrieval path (the electronic address) and the date of your last access of the material.

Electronic Book   Begin with the author's name, reversed, followed if possible by date of publication, then the title of the work, the retrieval path, and the date of your last access to the work, in parentheses.

Amshiral, Sretas. 2014. *Aviation in the Far East.* http://www.flight_easthist.org (January 3, 2016).

Chapter in an Electronic Book

Burris, Akasha. 2013. "Experiments in Transubstantiation." *Surviving Global Disaster*. http://www.meekah/exit/paleoearth.html (March 5, 2016).

You may continue a lengthy URL on the next line of the reference. Do not add a hyphen at the end of the first line.

Electronic Journals

Include all of the following information that you can find, in this order: name of author, reversed; year of publication; title of article, in quotation marks; title of journal, in italics; any further publication information, such as volume number, day or month; full retrieval path; and date of your last access, in parentheses:

Zoheret, Jeanie. 2013. "The Politics of Social Deprivation." *B & N Digest* 3 (February). http://postmodern/tsu/b&n.edu (December 5, 2014).

Material from a Website

The author's name (reversed) and year of publication are followed by the title of the article, in quotation marks; the title, if applicable, of the complete work or Web page, in italics; the full Web address (URL); and, finally, the date on which you last accessed the page, in parentheses:

Squires, Lawrence. 2012. "A Virtual Tour of the White House, circa 1900." *National Landmarks: Then and Now*. http://www.natlandmk.com/hist (August 21, 2014).

e-Mail Material

The revised 2006 edition of the APSA *Style Manual* suggests that e-mail, bulletin board, and electronic discussion group messages be cited as personal communication in the text and left out of the reference list.

Interviews

Published Interviews

Untitled Interview in a Book

Jorgenson, Mary. 2004. Interview by Alan McAskill. In *Hospice Pioneers*. Ed. Alan McAskill, 62–86. Richmond: Dynasty Press.

Titled Interview in a Periodical

Simon, John. 2014. "Picking the Patrons Apart: An Interview with John Simon." By Selena Fox. *Media Week*, March 14, 40–46.

Interview on Television

Snopes, Edward. 2004. Interview by Klint Gordon. *Oklahoma Politicians*. WKY Television, 4 June.

Unpublished Interview

According to *CMS* 15 (17.208), unpublished interviews should be identified within the running text or in a note rather than in a parenthetical citation and left out of the reference list.

Unpublished Sources

Theses and Dissertations

If the work has a sewn or glued binding, place the title in italics, like a book; otherwise designate the title by quotation marks:

Hoarner, Art. 2005. *Populism and the Free Soil Movement*. Ph.D. diss. University of Virginia.

Sharpe, Ellspeth Stanley. 2003. "Black Women in Politics: A Troubled History." Master's thesis. Oregon State University.

Paper Presented at a Meeting

Zelazny, Kim, and Ed Gilmore. 2005. "Art for Art's Sake: Funding the NEA in the Twenty-First Century." Presented at the Annual Meeting of the Conference of Metropolitan Arts Councils, San Francisco.

Manuscript in the Author's Possession

Borges, Rita V. 1979. "Mexican-American Border Conflicts, 1915–1970." University of Texas at El Paso. Photocopy.

The entry includes the institution with which the author is affiliated and ends with a description of the format of the work (typescript, photocopy, etc.).

Personal Communications   Handle such items as personal email messages and texts from bulletin board discussions within the text or in a note instead of in a parenthetical reference. There is no need to provide a citation for such material in the reference list.

Note: Most of the sources used as models in this chapter are not references to actual publications.

Sample Bibliography: APSA Author-Date System

Ariès, Philippe. 1962. *Centuries of Childhood: A Social History of Family Life.* Trans. Robert Baldock. New York: Knopf.

Cesbron, Henry. 1909. *Histoire critique de l'hystérie.* Paris: Asselin et Houzeau.

Farmer, Susan A. 2004. "Tax Shelters in the New Dispensation: How to Save Your Income." In *Making Ends Meet: Strategies for the Nineties,* ed. Susan A. Farmer. Nashville: Burkette and Hyde.

Herring, Ralph, et al. 2004. *Funding City Projects.* Atlanta: Jessup Institute for Policy Development.

Hunzecker, Joan. 2014. "Teaching the Toadies: Cronyism in Municipal Politics." *Review of Local Politics* 4: 250–62.

Moore, J. B., Jeannine Macrory, and Natasha Traylor. 2016. *Down on the Farm: Renovating the Farm Loan.* Norman: Univ. of Oklahoma Press.

Northrup, Alan K. 2015. *Living High Off the Hog: Recent Pork Barrel Legislation in the Senate.* Cleveland: Johnstown.

Skylock, Browning. 2009. "'Fifty-Four Forty or Fight!': Sloganeering in Early America." *American History Digest* 28(3): 25–34.

Squires, Lawrence. 2012. "A Virtual Tour of the White House, circa 1900." *National Landmarks: Then and Now.* http://www.natlandmk.com/hist (21 August 2014).

Stapleton, Bonnie. 1981. "How It Was: On the Campaign Trail with Ike." *Lifetime Magazine,* April.

U.S. Securities and Exchange Commission. 1984. *Annual Report of the Securities and Exchange Commission for the Fiscal Year.* Washington, 2005.

Read&Write 3.4 Create an Actually Usable Bibliography

Create a bibliography for a paper on a topic of your choosing using twelve or more high quality actually published print and online sources.

3.5 AVOID PLAGIARISM

You want to use your source material as effectively as possible. This will sometimes mean that you should quote from a source directly, whereas at other times you will want to express such information in your own words. At all times, you should work to integrate the source material skillfully into the flow of your written argument.

When to Quote

You should quote directly from a source when the original language is distinctive enough to enhance your argument, or when rewording the passage would lessen its impact. In the interest of fairness, you should also quote a passage to which you will take exception. Rarely, however, should you quote a source at great length (longer than two or three paragraphs). Nor should your paper, or any substantial section of it, be merely a string of quoted passages. The more language you take from the writings of others, the more the quotations will disrupt the rhetorical flow of your own words. Too much quoting creates a choppy patchwork of varying styles and borrowed purposes in which your sense of your own control over your material is lost.

Quotations in Relation to Your Writing

When you do use a quotation, make sure that you insert it skillfully. According to *CMS* 16 (13.9–10), quotations of fewer than 100 words (approximately eight typed lines) should generally be integrated into the text and set off with quotation marks:

"In the last analysis," Alice Thornton argued in 2006, "we cannot afford not to embark on a radical program of fiscal reform" (12).

A quotation of 100 words or longer (eight typed lines or longer) should be formatted as a *block quotation*; it should begin on a new line, be indented from the left margin, and not be enclosed in quotation marks.

Blake's outlook for the solution to the city's problem of abandoned buildings is anything but optimistic:

> If the trend in demolitions due to abandonment continues, the cost of doing nothing may be too high. The three-year period from 2016 to 2007 shows an annual increase in demolitions of roughly twenty percent. Such an upward trend for a sustained period of time would eventually place a disastrous hardship on the city's resources. And yet the city council seems bent on following the tactic of inaction. (2016, 8)

Acknowledge Quotations Carefully

Failing to signal the presence of a quotation skillfully can lead to confusion or choppiness:

The U.S. Secretary of Labor believes that worker retraining programs have failed because of a lack of trust within the American business culture. "The American business community does not visualize the need to invest in its workers" (Winn 2016, 11).

The first sentence in the above passage seems to suggest that the quote that follows comes from the Secretary of Labor. Note how this revision clarifies the attribution:

According to reporter Fred Winn, the U.S. Secretary of Labor believes that worker retraining programs have failed because of a lack of trust within the American business culture. Summarizing the secretary's view, Winn writes, "The American business community does not visualize the need to invest in its workers" (2016, 11).

The origin of each quote must be indicated within your text at the point where the quote occurs as well as in the list of works cited, which follows the text.

Quote Accurately

If your transcription of a quotation introduces careless variants of any kind, you are mis-representing your source. Proofread your quotations very carefully, paying close attention to such surface features as spelling, capitalization, italics, and the use of numerals.

Occasionally, in order to make a quotation fit smoothly into a passage, to clarify a reference, or to delete unnecessary material, you may need to change the original wording slightly. You must, however, signal any such change to your reader. Some alterations may be noted by brackets:

"Several times in the course of his speech, the attorney general said that his stand [on gun control] remains unchanged" (McAffrey 2016, 2).

Ellipses indicate that words have been left out of a quote:

"The last time voters refused to endorse one of the senator's policies . . . was back in 1982" (Laws 2005, 143).

When you integrate quoted material with your own prose, it is unnecessary to begin the quote with ellipses:

Benton raised eyebrows with his claim that "nobody in the mayor's office knows how to tie a shoe, let alone balance a budget" (Williams 2006, 12).

Paraphrasing

Your writing has its own rhetorical attributes, its own rhythms, and structural coherence. Inserting several quotations into one section of your paper can disrupt the patterns of your prose and diminish its effectiveness. Paraphrasing, or recasting source material in your own words, is one way to avoid the choppiness that can result from a series of quotations.

Remember that a paraphrase is to be written in your language; it is not a near-copy of the source writer's language. Merely changing a few words of the original does justice to no one's prose and frequently produces stilted passages. This sort of borrowing is actually a form of plagiarism. To integrate another's material into your own writing fully, use your own language.

Paraphrasing may actually increase your comprehension of source material, because in recasting a passage you will have to think very carefully about its meaning—more carefully, perhaps, than if you had merely copied it word for word.

Avoiding Plagiarism When Paraphrasing

Paraphrases require the same sort of documentation as direct quotes. The words of a paraphrase may be yours, but the idea belongs to someone else. Failure to give that person credit, in the form of references within the text and in the bibliography, may make you vulnerable to a charge of plagiarism.

Plagiarism is the use of someone else's words or ideas without proper credit. Although some plagiarism is deliberate, produced by writers who understand that they are guilty of a kind of academic thievery, much of it is unconscious, committed by writers who are not aware of the varieties of plagiarism or who are careless in recording their borrowings from sources. Plagiarism includes

- Quoting directly without acknowledging the source
- Paraphrasing without acknowledging the source
- Constructing a paraphrase that closely resembles the original in language and syntax

One way to guard against plagiarism is to keep careful notes of when you have directly quoted source material and when you have paraphrased—making sure that the wording of the paraphrases is yours. Be sure that all direct quotes in your final draft are properly set off from your own prose, either with quotation marks or in indented blocks.

What kind of paraphrased material must be acknowledged? Basic material that you find in several sources need not be documented by a reference. For example, it is unnecessary to cite a source for the information that Franklin Delano Roosevelt was elected to a fourth term as President of the United States shortly before his death, because this is a commonly known fact. However, Professor Smith's opinion, published in a recent article, that Roosevelt's winning of a fourth term hastened his death is not a fact, but a theory based on Smith's research and defended by her. If you wish to use Smith's opinion in a paraphrase, you need to credit her, as you should all judgments and claims from another source. Any information that is not widely known, either factual or open to dispute, should be documented. This includes statistics, graphs, tables, and charts taken from sources other than your own primary research.

Read & Write 3.5 Properly Summarize an Article from *The Economist* or *Mother Jones*

Select an article from a recent copy of *The Economist* or *Mother Jones* and summarize it properly in your own words, without plagiarizing, in approximately 500 words. Attach the article itself to your summary.

4

BECOME FAMILIAR WITH GOVERNMENT DOCUMENTS

4.1 WELCOME TO THE NATIONAL ARCHIVES

Famous astronomer Carl Sagan expressed his awe of the universe, admiring a night sky full of "billions and billions of stars." One may well be awed exploring the remarkable United States National Archives online (www.archives.gov), with its billions of various photographs, documents, and other items.

Despite an increasing amount of material available online, the archives headquarters in Washington, DC, and at other branch locations throughout the country offer much more. To find a branch location near you, visit http://www.archives.gov/locations.

According to http://www.archives.gov/locations/why-visit.html, the archives provide the following:

> We have historical documents that tell the stories of America's history as a nation and as a people, available to you in 33 locations nationwide. These valuable records are evidence of our national experience.

> Each year, our staff serves our visitors billions of letters, photographs, video and audio recordings, drawings, maps, treaties, posters, and other items that we have preserved. The materials are not for loan to the public, as a library loans material; they are protected, but are available for you to use in-person at our facilities and affiliated archives.

> You can visit the National Archives, nationwide, to:

> - View exhibits of historical records and presidential papers:
>   - The Public Vaults and the Charters of Freedom (the Declaration of Independence, The Constitution, and the Bill of Rights), located in Washington, DC
>   - Exhibits about American Presidents (each one since Herbert Hoover) in our Presidential libraries.
>   - Records of local importance to geographical regions of America in our regional facilities.
> - Request records for your examination in our research rooms. Please note: Records are located in specific facilities. Learn about how to determine which records are located where.

- Attend public programs, including film presentations, workshops, and lectures. See our Washington, DC Calendar of Events. For events around the country, see the calendars for each National Archives facility.[1]

Furthermore, this website provides

Examples of what you can find at the National Archives . . .

- President Ronald Reagan's speech card from remarks made in Berlin, Germany, in June 1987 (when the infamous Berlin Wall was still standing), which is marked up to indicate points of emphasis.
- Photographs of child labor conditions at the turn of the 19th century. Children did everything from selling newspapers to shucking oysters to make a few pennies.
- The Zimmermann Telegram, named for German foreign minister Arthur Zimmermann, secretly offered U.S. lands to Mexico in exchange for Mexican support during World War I. The British were able to decipher the code. The telegram helped convince the United States to enter the war in 1917.
- The arrest warrant for Lee Harvey Oswald, the man who was accused of assassinating President John F. Kennedy in Dallas, Texas.

To appreciate the value of these archives, read

Who Uses the National Archives and Why?

Every year, hundreds of thousands of people contact us or come to our research facilities and Presidential libraries, and millions use our web site. Their purposes are many and varied.

Genealogists

Most people who come to the National Archives to conduct research are genealogists or family historians. They are trying to find information about their ancestors in order to fill in their family tree or write a family history. They use census records to learn people's names, ages, and who lived where, when. They check passenger arrival lists from boats that originated in Europe to prove when an immigrant landed in the United States. Genealogists also often look at military service records, as well as land, naturalization, and passport records, and more.

In addition to conducting this research at the National Archives Building in Washington, DC, the Regional Archives also have most of the main genealogical-related records on microfilm as well.

Veterans

Veterans and next-of-kin of deceased veterans contact the National Archives to obtain copies of military service records, including the DD Form 214, Report of Separation, which is used to determine eligibility for Government benefits and employment. Veterans and next-of-kin of deceased veterans have the same rights for full access to the record. Next-of-kin include the widow or widower (not remarried), son or daughter, father or mother, brother or sister of the deceased veteran. More than 70 million veterans service records are on file at NARA's National Personnel Records Center in St. Louis, Missouri. Pre-WWI military records can primarily be found in Washington, DC, at the National Archives Building. Post-WWI records are generally

[1] All excerpts reprinted here can be found at "Why Visit the National Archives?" National Archives. http://www.archives.gov/locations/why-visit.html (March 7, 2016).

in St. Louis, and must be ordered through the mail. However, a small research room is opening this . . . in St. Louis for the public to view select military records.

Educators and Students

Educators frequently employ the National Archives to develop primary-source, document-based lesson plans and to help bring history alive for their students. Many students use the archives for research projects. While researchers must be at least 14 years old to conduct research at the National Archives' facilities, all ages can use the National Archives website to find information.

Museum Visitors

American citizens and foreign visitors come to the National Archives to see historical documents and discover how they reflect our history. We also offer tours for school groups. Our museums include the National Archives Building in Washington, DC and our Presidential libraries located nationwide. Exhibits are often on display as well at our regional locations.

Environmentalists and Land Researchers

Over the years, the U.S. Geological Survey, Soil Conservation Service, and other government agencies have used aerial photography to study and map the land. Environmentalists look at these photos to trace changes in land use. Other people use the photos to settle land–boundary disputes.

Archaeologists

Maps that were created by the U.S. Army during the War of 1812 are being utilized today by archaeologists to help locate the remains of buildings and sunken ships and to plan excavations.

Architects

Many of the designs used by the Federal Government to build forts, post offices, lighthouses, and offices across the country are housed in the National Archives. As a result, architectural historians and preservationists look at these records when exploring different building styles and in helping city planners save important historic buildings.

Museum Curators

Museum curators develop displays based on research or fascinating discoveries from the National Archives. Even hobbyists find the Archives useful. Model airplane and ship builders can find the designs for hundreds of military planes and ships that have been built for the United States since the Revolutionary War.

Writers

Biographers, novelists, software developers, and movie and television screenwriters sometimes enlist the help of the National Archives to make their books, shows, and computer games more accurate and enjoyable.

Read&Write 4.1 Describe Five Images from the Digital Vaults

The National Archives Digital Vaults (http://www.digitalvaults.org/) are a wonderful resource even if you merely wish to satisfy your curiosity. From the original document in which Pennsylvania officially rejected slavery, to photographs of Elvis Presley meeting President Nixon at the White House, to photos of World War II code talkers, the archives have online a 1,200-item sample of the *ten billion* photographs and documents it has in store. As you peruse the collection, construct with clear, insightful prose a two-to-three-page essay in which you bring to life for your reader five images you have chosen, explaining their meaning and significance.

4.2 WELCOME TO THE LIBRARY OF CONGRESS

The large collections of the Library of Congress (www.loc.gov) are remarkable as well. The library provides access to millions of documents of every source.

The manuscripts section alone declares: "The Library of Congress holds approximately sixty million manuscript items in eleven thousand separate collections, including some of the greatest manuscript treasures of American history and culture."[2]

Although massive today, the library's collections had a more modest beginning, as the website's history link (http://www.loc.gov/about/history-of-the-library/) describes:

> The Library of Congress was established by an act of Congress in 1800 when President John Adams signed a bill providing for the transfer of the seat of government from Philadelphia to the new capital city of Washington. The legislation described a reference library for Congress only, containing "such books as may be necessary for the use of Congress—and for putting up a suitable apartment for containing them therein…"
>
> Established with $5,000 appropriated by the legislation, the original library was housed in the new Capitol until August 1814, when invading British troops set fire to the Capitol Building, burning and pillaging the contents of the small library.
>
> Within a month, retired President Thomas Jefferson offered his personal library as a replacement. Jefferson had spent 50 years accumulating books, "putting by everything which related to America, and indeed whatever was rare and valuable in every science"; his library was considered to be one of the finest in the United States. In offering his collection to Congress, Jefferson anticipated controversy over the nature of his collection, which included books in foreign languages and volumes of philosophy, science, literature, and other topics not normally viewed as part of a legislative library. He wrote, "I do not know that it contains any branch of science which Congress would wish to exclude from their collection; there is, in fact, no subject to which a Member of Congress may not have occasion to refer."

---

[2] "Collections with Manuscripts." Library of Congress. https://www.loc.gov/manuscripts/ collections/ (March 7, 2016).

In January 1815, Congress accepted Jefferson's offer, appropriating $23,950 for his 6,487 books, and the foundation was laid for a great national library. The Jeffersonian concept of universality, the belief that all subjects are important to the library of the American legislature, is the philosophy and rationale behind the comprehensive collecting policies of today's Library of Congress.[3]

Read & Write 4.2 Recall Some Actual American Slave Narratives

The library's manuscript collections (http://www.loc.gov/manuscripts/collections/) cover many fascinating themes. Consider the Library's descriptions of two collections:

Born in Slavery: Slave Narratives from the Federal Writers' Project, 1936–1938, contains more than 2,300 first-person accounts of slavery and 500 black-and-white photographs of former slaves. These narratives were collected in the 1930s as part of the Federal Writers' Project of the Works Progress Administration (WPA) and assembled and microfilmed in 1941 as the seventeen-volume *Slave Narratives: A Folk History of Slavery in the United States from Interviews with Former Slaves*. This online collection is a joint presentation of the Manuscript and Prints and Photographs Divisions of the Library of Congress and includes more than 200 photographs from the Prints and Photographs Division that are now made available to the public for the first time. *Born in Slavery* was made possible by a major gift from the Citigroup Foundation.[4]

"I Do Solemnly Swear . . .": Presidential Inaugurations is a collection of approximately 400 items or 2,000 digital files relating to inaugurations from George Washington's in 1789 to Barack Obama's inauguration of 2009. This presentation includes diaries and letters of presidents and of those who witnessed inaugurations, handwritten drafts of inaugural addresses, broadsides, inaugural tickets and programs, prints, photographs, and sheet music. The selections are drawn from the Presidential Papers in the Manuscript Division and from the collections of the Prints and Photographs Division, Rare Book and Special Collections Division, Music Division, and the General Collections of the Library of Congress. Additional material has been included from the photography collections of the Architect of the Capitol, the White House, and the United States Senate Office of the Sergeant at Arms. Some items, from records of early sessions of Congress to early films, that are already online in American Memory, have been incorporated. An important component is the collaboration with the Avalon Project at the Yale Law School, which permits the site to offer Yale's online presentations of the inaugural addresses from Presidents Washington to Obama with associated searchable text transcriptions.[5]

Your task in this exercise is to peruse the Library of Congress manuscript collections, select five items from one of them, and, for each item write a separate paragraph of approximately 400 words explaining why it is of interest to you.

---

[3] "History of the Library." Library of Congress. https://www.loc.gov/about/history-of-the-library/ (March 7, 2016).

[4] "Born in Slavery: Slave Narratives from the Federal Writers' Project, 1936–1938." Library of Congress. http://memory.loc.gov/ammem/snhtml/snhome.html (March 7, 2016).

[5] "'I Do Solemnly Swear': Presidential Inaugurations." Library of Congress. http://memory.loc.gov/ammem/pihtml/pihome.html (March 7, 2016).

4.3   HOW TO READ THE *CONGRESSIONAL RECORD*

The Library of Congress website (www.congress.gov) provides a link to the *Congressional Record* (*CR*). The website also provides a link to a description of the CR:

> The Congressional Record is the most widely recognized published account of the debates, proceedings, and activities of the United States Congress.
>
> The *Journals* of the House and Senate, in which the daily actions of the respective chambers are recorded, are the official records of House and Senate proceedings. However, the Congressional Record—printed by the Government Printing Office on a daily, over-night basis, and after a session is over in bound form—is widely considered to be an essential, fuller record of legislative proceedings. Published under this title since 1873—and before that in three forms and under three titles (*Annals of Congress, Register of Debates*, and the *Congressional Globe*)—the *Record* records the daily floor proceedings of the House and Senate, substantially verbatim. Since 1947, each day's *Record* also contains at its close a Daily Digest, which recounts by chamber the day's activities, including the number of bills introduced, the floor actions taken that day, a summary of meetings held that day by committees and for what purpose, and a list of committee meetings scheduled for the next day and on what topics (at the end of each week, a list of committee meetings scheduled for the following week, and their topics, is printed).[6]

The National Archives provides detailed information on research strategies for the use of CR (http://www.archives.gov/legislative/guide/house/chapter-01-strategies.html). This site also presents a range of approaches to the CR. Our present purpose with respect to the CR *is* limited. We intend to show how to contact your representatives or senators on current legislation.

Read & Write 4.3   Correspond with Your Representative about Current Legislation

Writing to your senator or representative may have more effect than you might think. There is an old political adage that states that for every letter a member of Congress receives, another 100 people share the correspondent's opinion; they simply haven't taken time to write. Now you can take the time to write, and perhaps you will be the voice of 101 citizens.

First, select a piece of legislation. On www.congress.gov, select "Top 10 Most Viewed Bills." On January 10, 2016, this list included the following items:

1.	H.R.4269 [114th]	Assault Weapons Ban of 2015
2.	H.Res.569 [114th]	Condemning violence, bigotry, and hateful rhetoric towards Muslims in the United States
3.	H.R.2029 [114th]	Consolidated Appropriations Act, 2016
4.	H.R.1314 [114th]	Bipartisan Budget Act of 2015

[6] "About the *Congressional Record.*" Thomas. Library of Congress. http://thomas.loc.gov/home/abt.cong.rec.html (March 7, 2016).

5.	H.R.3762 [114th]	Restoring Americans' Healthcare Freedom Reconciliation Act of 2015
6.	H.R.1321 [114th]	Microbead-Free Waters Act of 2015
7.	H.R.3799 [114th]	Hearing Protection Act of 2015
8.	H.R.1002 [114th]	Mortgage Forgiveness Tax Relief Act of 2015
9.	H.R.22 [114th]	FAST Act
10.	S.1177 [114th]	Every Student Succeeds Act

A new top ten list appears every time Congress is in session, so this is your "hot topics" menu for the week. You can follow the links on the list to get more information about these bills. H.R bills are proceeding through the House of Representatives, and S. bills through the Senate. If none of these topics interests you, or you have a favorite topic in mind, you can return to www.congress.gov and enter into the search engine a topic of your choice. Make sure that the bill you choose is still in Congress and has not been killed or sent to the President.

How Do I Go About Writing the Letter?

First, address your letter properly. A table providing proper forms of address is printed at the end of this section of the chapter. Begin your letter by telling the representative exactly what you want him or her to do and which piece of legislation is affected. Be sure to include the following information, which you will find when you locate the bill in the online *Congressional Digest:*

- Short Number and Name of the bill (e.g., H.R.4269—Assault Weapons Ban of 2015)

- Subtitle or Full Title of the bill (To regulate assault weapons, to ensure that the right to keep and bear arms is not unlimited, and for other purposes.)

- Current status of the bill (e.g., referred to the Subcommittee on Commercial and Administrative Law)

Next, find out what members of Congress have already said about the bill so that you will have some arguments to use in your letter. In the search engine on www.congress.gov, select *Congressional Record* from the pull down menu next to the search line. Then enter the number of the bill. If members of Congress have made speeches on the bill they should appear here. Make up your own mind and make a stand.

Next, address two of the legislator's primary concerns. For every bill that comes to the representative's attention, he or she must answer two questions: (1) Is legislative action needed to deal with whatever problem or issue is at hand? and (2) If legislation is needed, is the specific legislation in question the best way to address the issue? To answer these two questions you will need to make the following two arguments: (1) That the issue or problem warrants (or does not warrant) legislative action, and (2) That the specific proposed legislation appropriately deals (or does not appropriately deal) with the issue or problem.

Provide at least a few facts and examples or anecdotes. Include any personal experience or involvement that you have in the issue or problem. You do not need to provide all the information the legislator will need to make a decision, but provide enough to get him or her interested in the issue enough to examine the matter further and give it serious thought. Format the letter as you do a standard business letter and, of course, proofread your final draft carefully. You will find a table of proper forms of address for letters to government officials in Appendix B of this Manual.

Back again on www.congress.gov you will find a link to MEMBERS OF CONGRESS. Select your home state and then the representative or senator to whom you want to write. If you do not know who your representative is, follow the link above to MEMBERS and then, selecting representatives, you will find a search engine where you can enter your zip code to find your representative. You can follow a link from this page to that person's web page, which contains a good deal of helpful information.

Sample Letter to a Representative

October 15, 2016
The Honorable Ben Ray Lujan
2446 Rayburn House Office Building
Washington, DC, 20515

Dear Representative Lujan:

I am writing to ask you to vote for the Environmental Justice Act of 2016 (H. R. 2200, currently under consideration by the Subcommittee on Commercial and Administrative Law), an act "To require Federal agencies to develop and implement policies and practices that promote environmental justice, and for other purposes." Native Americans, Latinos, and Blacks have suffered too long under unhealthy environmental conditions on reservations and in substandard neighborhoods across the country. In my neighborhood the toxic waste from old mining operations has caused illness in more than twenty children.

Across the country Superfund sites and pockets of polluted air and water are affecting most the people with the fewest resources and the least political clout to deal with the problem. In Los Angeles, for example, more than 70 percent of African-Americans and half of Latinos reside in the most highly polluted areas while only a third of the local whites live in these areas. Again, workers in the meatpacking plants of South Omaha, Nebraska, are battling to restore the vitality of city parks and improve unsanitary conditions in the plants. Too often people in these communities face greater exposure to toxins and dangerous substances because waste dumps, industrial facilities, and chemical storage facilities take fewer precautions in low-income communities than they do in high-income communities. Sadly, the captains of industry view these communities as expendable, denying the human beings who live in them the dignity and respect that is their constitutional right as American citizens.

What can be done? The first step is to solve a problem in and among federal agencies. Recent environmental and health policy studies have determined that most federal agencies, including the Environmental Protection Agency, do not adequately understand that environmental justice is being continuously denied to American citizens. Furthermore, there is currently no mechanism in place to coordinate and therefore make effective the environmental justice efforts that are currently under way.

The Environmental Justice Act of 2016 does much to correct these problems. In addition to focusing federal agency attention on the environmental and human health conditions in minority, low-income, and Native American communities, this legislation takes several positive steps in the direction of securing environmental justice for Native Americans. The Environmental Justice Act of 2016:

- Ensures that all federal agencies develop practices that promote environmental justice
- Increases cooperation and coordination among federal agencies
- Provides minority, low-income, and Native American communities greater access to public information and opportunity for participation in environmental decision-making
- Mitigates the inequitable distribution of the burdens and benefits of federal programs having significant impact on human health and the environment
- Holds federal agencies accountable for the effects of their projects and programs on all communities.

Your support in this urgent matter is much appreciated.

Sincerely,

P. Henry Gibson III

18 Lake Charles Way

Passamadumcott, SD 57003

4.4 HOW TO READ THE *FEDERAL REGISTER*

The *Federal Register* information page (http://www.archives.gov/federal-register/the-federal-register/about.html) describes the *Federal Register* as follows:

> The Federal Register (the daily newspaper of the Federal government) is a legal newspaper published every business day by the National Archives and Records Administration (NARA).

> The *Federal Register* contains:

> - Federal Agency Regulations
> - Proposed Rules and Public Notices
> - Executive Orders
> - Proclamations
> - Other Presidential Documents

> NARA's Office of the Federal Register prepares the Federal Register for publication in partnership with the Government Printing Office (GPO). GPO distributes the Federal Register in paper, on microfiche, and on the World Wide Web.

Why should you read it? "The *Federal Register* informs citizens of their rights and obligations and provides access to a wide range of Federal benefits and opportunities for funding" (http://www.archives.gov/federal-register/the-federal-register/about.html#whysho).

The same page also provides the following information:

How is the *Federal Register* organized?

Each issue of the *Federal Register* is organized into four categories:

- Presidential Documents, including Executive orders and proclamations
- Rules and Regulations, including policy statements and interpretations of rules
- Proposed Rules, including petitions for rulemaking and other advance proposals
- Notices, including scheduled hearings and meetings open to the public, grant applications, and administrative orders

Documents published in the *Federal Register* as rules and proposed rules include citations to the *Code of Federal Regulations* (CFR) to refer readers to the CFR parts affected. The CFR contains the complete and official text of agency regulations organized into fifty titles covering broad subject areas. The CFR is updated and published once a year in print, fiche, and on-line formats.[7]

Furthermore, the "FDsys' *Federal Register* Search Page allows users to retrieve documents using a variety of different search criteria." The ADVANCED SEARCH option can be used to select a topic of your choice.

Read&Write 4.4 Contribute Comments to Pending Government Regulations

The purpose of this exercise is to acquaint you with your opportunity to comment upon pending government regulations. Continuing on the federal register information website (http://www.archives.gov/federal-register/the-federal-register/about.html#whysho), you will find the following information:

How can I use the *Federal Register* to affect Federal rulemaking?

Federal agencies are required to publish notices of proposed rulemaking in the *Federal Register* to enable citizens to participate in the decision making process of the Government. This notice and comment procedure is simple.

1. A proposed rule published in the *Federal Register* notifies the public of a pending regulation.
2. Any person or organization may comment on it directly, either in writing, or orally at a hearing. Many agencies also accept comments online or via e-mail. The comment period varies, but it usually is 30, 60, or 90 days. For each notice, the *Federal Register* gives detailed instructions on how, when, and where a viewpoint may be expressed. In addition, agencies must list the name and telephone number of a person to contact for further information.
3. When agencies publish final regulations in the *Federal Register*, they must address the significant issues raised in comments and discuss any changes made in response to them. Agencies also may use the notice and comment process to stay in contact with constituents and to solicit their views on various policy and program issues.

---

[7] Excerpts reprinted here can be found at "About the *Federal Register*." *Federal Register*. http://www.archives.gov/federal-register/the-federal-register/about.html#whysho (March 7, 2016).

Your next step is to visit regulations.gov. Here you will find lists of pending regulations on which you can comment and links to explanations of how to comment. On this page, under COMMENTS DUE SOON, select NEXT 30 DAYS. You will find here several hundred issues upon which you can comment. As you peruse the list you can get information about each proposed regulation by selecting the selected item's OPEN DOCUMENT FOLDER link. When you have selected a particular regulation, read the information in its document folder, and then, all in your own WORD file:

1. Copy the regulation's identifying information and paste it into your WORD file.
2. Write a page or less of comments to submit.
3. Select COMMENT NOW and paste your comment into the place provided.

In your WORD file you will have a copy of your submission that you can submit to your instructor.

5

INTRODUCTORY SKILLED OBSERVATIONS

5.1 PRESIDENTIAL CAMPAIGN COMMERCIALS

The Ghost of Willie Horton

It's a classic and infamous television campaign ad. A foreboding prison tower, somber and gray, sharply cuts through a gloomy stillness. The camera focuses on a rifle-toting guard patrolling a barbed-wire-topped wall. Next, marching in file, monochrome prisoners enter a revolving door that places them momentarily inside the prison, but then sweeps them immediately out to freedom. As the line of prisoners continues its bizarre liberation, the following banners sequentially appear on the screen:

The Dukakis Furlough Program

268 escaped

Many are still at large

Meanwhile, a resonant voice intones: "As governor, Michael Dukakis vetoed mandatory sentences for drug dealers. He vetoed the death penalty. His revolving door prison policy gave weekend furloughs to first-degree murderers not eligible for parole. While out, many committed other crimes like kidnapping and rape. And many are still at large. Now Michael Dukakis says he wants to do for America what he's done for Massachusetts. America can't afford that risk."[1]

It's all over in 30 seconds, and it's one of the most famous campaign ads in history. Having spent eight years as Ronald Reagan's Vice President, George Herbert Walker Bush was eager to retain Republican control in the 1988 election and was pulling no punches. His Democratic opponent, Michael Dukakis, Commonwealth of Massachusetts Governor, had, like virtually every state governor across the nation (including Ronald Reagan), furloughed prisoners who had later committed crimes.

---

[1] "Dukakis Furlough Program." YouTube.com. https://www.youtube.com/watch?v= Nch860E_Df0 (March 7, 2016).

Crime was a big issue in the 1980s. Major cities waged war on violence, and many, especially New York City, were successful. However, fear and anger remained ripe for political picking. The revolving door ad became known as the "Willie Horton" ad, although Horton, who was then well known, is never specifically mentioned. Horton had been convicted for murder before being furloughed, and, once out, committed rape and armed robbery. The Bush–Quayle campaign used Horton's infamy as a tool to portray Dukakis as soft on crime. The ad may have contributed to Dukakis's defeat, but was later criticized as veiled racism since it obliquely referred to an African-American convict. Campaign ads are rarely even-handed and fair. It was no mistake, therefore, that this one never mentioned a certain fact: the furlough program, under which Horton was released, had become law before Dukakis's inauguration, during a previous Republican administration.

If omitting pertinent facts is lying, do all campaign commercials lie? Probably. At least the vast majority. It seems fair to say that campaign ads, however entertaining they may be, are among the least reliable sources of information. The problem is not so much that they are misleading but that they are so effective. Campaigns and interest groups spend hundreds of millions of dollars on these ads because they work.

Read & Write 5.1 Analyze a Presidential Campaign Commercial

The instructions may require a bit of research, but they are quite simple. First, find an interesting political ad. They can be found all over the Internet and on YouTube. An especially good place to start is www.livingroomcandidate.org, which presents the most prominent ads in presidential campaigns from the present all the way back to the early 1950s.

Second, write an essay (about five pages long, but ask your instructor about the length) in which, in a series of clear, concise, and well-written paragraphs, you complete the following tasks: (You will find the information you want in the many news and political sites on the internet.)

1) Provide the political background for the ad. Briefly describe or explain each of the following:

> In which election year and in which race was the ad presented?
> Who were the contestants?
> What were the key issues in the race?
> What groups provided the strongest support for each contestant?

2) Describe the content of the ad. Describe the images presented in it. Write a transcript of the verbal content similar to the one for the revolving door ad.

3) Identify the message. What, exactly, is this ad trying to say?

4) Identify the goal of the ad. Of course all campaign ads are aimed at getting someone elected, but be more specific. Ads are always aimed at getting someone to vote, but most are aimed at some people in particular. Determine the audience for this ad—are they wealthy suburbanites, Latinos, men, women, older voters, environmentalists, or unemployed workers?

5) Identify the strategy. Studies show that people who actually make the effort to vote are more likely to vote *against* something than *for* something. If you can motivate people

to vote, you can win an election. Emotions motivate. What is it about the ad you select that *motivates* people to vote? Fear? Hope? Jealousy? Compassion? What artistic and psychological *techniques* does it use to generate the emotion it is after? Does the ad appeal to reason? Describe the emotional and intellectual content of the visual images. How is color used? Are the images "hard" or "soft," slow or rapid, cartoonish or sophisticated? Describe the emotional and intellectual content of the words spoken. Does it connect a particular candidate with popular symbols? With negative symbols? Was the ad largely positive (portraying the good qualities of a favored candidate) or negative (portraying a candidate's weaknesses)? Some commentators claim that all political ads are negative because even seemingly positive ones inherently portray the opposing candidate as inferior in comparison.

6) Evaluate the ad. What has been said about it on blogs or in editorials or other political commentary? What is your personal impression of the ad? In your opinion, how effective was it in achieving its goal?

Classroom Project: Create Your Own Campaign Commercial

Step 1: Identify your ideological inclination. There are no right or wrong answers. Indicate your opinion about each of the following statements by placing a number from 1 to 5 (whichever number most closely expresses your opinion) in the open column to the right of each statement as follows:

1 = strongly agree, 2 = agree, 3 = uncertain, 4 = disagree, 5 = strongly disagree.

Columns	1	2
The truly wealthy "one-percenters" do not pay their fair share of taxes.	■	
Our public schools need more funding.	■	
Strong penalties are the best way to reduce crime.		■
The unborn child has a fundamental right to life.		■
Racism is a serious problem in this country.	■	
Climate change demands swift and immediate action.	■	
Individuals should be able to own semiautomatic weapons.		■
Illegal immigrants pose a substantial threat to our society.		■
Public support for Planned Parenthood promotes healthy families.	■	
The minimum wage should be raised to $15 per hour.	■	
A lot of people on welfare could be earning their own living.		■
Obama Care should be repealed.		■
Total		

Total the numbers in each column. Calculate your score as follows:

Total for column 2 _____ minus total for column 1 _____ = score: _____

Now, select the viewpoint category into which your score falls:

18	to	25	Very conservative
10	to	17	Conservative
8	to	16	Moderate conservative
−7	to	7	Moderate
−8	to	−16	Moderate liberal
−10	to	−17	Liberal
−18	to	−25	Very liberal

Step 2: Form parties and write platforms. Depending upon the size of the class, divide the class into three (Democrat, Independent, and Republican) or five (Democrat, Green, Independent, Republican, and Libertarian) groups, combining neighboring categories. Each party must write a simple six-statement platform that states its stands on the issues that it considers most important.

Step 3: Script and video. Each party will write a one-minute script that either supports its own prospective or actual candidate for the next upcoming presidential election or attacks a prospective or actual candidate for that election. If possible, the commercial should have some "punch" to it, like that of the anti-Dukakis commercial.

After practicing the script and refining it, the group must video the commercial on cell phone or camera, and at the appointed time, all parties will show their commercials to the class and discuss them.

5.2   LOCAL GOVERNMENT POLICY

Ariel Kaminer, a contributor to the *New York Times*, calls himself the "City Critic." Like other New Yorkers, he is sometimes frustrated by the Big Apple's crowds and by how hard it is to get around the city. In the June 4, 2010, edition of the *Times* online, Kaminer did a bit of policy analysis. Noting that the streets and subways are overcrowded but the Hudson River is relatively unused, Kaminer examined the city's system of water taxis. He found that if the city provided more piers and some coordination, water taxis could be ferrying thousands more New Yorkers to their daily destinations.[2] This is called "policy analysis"—analyzing what a government is or is not doing and innovating ways to improve things. Similar to Ariel Kaminer, you too may come up with a good idea to improve your hometown.

A policy is a solution to a problem. Every day, governments, at all levels, encounter new problems and then formulate policies to solve them. Policies may result in many different actions being taken, such as laws being passed or new programs being established. For example, a small city may find that its population growth has placed new demands on its water supply. A city that needs more water might establish a policy to restrict certain types of water usage, build a new reservoir, or institute new water conservation measures. Most policies are periodically reviewed, evaluated, and altered to meet changing conditions. These reviews and evaluations are called policy analyses.

[2] Ariel Kaminer. 2010. "What New York Needs: More Water Taxis." *New York Times*, June 4. http://www.nytimes.com/2010/06/06/nyregion/06critic.html?_r=0 (March 7, 2016).

Read&Write 5.2 Analyze a Local Government Policy

In this assignment, you will be analyzing a specific, current policy of a specific local (city, town, or county) government. A local government policy analysis is advice. It is a document that guides a decision-maker on creating or revising a specific policy so that the community is served better. To write your local government policy analysis, follow these steps:

1. Identify a specific local government policy.
2. Identify the problem(s) the policy was created to solve.
3. Evaluate the effectiveness and efficiency of the policy.
4. Identify different alternative ways to solve the problem.
5. Identify ways in which the policy could be improved and make a recommendation.

1. Identify a specific local government policy.

Perhaps the most useful way to select a topic for a local government policy analysis is to tie your search to your own interests, perhaps one that relates to your future vocation. You may find a topic by asking yourself: "What are my career goals, and in what ways will government affect my ability to achieve them?" Local governments affect all of our lives by providing transportation, health, safety, and other services. If you want to be a teacher, you may want to investigate current problems in a local school, like lack of funding for textbooks or the lack of physical education programs. If you are an aspiring athlete, you may want to inquire about opportunities for developing your skills in your community. Are there enough soccer fields? Bicycle paths? If medical school is in your future, you may want to investigate accessibility to emergency medical services in your neighborhood. Every day your local newspaper, in print and online, contains viable topics for local government policy analysis, and Sunday editions usually discuss a variety of issues in detail. Sometimes newspapers highlight community problems and activities on a specific day of the week.

Remember that local government policy analysis topics should have an appropriate scope. A common mistake that students make is choosing topics that are too complex or that require special technical knowledge or skills beyond those readily available. Investigating parent/faculty conflict at your local high school, for example, could be interesting and accomplishable, while checking on the town's water quality standards might make you wish you were a chemistry major.

Once you have decided on a general topic of personal interest, an excellent way to narrow the topic is to contact a public administrator concerned with that subject and have that person identify a related problem currently facing his or her agency. Someone in your city planning office, for example, could tell you about plans for future parks and recreation facilities. At the police department, you may find a public relations officer who will tell you about crime rates and what his or her department is doing to keep the community safe.

2. Identify the problem(s) the policy was created to solve.

You will usually find it essential to interview public officials, representatives of interest groups, and/or technical experts to get all the information necessary to write a local government policy analysis. Information from news stories may help get you started on a topic, but they rarely have enough accurate information for a good analysis. As just mentioned, you will probably find that a local government official will be very helpful. Your local government website will identify people to call and their contact information. Call and make an appointment.

During your appointment, you will want to ask the public official to provide you with:

- General background information on the topic you have chosen
- A written copy of whatever policies may be in effect with respect to the topic
- An explanation about why particular policies were adopted, especially precisely what problem they were meant to solve
- A copy of any studies that have been conducted on the problem or the policies in place
- Information about other people and agencies who can provide you with more information

Once you have this information, identify a specific problem and a specific policy that has been created to solve that problem.

3. Evaluate the effectiveness and efficiency of the policy.

From the information provided during interview(s) and from your other sources of information, attempt to assess the policy. First, you will want to come to some conclusions about how *effective* the policy is. In other words, how well does the policy you have selected actually solve the problem it was intended to solve? If a city has created a program to encourage neighborhood watch plans for suburban neighborhoods, for example, find out if this program had any effect on crime rates in the area.

Second, attempt to estimate the *efficiency* of the policy. Efficiency is the relationship of a program's effectiveness to its cost. For example, if a city spent $10,000 to create a network of neighborhood watch programs, and crime in those neighborhoods was reduced by 50%, saving the involved suburbanites $500,000, then the program could be said to be highly efficient.

4. Identify different alternative ways to solve the problem.

If the policy has not completely resolved the problem at which it was aimed, are there other ways to solve the problem? You may want to do some online research to see what other cities and towns have done, to determine whether someone in another locality has a better idea.

5. Identify ways in which the policy could be improved and make a recommendation.

By now, you should be able to make a recommendation to the people responsible for creating or implementing the policy. Perhaps they should continue with the current policy exactly as it is. Perhaps a change in policy would be beneficial. In any case, be very clear and specific and state precisely what you believe ought to be done.

Read&Write 5.3 Report on a Local Government Agency Meeting

There is no better way to understand local government than to participate in it, and this is one fun and interesting way to do it. Just complete the following easy steps:

1. Select an upcoming meeting from your home city or town's internet home page.

For example, if you type www.northamptonma.gov in your web browser's search line, you will find the website for the city government of Northampton, Massachusetts. If you select "City Government" and then "City Council" and then "Calendar," you can see the schedule of the upcoming meetings. If you select "Councilors," you will find a list of current members, including (in January 2016) the following entry:

William H. Dwight
City Council

Title: City Council President/Councilor-At-Large
Phone: 413-262-6710
bdwight@comcast.net

2. Send an email to Mr. Dwight that contains something similar to the following:

Dear Mr. Dwight:

I am a first year student at UMass Amherst and am enrolled in a course in American Politics and Government. My assignment is to attend a local government meeting and write a short essay that includes my observations about the meeting.

It would be very helpful if you could identify particularly interesting topics that may be discussed at one of your upcoming meetings, and, if possible, suggest a good source of information about that topic and what has transpired in Northampton regarding that topic to date.

Any information you can provide will be much appreciated.

Yours truly,

Rita Hayworth

rhayworth973012@att.net

   If Mr. Dwight does not reply, try another member of the council. When you attend your chosen meeting, take notes so that you can include the following types of information in your three- to four-page essay.

1. Meeting details. Time, place, announcements, agenda.
2. Issues of interest discussed. Description of the issue(s). Identification of controversies, parties to the discussion, tenor or tone of the meeting, and so on.
3. Resolutions and decisions. Extent to which issues are decided or resolved.
4. General impressions. Your opinion, in this particular meeting, whether Northampton's government is operating effectively and efficiently. Add other impressions in your conclusion.

5.3 THE PRESIDENTIAL DECISION-MAKING PROCESS

Presidents make decisions with the help of many types of people including spouses, White House Staff members, informal advisors and trusted friends, councils and advisory boards, cabinets (heads of departments), members of Congress, and lobbyists. Every day, presidents face a myriad of decisions, some that every administration must confront and some that are peculiar to particular times and presidents. But every president soon settles into a unique style of decision-making. Perhaps the best people to describe the decision-making styles of presidents are those who spend the most time with them: their White House Chiefs of Staff. On June 2, 2014, Leon Panetta, former U.S. Secretary of Defense, and Chief of Staff for President Bill Clinton, hosted a discussion panel at the Panetta Institute for Public Policy on the topic of the decision-making styles of presidents Reagan, Clinton, George W. Bush, and Obama. The panel consisted of former chiefs of staff for each of these presidents.

Read&Write 5.4 Analyze Styles of Presidential Decision-Making

Your first task is to watch, listen, and take notes on the Panetta Institute discussion, which you can find at http://www.c-span.org/video/?319601-1/presidential-decision-making.

Based on your notes, write a summary of the decision-making styles of each of the four presidents. Be sure to comment, at least, on who each president trusted, what sources of information the president used, and the relative strengths and weaknesses of each person's decision-making process.

5.4 THE LAW-MAKING PROCESS

It is not surprising that making laws is a highly political business. Every aspect of the process is important to someone, and with more than 250,000 lobbyists working to persuade Congress and state legislators to favor their particular causes, we see why understanding the legislative process is a valuable skill in itself.

One of the best ways to develop this skill is to watch, while taking notes, a series of videos that Congress provides for this purpose. At the following address, part of the www.congress.gov site, you can access nine videos explaining each of the common legislative stages: https://www.congress.gov/legislative-process.

These excellent short videos provide the required information to complete the next writing exercise. The process of examining a bill under consideration by the legislature can teach us many things about how our government works and how those currently serving it think. Accessing the work of legislators, as we will discover, is simple. But finding work of value—a substantive bill that will reward our in-depth consideration—may, unfortunately, prove a more difficult task.

Read&Write 5.5 Analyze a Bill Currently before Congress

Step 1 Select a Substantive Bill to Analyze. Though the work of Congress is vital to the life of the nation, it is an unfortunate fact that many of the pieces of legislation submitted before either of its houses during the course of a typical session will seem frivolous to sizable portions of the country. A little experiment will demonstrate how a single topic can generate both serious, useful bills and bills that seem clearly to be a waste of time. Start at www.congress.gov. Select the link that says "Most-Viewed Bills Top Ten." On January 5, 2016, this list included the following items:

1.	H.R.4269 [114th]	Assault Weapons Ban of 2015
2.	H.Res.569 [114th]	Condemning violence, bigotry, and hateful rhetoric towards Muslims in the United States
3.	H.R.2029 [114th]	Consolidated Appropriations Act, 2016
4.	H.R.3799 [114th]	Hearing Protection Act of 2015
5.	H.R.1321 [114th]	Microbead-Free Waters Act of 2015
6.	H.R.1002 [114th]	Mortgage Forgiveness Tax Relief Act of 2015

7.	H.R.158 [114th]	Visa Waiver Program Improvement Act of 2015
8.	H.R.2393 [114th]	Country of Origin Labeling Amendments Act of 2015
9.	S.754 [114th]	Cybersecurity Information Sharing Act of 2015
10.	H.R.569 [114th]	To prohibit the Secretary of the Interior from issuing oil and gas leases on portions of the Outer Continental Shelf located off the coast of New Jersey

If one of the items in the Most-Viewed list appeals to you, follow the link for that bill. If you have another topic in mind, say "education," the search engine immediately above the Most-Viewed link will locate bills that address education for you. Avoid vacuous bills! A vacuous bill is one that, though it is actual legislation, does not do anything significant. A bill to designate January 30 as National Bagel Day, for example, has much less substance than a bill that funds health care programs.

If we choose to learn about the H.R.4269 [114th] Assault Weapons Ban of 2015 and select the link to that bill, we find further links to:

- the bill's sponsor
- the date the bill was introduced
- the committees to which it is assigned
- the latest action that has been taken on the bill
- a summary of the bill
- the full text of the bill
- actions that have been taken in Congress related to the bill
- short (Assault Weapons Ban of 2015) and official (To regulate assault weapons, to ensure that the right to keep and bear arms is not unlimited, and for other purposes.) titles
- amendments to bill
- cosponsors of the bill
- committees to which the bill has been assigned
- related bills

Step 2   Summarize and evaluate the importance of the bill you have selected and explain where it is in the legislative process. Writing a clear, accurate summary is an exercise in paraphrasing without plagiarizing. Using the information contained in the online bill's summary and text, tell your readers what this bill is all about. Explain to your reader what you see as the substantive effects of this legislation if it should become law. Then, using the information you have gained by watching the legislative process videos described above, explain where this bill is in the legislative process and comment about the prospects for this bill eventually becoming law.

Step 3   Identify and evaluate support for and opposition to this bill. Now, using the skills you have learned in Section 4.3 of this Manual ("How to Read the *Congressional Record*"), peruse the parts of the *Congressional Record* that refer to this bill. Continuing your essay, summarize why this particular bill has been presented to Congress and the main arguments for and against this bill as it stands today. Next, identify and describe the key individuals and groups supporting and opposing this bill and describe the political strength and support each side is able to muster.

Step 4 Summarize the main political, social, and economic implications of this proposed law. In a few paragraphs, explain what difference this bill will make in the lives of Americans if it is passed. Whom will it affect? Make both quantitative and qualitative evaluations. Will the bill affect a few people greatly, a lot of people in a minor way, a few people marginally? Or will it significantly change the lives of large numbers of Americans? How positive will these effects be? Will there be significant side effects to the bill? Consider social and economic impacts of the bill.

What interest groups will win or lose if this bill is passed? Will either of the two major political parties derive benefits? Will particular politicians gain or lose influence if this act is passed? As you conclude your analysis, provide your own assessment of the extent to which this bill will improve America's future.

6

READ AND WRITE PROFESSIONALLY AND CRITICALLY

6.1 HOW TO READ POLITICAL SCIENCE SCHOLARSHIP

To get the most out of anything you read, especially scholarship, ask yourself some questions as you begin. What am I reading? Why am I reading it? What, exactly, do I expect from it?

First of all, when you read an academic article, you are reading scholarship. Scholars are people on a quest for knowledge. They want to know *what* exists (detecting, identifying, and categorizing phenomena), *how* it came to be, or how it does what it does, and *why* it acts or reacts in a certain way. To qualify as scholarship accepted by the academic community, the article must make an *original contribution to knowledge*. When scholars achieve this goal, they participate in an ongoing discussion, by becoming members of a community of people who contribute to the ever-expanding universal storehouse of knowledge. Scholarship is rarely easy reading. Since its audience is scholars, it assumes that one has some basic and sometimes advanced knowledge of languages and practices that are employed in a particular discipline.

So, what is the best approach to reading scholarship? At this point it might be a good idea to revisit the reading tips given in Chapter 1. Here is a brief summary of those points, with new emphasis geared specifically to the reading of scholarship:

- Read slowly, carefully, deeply, and repeatedly.
- Read everything one section at a time.
- Reread everything one section at a time.
- Understand anything you encounter:
    Understand the article.
    Understand the article's implications.
    Imagine applications of the article's insights and discoveries.
- Question everything. Scholars are by no means infallible.
- Take lots of notes.

- Be sure to include important points, questions you can't answer, and interesting insights you have or the article provides.
- Create outlines as you go along that include the structure of the argument (logic) and the process by which information in the article unfolds.
- Before reading, check out the author. Find his or her web page, and identify his or her specialization and credentials.

You will find that most, if not all scholarly articles you read include the following elements:

- An *abstract*: a brief summary of what the article purports to have accomplished
- An *introduction* that includes reasons for conducting the research
- A *research question* revealing what the article intends to discover
- A discussion of the *methods* used to produce knowledge findings
- A statement of the *outcomes* of applying the methods
- A discussion of the *implications* of the findings
- A conclusion that explains the *significance* of the findings
- A list of *references*—sources of information used in the study

Scholarship always has an agenda, something the scholar or scholars who have written the paper are trying to prove. Precisely identify the agenda. Then identify the sequence of points in the argument employed to support the agenda. Is the pattern of points logical? Is it biased?

Read & Write 6.1 Explain the Content of a Recent Article from a Political Science Journal

Your library will most likely hold paper copies of recent issues of a variety of political science journals, as well as providing them to you online. The easiest and most satisfying way to select an article of interest to you is to peruse the shelved copies in the library.

Having selected an article, first read it slowly, attempting to understand what it is all about. Then re-read the article taking notes as described above. Using your notes, write an essay that includes a description in your own words of:

- What the author(s) attempted to do?
- Why the author(s) wanted to do it?
- How the author(s) went about doing it?
- What the author(s) claimed to have discovered?
- What the author(s) inferred about the importance and the benefits of knowing the discovery?

6.2 HOW TO CRITIQUE AN ACADEMIC ARTICLE

The previous section of the chapter explains how to effectively *read* and *describe* an academic article. This section takes that process a step further. An *article critique* is a paper that *evaluates* an article published in an academic journal. A good critique tells the reader what point the article is trying to make and how convincingly it makes that point. Writing an article critique achieves three purposes. First, it provides you with an understanding of the information contained in a scholarly article and a familiarity with other information written on the same topic. Second, it provides you with an opportunity to apply and develop your critical thinking skills as you attempt to evaluate critically a political scientist's work. Third, it helps you to improve your own writing skills as you attempt to describe the selected article's strengths and weaknesses so that your readers can clearly understand them.

The first step in writing an article critique is to select an appropriate article. Unless your instructor specifies otherwise, select an article from a scholarly journal (such as the *American Political Science Review, Journal of Politics,* or *Southeastern Political Science Review*) and not a popular or journalistic publication (such as *Time* or the *National Review*). Appendix A of this manual includes a substantial list of academic political science journals, but your instructor may also accept appropriate articles from academic journals in other disciplines, such as history, economics, or sociology.

Choosing an Article

Three other considerations should guide your choice of an article. First, browse for article titles until you find a topic that interests you. Writing a critique will be much more satisfying if you have an interest in the topic. Hundreds of interesting journal articles are published every year.

The second consideration in selecting an article is your current level of knowledge of the topic. Many political science studies, for example, employ sophisticated statistical techniques. You may be better prepared to evaluate them if you have studied statistics.

The third consideration is to select a current article, one that is written within the last 12 months. Most of the material in the study of political science is quickly superseded by new studies. Selecting a recent study will only ensure that you will be engaged in an up-to-date discussion of your topic.

Read&Write 6.2 Critique a Recent Article from a Political Science Journal

Once you have selected and carefully read your article, you may begin to write your critique, which will cover five areas:

1. Thesis
2. Methods
3. Evidence of thesis support
4. Contribution to the literature
5. Recommendation

Thesis

Your first task is to find and clearly state the thesis of the article. The thesis is the main point the article is trying to make. In a 2014 article published in the scholarly journal

PS: Political Science & Politics and titled "Transparency: The Revolution in Qualitative Research," Andrew Moravcsik of Princeton University states his thesis very clearly:

> Qualitative political science, the use of textual evidence to reconstruct causal mechanisms across a limited number of cases, is currently undergoing a methodological revolution . . . The cornerstone of this methodological revolution is enhanced *research transparency:* the principle that every political scientist should make the essential components of his or her work visible to fellow scholars. The most broadly applicable tool for enhancing qualitative research transparency is *active citation.*[1]

Many authors, however, do not present their theses this clearly. After you have read the article, ask yourself whether you had to hunt for the thesis. Comment about the clarity of the author's thesis presentation and state the author's thesis in your critique. Before proceeding with the remaining elements of your critique, consider the importance of the topic. Has the author written something that is important for us as citizens or political scientists to read?

Methods

In your critique, carefully answer the following questions:

1. What methods did the author use to investigate the topic? In other words, how did the author go about supporting the thesis?
2. Were the appropriate methods used?
3. Did the author's approach to supporting the thesis make sense?
4. Did the author employ the selected methods correctly?
5. Did you discover any errors in the way he or she conducted the research?

Evidence of Thesis Support

In your critique, answer the following questions:

1. What evidence did the author present in support of the thesis?
2. What are the strengths of the evidence presented?
3. What are the weaknesses of the evidence?
4. On balance, how well did the author support the thesis?

Contribution to the Literature

This step will probably require you to undertake some research of your own. Identify articles and books published on the subject of your selected article within the past five years. Browse the titles and read perhaps half a dozen of the publications that appear to provide the best discussion of the topic. In your critique, list the most important other articles or books that have been published on your topic and then, in view of these publications, evaluate the contribution that your selected article makes to a better understanding of the subject.

Recommendation

In this section of your critique, summarize your evaluation of the article. Tell your readers several things: Who will benefit from reading this article? What will the benefit be? How important and extensive is that benefit? Clearly state your evaluation of the article

---

[1] Andrew Moravcsik. 2014. "Transparency: The Revolution in Qualitative Research." *PS*, January. https://www.princeton.edu/~amoravcs/library/transparency.pdf (March 7, 2016).

in the form of a thesis for your own critique. Your thesis might be something like the following:

> In a 2014 article published in *PS: Political Science & Politics* and entitled "Transparency: The Revolution in Qualitative Research," Andrew Moravcsik of Princeton University provides the most concise and comprehensive discussion of the problem of maintaining high quality in quantitative research published in recent years. Political scientists should adopt enhanced *research transparency* because Moravcsik conclusively demonstrates that it will significantly improve the quality of quantitative research.

When writing this assignment, follow the directions for paper formats in Chapter 3 of this manual. Ask your instructor for directions concerning the length of the critique, but in the absence of further guidelines, your paper should not exceed five typed, double-spaced pages.

6.3   HOW TO WRITE A BOOK REVIEW

Successful book reviews answer three questions:

- What did the author of the book try to communicate?
- How clearly and convincingly did he or she get this message across to the reader?
- Was the message worth reading?

Capable book reviewers of several centuries have answered all these three questions well. People who read a book review want to know if a particular book is worth reading, for their own purposes, before buying or reading it. These potential readers want to know the book's subject and its strengths and weaknesses, and they want to gain this information as easily and quickly as possible. Your goal in writing a book review, therefore, is to help people efficiently decide whether to buy or read a book. Your immediate objectives may be to please your instructor and get a good grade, but these objectives are most likely to be met if you focus on a book review's audience: people who want help in selecting books to buy or read. In the process of writing a book review that reaches this primary goal, you will also:

- Learn about the book you are reviewing
- Learn about professional standards for book reviews in political science
- Learn the essential steps of book reviewing that apply to any academic discipline

This final objective, learning to review a book properly, has more applications than you may at first imagine. First, it helps you to focus quickly on the essential elements of a book, and then to draw from a book its informational value for yourself and others. Some of the most successful people in government, business, and the professions speed-read several books a week, more for the knowledge they contain than for enjoyment. These readers then apply this knowledge to substantial advantage in their professions. It is normally not wise to speed-read a book you are reviewing because you are unlikely to gain enough information to evaluate it fairly from such a fast reading. Writing book reviews, however, helps you become proficient in quickly sorting out valuable information from material that is not relevant. The ability to make such discriminations is a fundamental ingredient in management and professional success.

In addition, writing book reviews for publication allows you to participate in the discussions among the broader intellectual and professional community of which you are a part. People in the fields of law, medicine, teaching, engineering, administration, and other professions are frequently asked to write book reviews to help others assess newly released publications.

Before beginning your book review, read the following sample. It is Gregory M. Scott's review of *Political Islam: Revolution, Radicalism, or Reform?*, edited by John L. Esposito. The review appeared in volume 26 of the *Southeastern Political Science Review* (June 1998) and is reprinted here by permission:

Behold an epitaph for the specter of monolithically autocratic Islam. In its survey of Islamic political movements from Pakistan to Algeria, *Political Islam: Revolution, Radicalism, or Reform?* effectively lies to rest the popular notion that political expressions of Islam are inherently violent and authoritarian. For this accomplishment alone John L. Esposito and company's scholarly anthology merits the attention of serious students of religion and politics, and justifies the book's own claim to making a "seminal contribution." Although it fails to identify how Islam as religious faith and cultural tradition lends Muslim politics a distinctively Islamic flavor, this volume clearly answers the question posed by its title: yes, political Islam encompasses not only revolution and radicalism, but moderation and reform as well.

Although two of the eleven contributors are historians, *Political Islam* exhibits both the strengths and weaknesses of contemporary political science with respect to religion. It identifies connections between economics and politics, and between culture and politics, much better than it deciphers the nuances of the relationships between politics and religious belief. After a general introduction, the first three articles explore political Islam as illegal opposition, first with a summary of major movements and then with studies of Algeria and the Gulf states. In her chapter titled "Fulfilling Prophecies: State Policy and Islamist Radicalism," Lisa Anderson sets a methodological guideline for the entire volume when she writes:

> Rather than look to the substance of Islam or the content of putatively Islamic political doctrines for a willingness to embrace violent means to desired ends, we might explore a different perspective and examine the political circumstances, or institutional environment, that breeds political radicalism, extremism, or violence independent of the content of the doctrine. (18)

Therefore, rather than assessing how Islam as religion affects Muslim politics, all the subsequent chapters proceed to examine politics, economics, and culture in a variety of Muslim nations. This means that the title of the book is slightly misleading: it discusses Muslim politics rather than political Islam. Esposito provides the book's conclusion about the effects of Islamic belief on the political process when he maintains that "the appeal to religion is a two-edged sword. . . . It can provide or enhance self-legitimation, but it can also be used as a yardstick for judgment by opposition forces and delegitimation." (70)

The second part of the volume features analyses of the varieties of political processes in Iran, Sudan, Egypt, and Pakistan. These chapters clearly demonstrate not only that Islamic groups may be found in varied positions on normal economic and ideological spectrums, but that Islam is not necessarily opposed to moderate, pluralist politics. The third section of the anthology examines the international relations of Hamas, Afghani Islamists, and Islamic groups involved in the Middle East peace process. These chapters are especially important for American students because they present impressive documentation for the conclusions that the motives and demands of many Islamic groups are considerably more moderate and reasonable than much Western political commentary would suggest.

The volume is essentially well written. All the articles with the exception of chapter two avoid unnecessarily dense political science jargon. As a collection of method-ologically sound and analytically astute treatments of Muslim politics, *Political Islam: Revolution, Radicalism, or Reform?* is certainly appropriate for adoption as a supple-mental text for courses in religion and politics. By way of noting what it does not cover, readers may consider that although it is sufficient for its purposes as it stands, the volume could be a primary text in a course on Islamic politics if it included four additional chapters:

1. An historical overview of the origins and varieties of Islam as religion
2. A summary of the global Islamic political—ideological spectrum (from liberal to fundamentalist)
3. An overview of the varieties of global Islamic cultures
4. An attempt to describe in what manner, if any, Islam, in all its varieties, gives pol-itics a different flavor from the politics of other major religions.[2]

Elements of a Book Review

Your first sentence should entice people to read your review. A crisp summary of what the book is about entices your readers because it lets them know that you can quickly and clearly come to the point. They should know that their time and efforts will not be wasted in an attempt to wade through your vague prose in hopes of finding out something about the book. Notice Scott's opening line: "Behold an epitaph for the specter of monolithically autocratic Islam." It is a bit overburdened with large words, but it is engaging and precisely sums up the essence of the review. Your opening statement can be engaging and "catchy," but be sure that it provides an accurate portrayal of the book in one crisp statement.

Your book review should allow the reader to join you in examining the book. Tell the reader what the book is about. One of the greatest strengths of Scott's review is that his first paragraph immediately tells you exactly what he thinks the book has accomplished.

When you review a book, write about what is actually in the book, not what you think is probably there or ought to be there. Do not explain how you would have written the book, but instead how the author wrote it. Describe the book in clear, objective terms. Tell enough about the content to identify the author's major points.

Clarify the book's value and contribution to political science by defining (1) what the author is attempting to do and (2) how the author's work fits within current or similar efforts in the discipline of political science or other scholarly inquiry in general. Notice how Scott immediately describes what Esposito is trying to do: "This volume clearly answers the question posed by its title." Scott precedes this definition of the author's purpose by placing his work within the context of current similar writing in political science by stating that "for this accomplishment alone John L. Esposito and company's scholarly anthology merits the attention of serious students of religion and politics, and justifies the book's own claim to making a 'seminal contribution.'"

---

[2] Gregory M. Scott. 1998. Review of *Political Islam: Revolution, Radicalism, or Reform?* Ed. John L. Esposito. *Southeastern Political Review* 26(2): 512–24.

The elucidation portion of book reviews often provides additional information about the author. Scott has not included such information about Esposito in his review, but it would be helpful to know, for example, if Esposito has written other books on the subject, has developed a reputation for exceptional expertise on a certain issue, or is known to have a particular ideological bias. How would your understanding of this book be changed, for example, if you knew that its author were a leader of ISIS or the Taliban? Include information in your book review about the author that helps the reader understand how this book fits within the broader concerns of political science.

Once you explain what the book is attempting to do, you should tell the reader the extent to which this goal has been met. To evaluate a book effectively, you must establish an evaluation criteria and then compare the book's content to those criteria. There is no need to define your criteria specifically in your review, but they should be evident to the reader. Your criteria will vary according to the book you are reviewing, and you may discuss them in any order that is helpful to the reader. Consider, however, including the following among the criteria that you establish for your book review:

- How important is the subject to the study of politics and government?
- How complete and thorough is the author's coverage of the subject?
- How carefully is the author's analysis conducted?
- What are the strengths and limitations of the author's methodology?
- What is the quality of the writing? Is it clear, precise, and interesting?
- How does this book compare with others on the subject?
- What contribution does this book make to the field of political science?
- Who will enjoy or benefit from this book?

When giving your evaluations according to these criteria, be specific. If you write, "This is a good book; I liked it very much," you tell nothing of interest or value to the reader. Notice, however, how Scott's review helps to clearly define the content and the limitations of the book by contrasting the volume with what he describes as an ideal primary text for a course in Islamic politics: "By way of noting what it does not cover, readers may consider that although it is sufficient for its purposes as it stands, the volume could be a primary text in a course on Islamic politics if it included four additional chapters."

Read & Write 6.3 Review a New Political Science Book

Format and Content

The directions for writing papers provided in Chapters 1 through 3 apply to book reviews as well. Some further instructions specific to book reviews are needed, however. First, list on the title page, along with the standard information required for political science papers, data on the book being reviewed: title, author, place and name of publisher, date, and number of pages. As the sample that follows shows, the title of the book should be in italics or underlined, but not both:

Reflective or Analytical Book Reviews

Instructors in the humanities and social sciences normally assign two types of book reviews: *reflective* and *analytical*. Ask your instructor which type of book review you are to write.

The purpose of a reflective book review is for the student reviewer to exercise creative analytical judgment without being influenced by the reviews of others. Reflective book reviews contain all the elements covered in this chapter—enticement, examination, elucidation, and evaluation—but they do not include the views of others who have also read the book.

Analytical book reviews contain all the information provided by reflective reviews but add an analysis of the comments of other reviewers. The purpose is, thus, to review not only the book itself but also its reception in the professional community.

To write an analytical book review, insert a review analysis section immediately after your summary of the book. To prepare this section, use the *Book Review Digest* and *Book Review Index* in the library to locate other reviews of the book that have been published in journals and other periodicals. As you read these reviews:

1. List the criticisms of the book's strengths and weaknesses that are made in the reviews.
2. Develop a concise summary of these criticisms, indicate the overall positive or negative tone of the reviews, and mention some of the most commonly found comments.
3. Evaluate the criticisms found in these reviews. Are they basically accurate in their assessment of the book?
4. Write a review analysis of two pages or less that states and evaluates steps 2 and 3 above, and place it in your book review immediately after your summary of the book.

Length of a Book Review

Unless your instructor gives you other directions, a reflective book review should be three to five typed pages long, and an analytical book review should be five to seven pages long. In either case, a brief, specific, and concise book review is almost always preferred over one of greater length.

6.4 HOW TO WRITE A LITERATURE REVIEW

Your goal in writing a research paper is to provide an opportunity for your readers to increase their understanding of the subject you are addressing. They will want the most recent and precise information available. Whether you are writing a traditional library research paper, conducting an experiment, or preparing an analysis of a policy enforced by a government agency, you must know what has already been learned in order to give your readers comprehensive and up-to-date information or to add something new to what they already know about the subject. If your topic is about immigration reform, for example, you will want to find out precisely what national, state, and local government policies currently affect immigration, and the important details of how and why these policies have come to be adopted. When you seek this information, you will be conducting a *literature review*, a thoughtful collection and analysis of available information on the topic you have selected for study. It tells you, before you begin your paper, experiment, or analysis, what is already known about the subject.

Why do you need to conduct a literature review? It would be embarrassing to spend a lot of time and effort preparing a study, only to find that the information you are seeking has already been discovered by someone else. Also, a properly conducted literature review will tell you many things about a particular subject. It will tell you the extent of current knowledge, sources of data for your research, examples of what is *not* known (which in turn generate ideas for formulating hypotheses), methods that have been previously used for research, and clear definitions of concepts relevant for your own research.

Let us consider an example. Suppose that you have decided to research the following question: "How are voter attitudes affected by negative advertising?" First, you will need to establish a clear definition of "negative advertising"; then you will need to find a way to measure attitudes of voters; finally, you will need to use or develop a method of discerning how attitudes are affected by advertising. Using research techniques explained in this and other chapters of this manual, you will begin your research by looking for studies that address your research question or similar questions in the library, on the Internet, and from other resources. You will discover that many studies have been done on voters' attitudes and the effects of advertising on them. As you begin to read these studies, certain patterns will appear. Some research methods will seem to have produced better results than others. Some studies will be quoted in others many times—some confirming and others refuting what previous studies have done. You will constantly be making choices as you examine these studies, reading very carefully those that are highly relevant to your purposes, and skimming those that are only of marginal interest. As you read, constantly ask yourself the following questions:

- How much is known about this subject?
- What is the best available information, and why is it better than other information?
- What research methods have been used successfully in relevant studies?
- What are the possible sources of data for further investigation of this topic?
- What important information is still not known, in spite of all previous research?
- Of the methods that have been used for research, which are the most effective for making new discoveries? Are new methods needed?
- How can the concepts that are being researched be more precisely defined?

You will find that this process, like the research process as a whole, is recursive. Insights related to one of the above questions will spark new investigations into others, and these investigations will then bring up a new set of questions, and so on.

Read & Write 6.4   Write a Political Science Literature Review

Your instructor may request that you include a literature review as a section of the paper you are writing. Your written literature review may be from one to several pages in length, but it should always tell the reader the following information:

1. Which previously compiled or published studies, articles, or other documents provide the best available information on the selected topic?
2. What do these studies conclude about the topic?
3. What are the apparent methodological strengths and weaknesses of these studies are?

4. What remains to be discovered about the topic?
5. What appear to be, according to these studies, the most effective methods for developing new information on the topic?

Your literature review should consist of a written narrative that answers—not necessarily consecutively—the above questions. The success of your own research project depends in large part on the extent to which you have carefully and thoughtfully answered these questions.

PRELIMINARY SCHOLARSHIP

Research Effectively

7.1 INSTITUTE AN EFFECTIVE RESEARCH PROCESS

Your skills as an interpreter of details, an organizer of facts and theories, and a writer of prose come together in a research paper. Building logical arguments on the basis of fact and hypothesis is a way of achieving things in political science, and mastering the art of research makes one a successful political scientist.

Students new to the writing of research papers are sometimes intimidated by the job ahead of them. After all, the research paper adds what seems to be an extra set of complexities to the writing process. Just like an expository or persuasive paper, a research paper must present an original thesis that has a carefully organized and logical argument. But it also investigates a topic that is outside the writer's own experience. This means that writers must locate and evaluate information that is new and in the process educate themselves as they explore their topics of research. Sometimes, a beginning researcher may be overwhelmed by the basic requirements of the assignment or by the authority of the source material being investigated.

As you begin a research project, it may be difficult to establish a sense of control over the different tasks you are undertaking. You may have little notion of where to search for a thesis or even for the most helpful information. If you do not carefully monitor your work habits, you may find yourself unwittingly abdicating responsibility for the paper's argument by borrowing it wholesale from one or more of your sources.

Who is in control of your paper? The answer must be "you"—not the instructor who has assigned you the paper, and certainly not the published writers and interviewees whose opinions you will solicit. Your paper has little use if all it presents is the opinions of others. It is up to you to synthesize an original idea from a judicious evaluation of your source material. Initially, you will, of course, be unsure of the many elements of your paper. For example, you may not yet have a definitive thesis sentence or a clear understanding of the shape of your argument. But you can establish a measure of control over the process involved in completing the paper. And, if you work regularly and systematically, welcoming new ideas as they present themselves, your sense of control will grow. Here are some suggestions to help you establish and maintain control of your paper:

1. **Understand your assignment**. A research assignment can go wrong simply because the writer did not read the assignment carefully. Considering the time and effort you are investing in your project, it is good to ensure that you have a clear understanding of what your instructor wants you to do. Ask your instructor about any aspect of the assignment that is unclear to you—but only after reading it carefully. Recopying the assignment in your own handwriting is a good way to start, even though your instructor may have already given it to you in writing. Before diving into the project, consider the following questions:

2. **What is your topic?** The assignment may give you a great deal of specific information about your topic, or you may be allowed considerable freedom in establishing one for yourself. In a government class in which you are studying issues affecting American foreign policy, your professor might give you a very specific assignment—a paper, for example, examining the difficulties of establishing a viable foreign policy in the wake of the collapse of international communism— or he or she may allow you to choose for yourself the issue that your paper will address. You need to understand the terms, as set up in the assignment, by which you will design your project.

3. **What is your purpose?** Whatever the degree of latitude you are given in the matter of your topic, pay close attention to the way your instructor has phrased the assignment. Ask if your primary job is to *describe* a current political situation or to *take a stand* on it. Must you *compare* political systems, and if so, to what extent? Must you *classify*, *persuade*, *survey*, or *analyze*? Look for such descriptive terms in the assignment to determine the purpose of your project.

4. **Who is your audience?** Your orientation towards the paper is profoundly affected by your conception of the audience for whom you are writing. Of course, your main reader is your instructor, but see who else would be interested in your paper. Are you writing for the voters of a community, a governor, or a city council? A paper that describes the proposed renovation of city buildings may justifiably contain much more technical jargon for an audience of contractors than for a council of local business and civic leaders.

5. **What kind of research are you doing?** You will be doing one, if not both, of the following kinds of research:

   - *Primary research*, which requires you to discover information firsthand, often by conducting interviews, surveys, or polls. Here, you collect and sift through raw data—not already interpreted by researchers—that you will later study, select, arrange, and speculate on. These raw data may be the opinions of experts or of laypersons, historical documents, published letters of a famous politician, or material collected from other researchers. It is important to set up carefully the methods used to collect your data. Your aim must be to gather credible information, from which sound observations may be made later, either by you or by other writers using the material you have unearthed.

   - *Secondary research*, which uses published accounts of primary materials. If a primary researcher polls a community for its opinion on the result of a recent bond election, the secondary researcher uses the information from the poll to support a particular thesis. Secondary research, in other words, focuses on interpretations of raw data. Most of your college papers will be based on your use of secondary sources.

Primary Source	Secondary Source
A published collection of Thurgood Marshall's letters	A journal article arguing that the volume of letters illustrates Marshall's attitude toward the media
An interview with the mayor	A character study of the mayor based on the interview
Material from a questionnaire	A paper basing its thesis on the results of the questionnaire

6. **Keep your perspective**. Whichever type of research you perform, you must keep your results in perspective. As a primary researcher, you cannot be completely objective in your findings. It is not possible to design a question-naire that will net you absolute truth, nor can you be sure that the opinions of the people questioned during interviews are accurate and unchanging. Likewise, if you are conducting secondary research, you must remember that the articles and journals you are using are shaped by the aims of their writers, who are interpreting primary materials for their own ends. The farther you are removed from a primary source, the greater the possibility for distortion. As a researcher, you must be as accurate as possible, which means keeping in view the limitations of your methods and their conclusions.

In any research project, there will be some moments of confusion; by establishing an effective research procedure, you can prevent the confusion from overwhelming you. Design a schedule that is as systematic as possible, yet flexible enough so that you do not feel trapped by it. By always showing you what to do next, a schedule will help keep you from running into dead ends. At the same time, the schedule helps in retaining the focus necessary to spot new ideas and strategies as you work.

Give Yourself Plenty of Time

You may feel like delaying your research for various reasons: unfamiliarity with the library, the urgency of other tasks, or a deadline that seems comfortably far away. Never allow such factors to deter you. Research takes time. Working in a library seems to speed up the clock; the time you expected it would take you to find a certain source may double. You must allow yourself the time needed not only to find material but also to read it, assimilate it, and set it in the context of your own thoughts. If you delay starting, you may be distracted by the deadline, having to keep an eye on the clock while trying to make sense of a writer's complicated argument.

The following schedule lists the steps of a research project in the order in which they are generally accomplished. Remember that each step is dependent on the others and you may have to revise earlier decisions in light of later discoveries. After some background reading, for example, your notion of the paper's purpose may change, a fact that may in turn alter other steps. One of the strengths of a good schedule is its flexibility. Note that this schedule lists tasks for both primary and secondary research; you must use only those steps that are relevant to your project.

7.2   FIND AND EVALUATE THE QUALITY OF ONLINE AND PRINTED INFORMATION

Do Background Reading

Whether you are doing primary or secondary research, you need to know what kinds of work have already been done in your field. **Warning:** Be very careful not to rely too heavily on material in general encyclopedias such as *Wikipedia* or *Encyclopedia Britannica.* You may wish to consult one for an overview of a topic with which you are not familiar, but students who are new to research are often tempted to import large sections, if not entire articles, from such volumes, and this practice is not good scholarship. One major reason your instructor has assigned a research paper is to let you experience the kinds of books and journals in which the discourse of political science is conducted. Encyclopedias are good places for instant introductions to subjects; some even include bibliographies of reference works at the end of their articles. But to write a useful paper, you will need much more detailed information about your subject. Once you have learned what you can get from a general encyclopedia, move on to the academic articles that you will find by following links on your college library's web page. When you find two or three good articles on your topic, you will find that the bibliographies at the end of each article will be rich sources of other articles and books of academically acceptable quality.

Narrow Your Topic and Establish a Working Thesis

The process of coming up with a viable thesis for a paper involving academic research is pretty much the same one to use for a paper that doesn't require formal research, though the need to consult published sources may seem to make the enterprise more intimidating. (Chapter 1 offers general tips for finding a successful thesis for a paper.) For a research paper in a course in American government, Charlotte Goble was given the topic category of grassroots attempts to legislate morality in American society. She chose the specific topic of textbook censorship. Here is the path she took as she looked for ways to limit the topic effectively and find a thesis.

General Topic	Textbook Censorship
Potential Topics	How a local censorship campaign gets started
	Funding censorship campaigns
	Reasons behind textbook censorship
	Results of censorship campaigns
Working Thesis	It is disconcertingly easy in our part of the state to launch a textbook censorship campaign

As with any paper, it is unlikely that you will come up with a satisfactory thesis at the beginning of your research project. You need a way to guide yourself through the early stages of research as you work toward discovering the main idea that is both useful and manageable. Having in mind a *working thesis*—a preliminary statement of your purpose—can help you select the material that is of greatest interest to you as you examine potential sources. The working thesis will probably evolve as your research progresses, and you should be ready to accept such change. You must not fix on a thesis too early in the process, or you may miss opportunities to refine it later.

Conduct an Interview Establish a purpose for each interview, bearing in mind the requirements of your working thesis. In what ways might your interview benefit your paper? Write down your description for the purpose of the interview. Estimate its length, and inform your subject. Arrive for your interview on time and dressed appropriately. Be courteous.

Before the interview, learn as much as possible about your topic by researching published sources. Use research material to design your questions. If possible, learn something about the backgrounds of the people whom you will interview. This knowledge may help you establish rapport with your subjects and will also help you tailor your questions. Take a printout of the list of interview questions that you have prepared. However, be ready to digress during the interview from your own list in order to follow any potentially useful direction that the questioning may take.

Take notes. Make sure you have extra pens. Do not use a tape recorder because it will inhibit most interviewees. If you must use tape, *seek prior permission from your subject* before beginning the interview. Follow up your interview with a thank-you letter and, if feasible, a copy of the paper in which the interview is used.

Design and Conduct a Survey If your research study requires a survey, see Chapter 8 for instructions on designing and conducting surveys, polls, and questionnaires.

Draft a Thesis and Outline

No matter how thoroughly you may hunt for data or how fast you read, you will not be able to find and assimilate every source pertaining to your subject, especially if it is popular or controversial, and you should not unduly prolong your research. You must bring this phase of the project to an end—with the option of resuming it, if the need arises—and begin to shape both the material you have gathered and your thoughts about it into a paper. During the research phase of your project, you have been thinking about your working thesis, testing it against the material you have discovered, and considering ways to improve it. Eventually, you must formulate a thesis that sets out an interesting and useful task, one that can be satisfactorily managed within the limits of your assignment and that effectively employs much, if not all, of the material you have gathered.

Once you have formulated your thesis, it is a good idea to make an outline of the paper. In helping you to determine a structure for your writing, the outline is also testing the thesis, prompting you to discover the kind of work your paper will need to complete the task set out by the main idea. Chapter 1 discusses the structural requirements of the formal and the informal outline. If you have used note cards, you may want to start outlining by organizing your cards according to the headings you have given them and looking for logical connections among the different groups of cards. Experimenting with structure in this way may lead you to various discoveries that will further improve your thesis.

No thesis or outline is written in stone. There is always time to improve the structure or purpose of your paper after you have begun to write your first draft or, for that matter, your final draft. Some writers actually prefer to write a first draft before outlining, and then study the draft's structure to determine what revisions need to be made. *Stay flexible*, always looking for a better connection—a sharper wording of your thesis. All the time while you are writing, the testing of your ideas continues.

Write a First Draft

Despite all the preliminary work you have done on your paper, you may be reluctant to begin your first draft. Integrating all your material and your ideas into a smoothly flowing argument is indeed a complicated task. It may help to think of your first attempt as only a rough draft, which can be changed as and when it is necessary. Another strategy for reducing reluctance to start is to begin with the part of the draft about which you feel most confident, instead of with the introduction. You may write sections of the draft in any order, piecing the parts together later. But however you decide to start writing—START.

Obtain Feedback

It is not enough that you understand your argument; others have to understand it, too. If your instructor is willing to look at your rough draft, you should take advantage of the opportunity and pay careful attention to any suggestions made for improvement. Other readers may also be of help, although having a friend or a relative read your draft may not be as helpful as having it read by someone who is knowledgeable in your field. In any event, be sure to evaluate any suggestions carefully. Remember, the final responsibility for the paper rests with you.

Read&Write 7.1   Write a Research Proposal

Do you aspire to a professional career? Entrepreneur? Doctor? Lawyer? Engineer? School Principal? Professor? Nurse? Architect? Marketing Director? Executive Director, Non-profit Organization? Research Director? The ability to write a high-quality research proposal may well be one of the most useful, and profitable skills you acquire on route to your B.A. or B.S. Research proposals are written by the hundreds in public and private agencies and by innovators and entrepreneurs every day. A long-standing motto of entrepreneurs of all sorts is a simple guide to commercial success: "Find a need and fill it." From the light bulb to the iPhone, this principle has been a guiding motivation for thousands of successful inventors, entrepreneurs, CEOs, volunteers and medical missionaries. Remember that a *need* is both a problem that someone wants to solve and an opportunity for you to make a contribution by solving it.

How does writing a research proposal foster success in this process? Simple. Most new ventures require *funding*. Most sources of funding (government agencies, nonprofit organizations, investors) require you to submit a *plan or feasibility study* that demonstrates: (1) the need for a particular project, (2) the economic viability of the project, and (3) the inclusion of the talent, expertise, and experience needed to successfully undertake the project.

The first step in acquiring funding is a *research proposal* to acquire funds and/or authorization to conduct the research necessary to affirm the need for and feasibility of the project.

Research proposals, therefore, are sales jobs. Their purpose is to "sell" the belief that a research study needs to be done. Before conducting a research study for a government agency, you must convince someone in authority that a study is necessary, by accomplishing the following tasks:

1. Prove that the study is necessary.
2. Describe the objectives of the study.
3. Explain how the study will be done.
4. Describe the resources (time, people, equipment, facilities, etc.) that will be needed to do the job.
5. Construct a schedule that states when the project will begin and end, and gives important dates in between.
6. Prepare a project budget that specifies the financial costs and the amount to be billed (if any) to the government agency.
7. Carefully define what the research project will produce, what kind of study will be conducted, how long it will be, and what it will contain.

The Content of Research Proposals

An Overview

In form, research proposals contain the following four parts:

1. Title page
2. Outline page
3. Text
4. Reference page

An outline of the content of research proposals appears as shown below:

I. Need for a study
   A. An initial description of the current problem
      1. A definition of the problem
      2. A brief history of problem
      3. The legal framework and institutional setting of the problem
      4. The character of the problem, including its size, extent, and importance

   B. Imperatives
      1. The probable costs of taking no action
      2. The expected benefits of study

II. Methodology of the proposed study
    A. Project management methods to be used
    B. Research methods to be used
    C. Data analysis methods to be used

III. Resources necessary to conduct the study
     A. Material resources
     B. Human resources
     C. Financial resources

V. Schedule for the study
VI. Budget for the study
VII. Product of the study

A Note on Research Process and Methods

Your research proposal will briefly describe the steps you will take to find, evaluate, and draw conclusions from the information that is pertinent to your study. The research process normally proceeds in these steps:

1. Data (information) collection: Gathering the appropriate information
2. Data analysis: Organizing the data and determining its meaning or implications
3. Data evaluation: Determining what conclusions may be drawn from the data
4. Recommendation: Formulating a concise description of the study that needs to be undertaken

A Note on the Anticipated Product of the Study

In the final section of the proposal, you will describe the anticipated product of your study. In other words, you will tell the persons for whom you are writing the proposal exactly what they will receive when the project is done. If you are writing this paper for a class in public, you will probably write something like the following:

The final product will be a research study from 25 to 30 pages in length, which will provide an analysis of the problem and an evaluation of alternative new policies that may solve the problem.

The quote "Winning isn't everything, it's the only thing" may not have originated with Vince Lombardi, the famous coach of the Green Bay Packers, but he certainly popularized it. In terms of academic scholarship, it is not an exaggeration to say, "Credibility isn't everything, it's the only thing" because the importance of the acceptance of what is written cannot be underestimated. Similarly, as you write political science scholarship, assume correctly that your work has no value if it lacks credibility. With this in mind, understand that the credibility of your writing depends, on the credibility of your sources more than anything else. Therefore, here are some guidelines to assess the credibility of the sources you employ in your paper.

You may have already read the news article appraisal checklist in Section 1.3 of this manual. Almost the same principles are applied to both reading other sources of information and reading news articles, but for the more complex information sources, the following additional suggestions would be helpful.

Reputation In general, reputation of information conforms to a clear hierarchy, described here in descending order of credibility. Here is a list of high-quality sources:

- Articles in academic journals, though not foolproof, have a huge credibility advantage. They conform to the research and writing standards explained throughout this manual. They often require months, if not years, to write, allowing for revision and refinement. They often employ a team of several authors, each of whom can assess the quality and accuracy of the others' work. Once submitted to a journal for publication, they are distributed (blind) to experts in the articles' topics for review and comments. Once published they are exposed to widespread readership, providing an additional quality filter.

- Research studies by recognized think tanks (research institutes) are often of exceptionally high quality. They are not exposed to the same extent of external review before publication as academic journals, and the institutions that produce them often have a known ideological perspective. Yet whether they are conservative, liberal, or libertarian in orientation, their writers know that the credibility of their work depends on maintaining consistency.

- Research studies by government agencies are much like think tank papers but are likely to be controversial because their findings will always annoy people who are unhappy with their conclusions. They can be very powerful, however, if they are used by presidents or by Congress to adopt particular public policies.

- Reports in high-quality nonpartisan magazines and television journalism are often highly reliable in both research and reporting. Some examples are periodicals like *The Economist, The Atlantic Monthly, The New Yorker, The American Scholar, Foreign Affairs, Foreign Policy,* and Public Broadcasting Service (PBS) journalism in features such as *Frontline* and *The American Experience.*

- Articles in high-quality newspapers, like the *New York Times, Wall Street Journal, Washington Post,* and the *Christian Science Monitor* cite authoritative sources.

- Pieces in high-quality partisan magazines like *The Nation* and *The National Review* can provide relatively reliable, if slanted and selective information.

Low-quality sources are of several sorts, and all are to be read for quickly secured unverified "facts" and amusement rather than education. Here are some low-quality sources:

- Wikipedia provides much information quickly, and some tolerable overviews of topics, but is notoriously vulnerable to people who provide unverified and even false information.

- Partisan blogs, like the *Huffington Post* are fun and provide an interesting array of perspectives and insights, but any information you find on them must be verified by more credible sources.

- Commercial TV news sources, like CNN and especially Fox News are so sensational and clearly biased that their value is little more than entertainment.

As with newspapers, the following elements of information sources are essential to assessing content quality.

- *Author.* What are the credentials and reputation of the author of the publication?
- *Information sources.* What sources of information are used by the author of a particular article? Are they recognized individuals or institutions?
- *Writing quality.* Is the article well written? Is it clear and cogent? Does it use a lot of jargons? Can you understand it?
- *Quantity of information.* Is the article sufficiently comprehensive to substantiate its thesis?
- *Unsupported assumptions.* Beware of statements like this: "Statistics prove that hospitals in urban areas provide better care than rural facilities." What statistics? Does the article identify them?
- *Balance.* Does the article cover all relevant aspects of a subject?

Develop a Working Bibliography

As you begin your research, you will look for published sources—essays, books, or interviews with experts—that may help you. This list of potentially useful sources is your *working bibliography*. There are many ways to develop this bibliography. The cataloging system in your library gives you sources, as will the published bibliographies in your field. (Some of these bibliographies are listed below.) The general references used for your background reading may also list such works, and each specialized book or essay will have a bibliography that its writer used, which may be helpful to you.

It is from your working bibliography that you will select the items that will appear in the final draft of your paper. Early in your research, you will not know which of the sources will help you and which will not; therefore, it is important to keep an accurate description of each entry in your working bibliography so that you can tell clearly which items you have investigated and which you will need to consult again. Establish your working bibliography in the format that you are required to follow in your final draft. Ensure that all the information about each of your potential sources is in the proper format and punctuation. (Chapter 3 describes in detail the bibliographical formats most often required for political science papers.)

Request Needed Information

In the course of your research, you may need to consult a source that is not immediately available to you. For example, while working on a textbook censorship paper, you might find that a packet of potentially useful information may be obtained from a government agency or public interest group in Washington, DC. Or you may discover that a needed book is not owned by your university library or by any other local library, or that a successful antidrug program has been implemented in the school system of a city of comparable size in another state. In such situations, it may be tempting to disregard potential sources because of the difficulty of consulting them. If you ignore this material, however, you are not doing your job.

It is vital that you take steps to acquire the needed data. In the first case mentioned above, you can simply write to the Washington, DC, agency or interest group; in the second, you may use your library's interlibrary loan procedure to obtain the book; in the third, you can track down the council that manages the antidrug campaign by e-mail, phone, or Internet, and ask for information. Remember that many businesses and government agencies want to share their information with interested citizens; some have employees or entire departments whose job is to facilitate communication with the public. Be as specific as possible when asking for such information. It is a good idea to outline your own project briefly—in no more than a few sentences—to help the respondent determine the types of information that will be useful to you.

Never let the immediate unavailability of a source stop you from trying to consult it. And be sure to begin the job of locating and acquiring such long-distance material as soon as possible, to allow for the various delays that often occur.

Read & Write 7.2   Locate a Dozen High-Quality Sources

Assume you are going to write a 10-page paper on a topic of your choice. Locate and list, in APSA bibliographical format, a dozen high-quality sources for your paper.

8

ANALYZE PUBLIC OPINION

LEARN THE STEPS IN WRITING A SURVEY PAPER

The Skill of Conducting Accurate Surveys

A poll is a device for counting preferences. On election days electoral polls calculate the votes of candidates and determine which candidates will assume office. Voter preference polls are conducted during election campaigns to track changes in voter preferences over a period of time.

A survey is a series of statements or questions that define a set of preferences to be polled. If a poll is conducted on the subject of immigration policy, for example, a survey will be constructed consisting of a series of questions, such as "Should illegal immigrants be deported?" or "Should children of illegal immigrants born in the U.S. be deprived their constitutional right to American citizenship?"

Writing your own public opinion survey paper will serve two purposes. First, you will learn how to construct, conduct, and interpret a public opinion poll, the means by which much research is done within the discipline. You will thus begin to learn a skill that you may actually use in your professional life. Large and small public and private organizations often conduct polls on the public's needs and preferences, in order to make their services more effective and desirable. Second, by writing a survey paper, you will understand how to evaluate polls thoughtfully and critically by knowing the strengths and weaknesses of the polling process.

In this chapter, you will learn how to construct and conduct a simple public opinion poll and how to apply some elementary data analysis and evaluation techniques to your poll results. Your instructor may want to add a few supplemental tasks, such as other statistical procedures, and your text in political science methods will tell you much more about the process of public opinion research. The following set of directions, however, will provide the information needed to create and interpret a public opinion poll.

Focus on a Specific Topic

The first step in writing a public opinion survey paper is to select a topic that is focused on one specific issue. Although nationally conducted polls sometimes cover a broad variety of topics, confining your inquiry to one specifically defined issue will allow you to gain an appreciation for even a single topic's complexity and the difficulties inherent in clearly identifying opinions. Precision is important in clearly understanding public opinion.

Public opinion surveys are conducted on topics pertaining to local, state, national, or international politics, topics nearly as numerous as the headlines/titles of articles that appear in a daily newspaper. You will usually increase the interest of the audience of your paper if you select an issue that is currently widely discussed in the news.

Formulate a Research Question and a Research Hypothesis

Once you have selected a topic, your task is to determine what you want to know about people's opinions concerning that topic. If you choose tax policy, for example, you may want to know the extent to which people are concerned about tax policy and what changes in current policy they will support. You need to phrase your questions carefully. If you ask, simply, "Are you concerned about tax quality?" you will probably receive a positive reply from a substantial majority of your respondents. But what does this actually tell you? Does it reveal the intensity and strength of people's concern about taxes? Do you know how the respondents will vote on any particular tax proposal? Do people have different attitudes toward tax rates, tax loopholes, and the complexity of the tax code? To find out, you have to design more specific questions. The following sections of this chapter will help you to do this.

A research question asks exactly what the researcher wants to know. Research questions posed by national polls include the following:

- What is the president's current approval rating?
- What types of voters are likely to favor immigration reform?
- What are the dominant current attitudes towards the national debt?

Research questions for papers for political science classes, however, should be more specific and confined to a narrowly defined topic. Consider the following:

- Is the population to be surveyed in favor of banning private ownership of assault weapons?
- To what extent do the people polled believe that their personal political actions, such as voting or writing to a representative, will actually make a difference in the political process (a sense of political efficacy)?

Select a Sample

Surveys of public opinion are usually conducted to find out what large groups of people, such as American voters, members of labor unions, or religious fundamentalists, think about a particular problem. It is normally unnecessary and too costly to obtain the views of everyone in these groups. Most surveys therefore question a small but representative percentage of the group that is being studied. The elements of surveys are the individual units being studied. These elements may be interest groups, corporations, or church denominations, but they are most often individual voters. The population is the total number of elements covered by the research question. If the research question is "Are voters in Calaveras County in favor of a 1 percent sales tax to pay for infrastructure improvements to encourage economic development?" then the population is the voters of Calaveras County. The sample is the part of the population that is selected to respond to the survey. A representative sample includes numbers of elements in the same proportions as they occur in the general population. In other words, if the population of Calaveras County is 14 percent Latino and 52 percent female, a representative sample will also be 14 percent Latino and 52 percent female. A nonrepresentative sample does not include the number of elements in the same proportions as they occur in the general population.

All samples are drawn from a sampling frame, which is the part of the population being surveyed. To represent the population accurately, a sampling frame should include all types of elements (e.g., youth, women, Latinos) of interest to the research question. If the population is the voters of Calaveras County, a sampling frame might be the parents of children in an elementary school who are registered to vote. Strata are groups of similar elements within a population. Strata of the voters of Calaveras County may include voters under 30, women, labor union members, or Latinos. Stratified samples include numbers of respondents in different strata that are not in proportion to the general population. For example, a stratified sample of the population of Calaveras County might purposely include only Latino women if the purpose of the survey is to determine the views of this group.

A survey research design of the Calaveras County issue would thus be constructed as follows:

Research question: Are voters in Calaveras County in favor of a 1 percent sales tax to pay for infrastructure improvements to encourage economic development?"

Research hypothesis: Fifty-five percent of the voters in Calaveras County will favor a 1 percent sales tax to pay for infrastructure improvements to encourage economic development.

Elements: Individual registered voters

Population: Registered voters in Calaveras County

Sampling frame: Five hundred registered voters in Calaveras County selected at random from voter registration lists

Sample: Of the 500 registered voters in Calaveras County selected at random from voter registration lists, those who answer the survey questions when called on the telephone.

How large must a sample be to represent the population accurately? This question is difficult to answer, but two general principles apply. First, a large sample is more likely, simply by chance, to be more representative of a population than a small sample. Second, the goal is to obtain a sample that includes representatives of all of the strata within the whole population.

You will find it most convenient if you use as your sample the class for which you are writing your survey paper. The disadvantage of this sample selection is that your class may not be representative of the voters of the county in which your survey is conducted. Even if this is the case, however, you will still be learning the procedures for conducting a survey, which is the primary objective of this exercise.

> **Note:** Public opinion surveys ask people for their opinions. The people whose opinions are sought are known as human subjects of the research. Most colleges and universities have policies concerning research with human subjects. Sometimes administrative offices known as institutional review boards are established to review research proposals in order to ensure that the rights of human subjects are protected. It may be necessary for you to obtain permission from such a board or from your college to conduct your survey. Be sure to comply with all policies of your university with respect to research with human subjects.

Construct the Survey Questionnaire

Your research question will be your primary guide for constructing your survey questions. As you begin to write your questions, ask yourself what it is that you really want to know about the topic. Suppose that your research question is, "What are the views of political science students regarding the role of the government in regulating abortions?" If you ask, for example, "Are you for abortion?" you may get a negative answer from 70 percent of the respondents. If you then ask, "Are you for making abortion illegal?" you may get a negative answer from 81 percent of your respondents. These answers seem to contradict each other. By asking additional questions, you may determine that, whereas a majority of the respondents finds abortion regrettable, only a minority wants to make it illegal. But even this may not be enough information to get a clear picture of people's opinions. The portion of the population that wants to make abortion illegal may be greater or smaller according to the strength of the legal penalty to be applied. In addition, some of the students who want no legal penalty for having an abortion may want strict medical requirements imposed on abortion clinics, while others may not. You must design additional specific questions to determine accurately respondents' views on these issues.

The number of questions to include in your questionnaire is a matter to be carefully considered. The first general rule, as mentioned earlier, is to ask a sufficient number of questions to find out precisely what it is you want to know. A second principle, however, conflicts with this first rule. This principle, which may not be a problem in your political science class, is that people in general do not like to fill out surveys. Survey information can be very valuable, and pollsters are found on street corners, in airports, and on the telephone. Short surveys with a small number of questions are more likely to be answered completely than long questionnaires. The questionnaire for your paper in survey research methods should normally contain between 10 and 25 questions.

Surveys consist of two types of questions: closed and open. Closed questions restrict the response of the respondent to a specific set of answers. Many types of closed questions are used in public opinion surveys, but they may be grouped into three categories:

- Two-choice questions
- Three-choice questions
- Multiple-choice questions

Two-choice questions may ask for a simple preference between candidates, such as if the election were held today, for whom would you vote: Donald Trump or Hillary Clinton?

Issue-centered, two-choice questions offer respondents a choice of one of two answers, most often "yes" and "no," or "agree" and "disagree," as shown below:

Is a mandatory five-day waiting period for the purchase of a handgun desirable?

☐ Yes   ☐ No

A balanced budget amendment to the Constitution should be passed.

☐ Agree   ☐ Disagree

Two-choice questions ask respondents to choose between two statements, neither of which they may entirely support. To find out how many people are ambivalent on these issues, three-choice questions are often asked, giving respondents a third selection, which is most often "undecided," "no opinion," "uncertain," "do not know," "does not apply," or "not sure":

The political party that does the most for Latino people is

☐ Republican ☐ Democratic ☐ Libertarian ☐ Uncertain

Simple multiple-choice questions are sometimes constructed to provide a wider range of choices, such as in the following:

If the Republican primary election were held today, for whom would you vote?

☐ Donald Trump   ☐ Hillary Clinton

☐ Marco Rubio   ☐ Bernie Sanders

Just as often, however, multiple-choice questions are constructed to discriminate more clearly between positions in a range of attitudes. For example, Likert scale multiple-choice questions are used to distinguish among degrees of agreement on a range of possible views on an issue. A Likert-scale question might be stated like this:

"American military expenditures should be reduced by an additional 10 percent to provide funds for domestic programs." Select one of the following responses to this statement:

☐ Strongly agree   ☐ Agree   ☐ Not sure

☐ Disagree   ☐ Strongly disagree

Guttmann-scale multiple-choice questions allow discrimination among a range of answers by creating a series of statements with which it is increasingly difficult to agree or disagree. A respondent who selects one item on the scale of questions is also likely to agree with the items higher on the scale. Consider this example.

Select the answer with which you agree most completely:

1. Citizen ownership of military weapons such as rocket launchers should be restricted.
2. Citizen ownership of fully automatic weapons such as machine guns should be restricted.
3. Citizen ownership of semiautomatic weapons should be restricted.
4. Citizen ownership of handguns and concealed weapons should be restricted.
5. Citizen ownership of hunting rifles should be restricted.

Closed questions have the advantage of being easy to quantify. A number value can be assigned to each answer, and totals can be made of answers of different types.

By contrast, open questions, or open-ended questions, are not easy to quantify. In open questions, respondents are not provided a fixed list of choices but may answer anything they want. The advantage of using open questions is that your survey may discover ideas or attitudes of which you were unaware. Suppose, for example, that you ask the following question and give space for respondents to write their answers:

What should be done about gun control?

You might, for example, get a response like the following:

All firearms should be restricted to law enforcement agencies in populated areas. Special, privately owned depositories should be established for hunters to store their rifles for use in target practice or during hunting season.

Open questions call for a more active and thoughtful response than do closed questions. The fact that more time and effort are required may be a disadvantage because in general the more time and effort a survey demands, the fewer responses it is likely to get. Despite this disadvantage, open questions are to be preferred to closed questions when you want to expand the range of possible answers in order to find out how much diversity there is among opinions on an issue. For practice working with open questions, you should include at least one in your survey questionnaire.

Perhaps the greatest difficulty with open questions is that of quantifying the results. The researcher must examine each answer and then group the responses according to their content. For example, responses clearly in favor, clearly opposed, and ambivalent to gun control might be differentiated. Open questions are of particular value to researchers who are doing continuous research over time. The responses they obtain help them to create better questions for their next survey.

Besides the regular open and closed questions on your survey questionnaire, you will want to add identifiers, which ask for personal information about the respondents, such as gender, age, political party, religion, income level, or other items that may be relevant to the particular topic of your survey. If you ask questions about gun control, for example, you may want to know if men respond differently than women, if Democrats respond differently than Republicans, or if young people respond differently than older people.

Once you have written the survey questionnaire, you need to conduct the survey. You must distribute it to the class or other group of respondents. Be sure to provide clear directions for filling out the questionnaire on the survey form. If the students are to complete the survey in class, read the directions aloud and ask if there are any questions before they begin to fill in the form.

Collect the Data

If your sample is only the size of a small political science class, you will be able to tabulate the answers to the questions directly from the survey form. If you have a larger sample, however, you may want to use data collection forms such as those from the Scantron Corporation. You may be using such forms (on which respondents use a number 2 pencil to mark answers) when you take multiple-choice tests in some of your classes. The advantage of Scantron forms is that they are processed through computers that tabulate the results and sometimes provide some statistical measurements. If you use Scantron sheets, you will need access to computers that process the results, and you may need someone to program the computer to provide the specific statistical data that you need.

Analyze the Data

Once you have collected the completed survey forms, you will need to analyze the data that they provide. Statistical procedures are helpful here to perform three tasks:

1. Describe the data
2. Compare components of the data
3. Evaluate the data

There are many statistical procedures especially designed to carry out each of these tasks. This chapter provides only a few examples of the methods that may be used in each category. Consult your instructor or a survey research methods textbook to learn about other types of statistical measurement tools.

Statistics designed to describe data may be very simple. We will start our discussion with two example questions, both employing the Likert scale:

Question 1

"Immigration reform should include amnesty for all illegal immigrants living in the United States today." Select one of the following responses to this statement:

☐ Strongly agree   ☐ Agree   Not sure   ☐ Disagree   ☐ Strongly disagree

Question 2

"Immigration reform must include strengthening the security of our borders." Select one of the following responses to this statement:

☐ Strongly agree   ☐ Agree   ☐ Not sure   ☐ Disagree   ☐ Strongly disagree

Our objective in describing the data is to see how our hypothetical respondent sample of 42 students, as a group, answered these questions. The first step is to assign a numerical value to each answer, as follows:

Answer	Points
Strongly agree	1
Agree	2
Not sure	3
Disagree	4
Strongly disagree	5

Our next step is to count our survey totals to see how many respondents in our hypothetical sample marked each answer to each question:

TABLE 8.1

Survey Totals

Answer	Points	Q1 Responses	Q2 Responses
Strongly Agree	1	8	13
Agree	2	16	10
Not Sure	3	12	1
Disagree	4	4	12
Strongly Disagree	5	2	6

We may now calculate the mean (numerical average) of responses by performing the following operations for each question:

1. Multiply the point value by the number of responses to determine the number of value points.
2. Add the total value points for each answer.
3. Divide the total value points by the number of respondents (42 in this case).

To see how this procedure is done, examine the chart below, which analyzes the responses to Question 1. Notice that column 1 contains the answer choices provided to the respondents, column 2 contains the point value assigned to each choice, column 3 contains the number of respondents who selected each answer, and column 4 contains the value points assigned for each answer choice, multiplied by the number of responses.

TABLE 8.2

Value Points

Answer Choices	Assigned Point Value	Number of Responses	Point Value x Number of Responses
Strongly agree	1	8	8
Agree	2	16	32
Not sure	3	12	36
Disagree	4	4	16
Strongly disagree	5	2	10
Total	42	102	
Mean			2.43

We can see that there are 42 total responses and 102 total value points. Dividing the number of value points (102) by the total number of responses (42), we get a mean of 2.43.

If we conduct the same operation for the responses to Question 2 in our survey, we get the following results:

TABLE 8.3

Value Points

Answer Choices	Assigned Point Value	Number of Responses	Point Value × Number of Responses
Strongly Agree	1	13	13
Agree	2	10	20
Not Sure	3	1	3
Disagree	4	12	48
Strongly Disagree	5	6	30
Total		42	114
Mean			2.71

We see from the above table that the mean of the responses for Question 2 is 2.71. Comparing the means of the two questions, we find that the mean for Question 1 (2.43) is lower than the mean for Question 2. Because the lowest value (1 point) is assigned to a response of "strongly agree," and the highest value (5 points) is assigned for a response of "strongly disagree," we know that a high mean score indicates that the sample surveyed tends to disagree with the statement made in the survey question. It is possible to conclude, therefore, that there is slightly more agreement with the statement in Question 1 than with the statement in Question 2. Comparing the mean values in this fashion allows us to compare easily the amount of agreement and disagreement on different questions among the people surveyed.

Standard Deviation Another frequently used statistical measure is the standard deviation, which provides a single number that indicates how dispersed the responses to the question are. It tells you, in other words, the extent to which the answers are grouped together at the middle ("agree," "not sure," and "disagree") or are dispersed to the extreme answers ("strongly agree" and "strongly disagree"). To calculate the standard deviation (S) for Question 1, we will follow these steps:

Step 1: Assign a value to each response and the frequency of each response.

Step 2: Find the mean for the question.

Step 3: Subtract the value from the mean.

Step 4: Square the results of Step 3.

Step 5: Multiply the results of Step 4 by the frequency of each value.

Step 6: Sum the values in Step 5.

Step 7: Divide the values in Step 6 by the number of respondents.

Step 8: Find the square root of the value in Step 7, which is the standard deviation.

Our calculation of the standard deviation of Question 1 therefore looks like this:

TABLE 8.4

Standard Deviation

Step 1	Step 2	Step 3	Step 4	Step 5	Step 6	Step 7	Step 8
Value (V) and frequency (F)	Mean	Mean minus value	Step 3 squared	Step 4 times the frequency	Sum of values in Step 5	Step 6 divided by no. of respondents	Square Root of Step 7: Standard Deviation
$V = 1, F = 8$	2.43	1.43	2.04	16.32			
$V = 2, F = 16$	2.43	0.43	0.18	2.88			
$V = 3, F = 12$	2.43	2.57	0.32	3.84			
$V = 4, F = 4$	2.43	21.57	2.46	9.84			
$V = 5, F = 2$	2.43	22.57	6.6	13.2			
					46.08	1.10	1.05

The standard deviation of Question 1 is 1.05. To understand its significance, we need to know that public opinion samples usually correspond to what is known as a normal distribution. In a normal distribution, 68.26 percent of the responses will fall between (1) the mean minus one standard deviation (2.43 − 1.05, or 1.38, in Question 1) and (2) the mean plus one standard deviation (2.43 + 1.05, or 3.48, in Question 1). In other words, in a normal distribution, about two-thirds of the respondents to Question 1 will express an opinion that is between 1.38 and 3.48 on the scale of assigned point values. Another one-third of the respondents will score less than 1.38 or more than 3.48.

For convenience, we will call the responses "strongly agree" and "strongly disagree" as extreme responses, and we will designate "agree," "not sure," and "disagree" as moderate responses. We see that a score of 1.38 is closest to our first extreme, "strongly agree." A score of 3.48 inclines to "disagree," but is "not sure." We may conclude that a substantial portion of the respondents (about one-third) tend to give extreme answers to Question 1. We may also notice that the score 1.38, which indicates strong agreement, is closer to its absolute extreme (1.38 is only 0.38 away from its absolute extreme of 1.0) than is the score 3.48 (which is 1.52 points from its absolute extreme of 5). This means that the responses are slightly more tightly packed toward the extreme of strong agreement. We may conclude that extreme respondents are more likely to strongly agree than to strongly disagree with the statement in Question 1. We can now see more completely the degree of extremism in the population of respondents. Standard deviations become more helpful as the number of the questions in a survey increases because they allow us to compare quickly and easily the extent of extremism in answers. You will find other measures of dispersion in addition to the standard deviation in your statistical methods textbooks.

After finding the amount of dispersion in responses to a question, you may want to see if different types of respondents answered the question in different ways; that is, you may want to measure relationships in the data. For example, from examining our political party identifier, we find, among our respondents to Question 1,

15 Democrats, 14 Republicans, and 13 independents. To compare their responses, we must construct a correlation matrix that groups responses by identifier:

TABLE 8.5

Responses

Answer	Democrat Responses	Republican Responses	Independent Responses	Total (Frequency)
Strongly Agree	4	2	2	8
Agree	8	4	4	16
Not Sure	3	5	4	12
Disagree	0	2	2	4
Strongly Disagree	0	1	1	2

Each number of responses in the matrix is found in a location known as a response cell. The numbers in the total (frequency) column are known as response total cells. From this matrix, it appears that Democrats are more likely to agree with the Question 1 statement than are either Republicans or independents. If this is true for the sample population, there is a correlation between party affiliation and opinion on the issue.

Read&Write 8.1   Write a Public Opinion Analysis

A public opinion survey paper is composed of five essential parts:

1. Title page
2. Abstract
3. Text
4. Reference page
5. Appendices

Title Page

The title page should follow the format directions in Chapter 3. The title of a public opinion survey paper should provide the reader with two types of information: the subject of the survey and the population being polled. Examples of titles for papers based on in-class surveys are "Baylor University Student Opinions on Welfare Reform," "Ohio Wesleyan University Student Attitudes about Sexual Harassment," and "The 2006 Gubernatorial Election and the University of Virginia Student Vote."

Abstract

Abstracts for a public opinion survey paper should follow the general format directions given for abstracts in Chapter 3. In approximately 100 words, the abstract should summarize the subject, methodology, and results of the survey. An abstract for the example used in this chapter might appear something like this:

A survey of attitudes of college students toward the amount of U.S. military expenditures was undertaken in October 2006 at Western State University. The sample was composed of forty-two students in a political science research methods class. The purpose of the survey was to determine the extent to which students are aware of and concerned about recent defense expenditure reductions, including those directly affecting the Seventh Congressional District, in which the university is located, and to determine student attitudes on related defense questions, such as germ warfare. The results indicate a weak correlation between political party affiliation and attitude toward expenditures, with Democrats favoring reductions more than Republicans.

The text of the paper should include five sections:

1. Introduction
2. Literature review
3. Methodology
4. Results
5. Discussion

Introduction

The introduction should explain the purpose of your paper, define the research question hypothesis, and describe the circumstances under which the research was conducted. Your purpose statement will normally be a paragraph in which you explain your reasons for conducting your research. You may want to say something like the following:

> The purpose of this paper is to define Howard University student attitudes toward federal student aid programs. In particular, this study seeks to understand how students view the criteria for aid eligibility and the efficiency of application procedures. Further, the survey is expected to indicate the amount of knowledge students have about the federal student aid process. The primary reason for conducting this study is that the results will provide a basis for identifying problems in the aid application and disbursement process, and facilitate discussion among administrative officers and students about solutions to problems that are identified.

Next, the introduction should state the research question and the research hypotheses. The research question in the above example might be "Is student knowledge of federal student aid programs related to student attitudes about the effectiveness of the programs?" A hypothesis might be "Student ratings of the effectiveness of federal student aid programs are positively correlated with student knowledge of the programs."

Literature Review

A literature review is written to demonstrate that you are familiar with the professional literature relevant to the survey and to summarize that literature for the reader. Your literature review for a public opinion survey paper should address two types of information: the subject and the methodology of the survey.

The subject of the survey, for example, may be a state's proposed secondary education reforms. In this case, the purpose of the subject section of your literature review would be to briefly inform your readers about (1) the history, content, and political implications of the proposed reforms and (2) the current status of the proposed reforms. In providing this information, you will cite appropriate documents, such as bills submitted to the legislature.

The purpose of the methodology section of your literature review will be to cite the literature that supports the methodology of your study. If you follow the directions in this manual or your course textbook to write your paper, briefly state the procedures and statistical calculations you use in the study and the source of your information (this manual or your text) about them.

Methodology

The methodology section of your paper describes how you conducted your study. It should first briefly describe the format and content of the questionnaire. For example, how many questions were asked? What kinds of questions (open, closed, Likert scale, Guttmann scale) were used, and why were these formats selected? What identifiers were selected? Why? What topics within the subject matter were given emphasis? Why? Here you should also briefly address the statistical procedures used in data analysis. Why were they selected? What information are they intended to provide?

Results

The results section of your paper should list the findings of your study. Here you report the results of your statistical calculations. You may want to construct a table that summarizes the numbers of responses to each question on the questionnaire. Next, using your statistical results, answer your research question; that is, tell your reader if your research question was answered by your results and, if so, what are the answers.

Discussion

In your discussion section, draw out the implications of your findings. What is the meaning of the results of your study? What conclusions can you draw? What questions remain unanswered? At the end of this section, provide the reader with suggestions for further research that are derived from your research findings.

Reference Page

Your reference page and source citations in the text should be completed according to the directions in Chapter 3.

Appendices

See Chapter 3 for further directions on placing appendices at the end of your text. Appendices for a public opinion survey paper should include the following:

- A copy of the questionnaire used in the study

- Tables of survey data not sufficiently important to be included in the text but helpful for reference

- Summaries of survey data from national polls on the same subject, if such polls are available and discussed in your text.

NOTE: Students and instructors should note that the applications of the mean and standard deviation suggested in this chapter are controversial because they are applied to ordinal data. In practice, however, such applications are common.

9

ANALYZE A DOMESTIC OR INTERNATIONAL GOVERNMENT POLICY

9.1 LEARN THE BASICS OF POLICY ANALYSIS

What Is Policy Analysis?

When President Obama took office, he faced a long list of problems, some of which seemed almost over-powering. The nation was in the trough of its deepest recession since the Great Depression of the 1930s. America was fighting wars in both Iraq and Afghanistan. The health care system was the worst among the world's great powers. Hundreds of medical bankruptcies, gaps in health insurance coverage, and soaring medical costs added to the many challenges to be faced. Governments solve problems by formulating *policies*, which are sets of principles or rules that guide government agencies in creating and running programs aimed at dealing with the problems. Confronted with a vast array of serious national predicaments, President Obama's administration developed and proposed to Congress a set of policies, some of which were eventually passed and became laws.

Domestic policies include matters *within* nations, such as issues related to highways, hospitals, schools, water treatment plants, law enforcement, public safety, and others. International policies related to trade, war, educational exchanges, disaster relief efforts, and so on, affect relations *between or among* nations.

Policy analysis is the examination of a policy (domestic or international) to determine its *effectiveness* (how well it solves the problem it was designed to solve) and its *efficiency* (the extent to which the cost of implementing the policy is reasonable, considering the size and nature of the problem to be solved). Every day, analysts, sometimes called policy wonks, at all levels of government, are writing policy analysis papers. Legislators, at the state and national levels, hire staff people who continually investigate public policy issues and seek ways to improve legislated policy. At the national level, the Congressional Research Service continually finds information for representatives and senators. Each committee of Congress employs staff members who help in reviewing current laws and defining options for making new ones. State legislatures also employ their own research agencies and committee staff. Legislators and other policymakers are also given policy information by hundreds of public interest groups and research organizations.

Public officials constantly face challenges to initiate new policies or change old ones. If they have a current formal policy at all, they want to know how effective it is. They then want to know the available options, the changes they might make to improve the current policy, and the possible consequences of those changes. Policies are reviewed under a number of circumstances. Policy analyses are sometimes conducted as part of the normal agency budgeting processes. They help decision makers in determining the policies that must be continued or discontinued. These policies under scrutiny may be very narrow in scope, such as deciding the hours of operation of facilities at city parks. Or they may be very broad, such as deciding how the nation will provide health care or defense for its citizens.

A good example of an organization that conducts policy analysis is the U.S. *Office of Management and Budget* (OMB), an agency within the White House that provides information to the President and the public servants in his administration. Within the OMB is the *Office of Information and Regulatory Affairs* (OIRA), which conducts policy analyses on many subjects. On the OIRA web page (https://www .whitehouse.gov/omb/policy_analyst/), you will find the following explanation of what OIRA analysts do:

Policy Analyst
Office of Information and Regulatory Affairs

Policy analysts oversee the Federal regulatory system so that agencies' regulatory actions are consistent with economic principles, sound public policy, and the goals of the President. They also review requests by agencies for approval of collections of information [including surveys, program evaluations, and applications for benefits] under the Paperwork Reduction Act of 1995. In addition, policy analysts review and analyze other Administration and Congressional policy initiatives. Policy analysts in OIRA work directly with high-level policy officials and have a great deal of responsibility in a wide array of policy areas. Major topic areas include virtually every domestic policy area including environment, natural resources, agriculture, rural development, energy, labor, education, immigration, health, welfare, housing, finance, criminal justice, information technology, and other related domestic policy issues.

Specifically, an OIRA policy analyst:

Oversees and evaluates the regulatory, information policies, and other policy initiatives of one or more government agencies, applying economics, statistics, and risk assessment.

Analyzes agency regulations prior to publication to ensure that the regulations adhere to sound analytical principles, and that agencies evaluate the need for, societal costs and benefits of, and alternatives to new regulations.

Reviews and approves agency collections of information in accordance with the Paperwork Reduction Act [PRA] of 1995. Ensures that agency collections reduce, minimize, and control paperwork burdens, and maximize the practical utility and public benefit of the information created, collected, disclosed, maintained, used, shared, and disseminated by or for the Federal government.

Coordinates the review of regulations and collections of information within OMB and the Executive Office of the President, as well as among other relevant Federal agencies.

Monitors and analyzes legislative and policy proposals and testimony for conformance with the policies and priorities of the President.

Performs special analyses and advises senior policy officials on specific issues.[1]

Become Familiar with Policy Analysis Institutions

In general, policy analysis institutions are of two sorts: public (government) and private (mostly nonprofit). Virtually every federal government agency conducts some sort of policy analysis, and there are many that specialize in this activity. The most important *federal* policy analysis organizations are:

- Congressional Budget Office (CBO)
- Congressional Research Service (CRS)
- National Council for Science and the Environment (NCSE)
- U.S. Department of State Office of Economic Policy Analysis & Public Diplomacy
- Office of Management and Budget (OMB)
- U.S. General Accountability Office (GAO)

Every state also has its own policy analysis offices. California's agencies, for example, include:

- California Senate Office of Research (SOR)
- California Office of the Governor, Legislative Analyst's Office

Private research institutes (think tanks) provide a great deal of often influential policy analysis and research upon which policy analysis can be conducted. Some of the most important are:

- American Enterprise Institute
- American Foreign Policy Council
- Battelle Memorial Institute
- Brookings Institution
- Carnegie Endowment for International Peace
- Cato Institute
- Center for Strategic and International Studies
- Claremont Institute

The Contents of a Policy Analysis Paper

Policy analysis papers contain six basic elements:

1. Title page
2. Executive summary
3. Table of contents, including a list of tables and illustrations

---

[1] "Office of Management and Budget." N.d. The White House. https://www.whitehouse.gov/omb/policy_analyst/ (March 7, 2016).

Read&Write 9.1 Write a Brief Domestic Policy Analysis

In writing a policy analysis paper, you should:

1. Select and clearly define a specific government policy.
2. Carefully define the social, governmental, economic, or other problem that the policy is designed to solve.
3. Describe the economic, social, and political environments in which the problem arose and in which the existing policy for solving the problem was developed.
4. Evaluate the effectiveness of the current policy or lack of policy in dealing with the problem.
5. Identify alternative policies that could be adopted to solve the selected problem, and estimate the economic, social, environmental, and political costs and benefits of each alternative.
6. Provide a summary comparison of all policies examined.

Successful policy analysis papers all share the same general purpose: to inform policy-makers about how public policy in a specific area may be improved. A policy analysis paper, like a position paper, is an entirely practical exercise. It is neither theoretical nor general. Its objective is to identify and evaluate the policy options that are available for a specific topic.

4. Text (or body)
5. References to sources of information
6. Appendices

Parameters of the Text   Ask your instructor for the number of pages required for the policy analysis paper assigned for your course. Such papers at the undergraduate level often range from 20 to 50 typed, double-spaced pages in length.

Two general rules govern the amount of information presented in the body of the paper. First, the content must be adequate to make a good policy evaluation. You must include all the facts necessary to understand the significant strengths and weaknesses of a policy and its alternatives. If your paper omits a fact that is critical to the decision, a poor decision is likely be made.

Never omit important facts merely because they tend to support a perspective other than your own. It is your responsibility to present the facts as clearly as possible, not to bias the evaluation in a particular direction.

The second guideline for determining the length of a policy analysis paper is to omit extraneous material. Include only the information that is helpful in making a particular decision at hand. For example, if you are analyzing the policy by which a municipal government funds a museum dedicated to the history of fishing in area lakes, how much information do you need to include about the specific exhibits in the museum?

The Format of a Policy Analysis Paper

Title Page   The title page for a policy analysis paper should follow the format provided for title pages in Chapter 3.

Executive Summary   A one-page, single-spaced executive summary immediately follows the title page. The carefully written sentences of the executive summary express the central concepts to be explained more fully in the text of the paper. The purpose of the summary is to allow the decision maker to understand, as quickly as possible, the major facts and issues under consideration. The decision maker should be able to get a clear and thorough overview of the entire policy problem and the value and costs of available policy options by reading the one-page summary.

Table of Contents   The table of contents of a policy analysis paper must follow the organization of the paper's text and should conform to the format shown in Chapter 3.

Text   The structure of a policy analysis paper's text may be outlined as follows:

  I. **Description of the policy currently in force**
      A. A clear, concise statement of the policy currently in force
      B. A brief history of the policy currently in force
      C. A description of the problem the current policy was aimed at resolving, including an estimate of its extent and importance

 II. **Environments of the policy currently in force**
      A. A description of the *physical* factors affecting the origin, development, and implementation of the current policy
      B. A description of the *social* factors affecting the origin, development, and implementation of the current policy
      C. A description of the *economic* factors affecting the origin, development, and implementation of the current policy
      D. A description of the *political* factors affecting the origin, development, and implementation of the current policy

III. **Effectiveness and efficiency of the current policy**
      A. How well the existing policy does what it was designed to do?
      B. How well the policy performs in relation to the effort and resources committed to it?

 IV. **Policy alternatives**
      A. Possible alterations of the present policy, with the estimated costs and benefits of each
      B. Alternatives to the present policy, with the estimated costs and benefits of each

  V. **Summary comparison of policy options**

Most public policy analysis textbooks describe in detail each of the policy analysis components listed in the above outline. The following sections of this chapter, however, provide further information with respect to Section II of this outline. Discuss the outline with your instructor to ensure that you understand what each section entails.

References   You must be sure to cite properly all sources of information in a policy analysis paper. Follow the directions for proper citation in Chapter 8.

Appendices Appendices can provide the reader of policy analysis papers with information that supplements the important facts contained in the text. For many local development and public works projects, a map and a diagram are often very helpful appendices. You should attach them at the end of the paper, after the reference page. You should not append entire government reports, journal articles, or other publications, but feel free to include selected charts, graphs, or other pages. The source of the information should always be evident on the appended pages.

9.2   FOREIGN POLICY ANALYSIS

Papers analyzing international policy issues—issues that occur substantially between and among nations—should proceed, much like domestic policy analysis papers, according to the outline presented in the foregoing section. One difference between domestic and international policy papers is that in Section I.B of international policy papers you will provide first a brief history of the country or countries involved in the policy issue you are analyzing, and then a brief history of the current problem or dispute.

But the main difference between the two types of papers is the range of factors they consider under Section II of the outline, "Environments of the policy currently in force." Having looked at how Section II of the outline helps to shape a typical domestic policy analysis paper, we will now explore how that section of the outline operates for an international policy analysis, and, as before, we will construct an example. Let's suppose that you have decided to write a policy analysis about the Obama administration's support for sanctions against Iran due to that country's suspected development of nuclear weapons. Your paper will analyze both the extent of the threat that Iranian nuclear weapons would pose and the options available to the Obama administration in meeting its goal of deterring Iran from developing nuclear offensive capability.

Note that the following outline, developed from Section II of the general outline provided above, makes use of many political concepts not defined in this chapter. These concepts will be well covered in your international relations text, and you will find definitions of them in the Glossary at the end of this manual.

Read & Write 9.2   Analyze a Specific Foreign Policy

To complete this assignment, use the directions in the "Domestic Policy Analysis" *Read & Write* found in Section 9.1.

Environments of the policy currently in force

A. *A description of the physical factors affecting the origin, development, and implementation of the current policy.* Physical factors to discuss in your analysis of the development of Iranian nuclear weapons might include these:

- Iran's geographic position in the world
- The countries that border Iran

- Strategically important countries in the region (Israel, Russia, etc.)
- Iran's chief natural resources
- Factors, such as ports, railways, and mountain ranges, that create either special advantages or disadvantages for Iran
- Factors tending to make Iran either especially powerful or vulnerable

B. *A description of the social factors affecting the origin, development, and implementation of the current policy.* Social factors to consider in your analysis of the development of Iranian nuclear weapons might include the following:

- Dominant ethnic groups
- Language (Farsi, not Arabic!)
- Religions
- Customs and traditions

C. *A description of the economic factors affecting the origin, development, and implementation of the current policy.* Your analysis of the development of Iranian nuclear weapons will need to explore such economic factors as the following:

- The level of Iran's economic development
- Commerce
- Iran's national wealth and debt
- Agriculture
- Banking
- Iran's currency
- Iran's natural resources
- The country's economic class system

D. *A description of the political factors affecting the origin, development, and implementation of the current policy.* The number of political factors affecting the development of an international policy is normally substantial, so the analyst's key chore is to identify the most important ones. Since many issues are so complex that it difficult to know where to start, we suggest that you first organize your survey of potential factors into three broad categories:

- The politics of the international political system
- The domestic politics of the states involved
- The politics of the specific policy issue (in our example, Iranian development of nuclear weapons)

For each of these categories, you will want to examine a number of factors. The entries below are by no means exhaustive, and each has a technical meaning within the specific discipline of International Relations (IR). You will find definitions and explanations of each entry in your IR textbook. For your convenience, we list here some of the most important entries in each category to help you begin a systematic review.

The Politics of the International Political System

What are the characteristics of the current international system? Is it unipolar, bipolar, or multipolar? How are the states involved in the issue under study affected by this system?

Is there a defined international regime? What factors affect the distribution of power within the international system? What international organizations, both governmental and nongovernmental (NGOs), are important in this particular issue? What processes (globalization, interdependence) play a key role? What formal and informal arrangements control interactions in the system (balances of power, issue linkages, terrorism)?

Domestic Politics of the States Involved

What are the key political characteristics of the states involved in this issue? What are their formal governmental structures? What are their formal and informal power structures? What internal forces shape the issue and politics in general within the states involved (nationalism, democratization, militarization, structural violence, fragmentation, religious authorities, drug lords or warlords, ethnic rivalries)? What doctrines affect the issue (flexible response, protectionism, preemption)?

Politics of the Specific Policy Issue

In our example of the Iranian development of nuclear weapons, several aspects of the specific policy issue readily come to mind:

Iranian national pride

American security and the imperative of nonproliferation

The American–Israeli alliance

Islamic Anti-Americanism

Iranian modernization and pro-Americanism

Russian dependence on Iranian oil

Of course, this is only the start of a list of relevant subtopics for this particular issue. As your research proceeds, you will gradually form an impression of the major factors in the issue you are studying and how they relate to one another. As you continue to follow the policy analysis outline provided earlier in this chapter, you will in the end produce the sort of analysis prepared by many people in governments and NGOs every day.

Foreign Policy and International Relations Agencies

As you research a foreign policy you will quickly become aware of the myriad of federal government agencies that play a role in international relations and in making foreign policy. You will find the following lists of agencies helpful in investigating the policy you have chosen.

The primary government agency involved in making foreign policy is the U.S Department of State (State). State advises the President of foreign policy issues, conducts international relations through its internal departments and its embassies and consulates throughout the world, and conducts a large number of programs that promote human welfare and strong relationships across the globe. The first Secretary of State was Thomas Jefferson, and his position today is held by John Kerry. Some of the key bureaus and offices of the Department of State include:

- African Affairs
- Arms Control, Verification, and Compliance

- Center for Strategic Counterterrorism Communications
- Chief Information Officer
- Chief Economist of the Department
- Chief of Staff
- Office of Civil Rights
- Conflict and Stabilization Operations
- Counterterrorism
- Democracy, Human Rights, and Labor
- Diplomatic Security
- East Asian and Pacific Affairs
- Economic and Business Affairs
- Educational and Cultural Affairs
- Energy Resources
- European and Eurasian Affairs
- Foreign Assistance (F)
- Foreign Missions
- Foreign Service Institute
- Global AIDS Coordinator (S/GAC)
- Global Criminal Justice
- Global Food Security
- Global Women's Issues (S/GWI)
- Global Youth Issues
- Intelligence and Research
- International Information Programs
- International Narcotics and Law Enforcement Affairs
- International Organization Affairs
- International Security and Nonproliferation
- Management Policy, Rightsizing, and Innovation
- Mission to the United Nations
- Near Eastern Affairs
- Oceans and International Environmental and Scientific Affairs
- Office of Terrorism Finance and Economic Sanctions Policy
- Policy, Planning, and Resources for Public Diplomacy and Public Affairs
- Policy Planning Staff (S/P)
- Political–Military Affairs
- Population, Refugees, and Migration
- South and Central Asian Affairs
- Trafficking in Persons
- Western Hemisphere Affairs

   Other U.S. government agencies that play a role in international relations include:

- Central Intelligence Agency
- Defense Intelligence Agency

- Defense Nuclear Facilities Safety Board
- Export–Import Bank of the United States
- Federal Bureau of Investigation
- Federal Trade Commission
- National Geospatial-Intelligence Agency
- National Reconnaissance Office
- National Security Agency
- Nuclear Regulatory Commission
- Office of the Director of National Intelligence
- Peace Corps
- United States Agency for International Development

Many think tanks and research institutes provide foreign policy analyses to their clients, government agencies, and the public. On the State's website (http://www.state.gov/s/p/tt/), you will find the following list of links to some of these organizations.

- American Enterprise Institute for Public Policy Research
- American Foreign Policy Council
- Arms Control Association
- Asia Society
- Aspen Institute
- Atlantic Council of the United States
- The Brookings Institution
- Canadian Institute of International Affairs
- Canadian Institute of Strategic Studies
- Carnegie Council on Ethics and International Affairs
- Carnegie Endowment for International Peace
- The Cato Institute
- Center for Defense Information
- Center for Global Development
- Center for Global Security Research
- Center for Strategic and Budgetary Assessments
- Center for Strategic and International Studies
- Center for the Study of Intelligence
- Centre d'Etudes et de Recherches Internationales (Center for International Studies and Research)
- Chemical and Biological Arms Control Institute
- Clingendael (Netherlands Institutes of International Relations)
- Council on Foreign Relations
- Deutsche Gesellschaftfuer Auswaertige Politik (German Council on Foreign Relations)
- East–West Institute
- Eisenhower Institute
- Federation of American Scientists

- Foreign Policy Association
- Foreign Policy Research Institute
- Freedom House
- German Marshall Fund of the United States
- Henry L. Stimson Center
- The Heritage Foundation
- Hudson Institute
- Institut Francais des Relations Internationales (French Institute of International Relations)
- Institute for International Economics
- Institute for Policy Studies
- Inter-American Dialogue
- International Centre for Trade and Sustainable Development
- International Crisis Group
- International Institute for Strategic Studies
- International Peace Academy
- Lexington Institute
- Middle East Media Research Institute
- National Bureau of Asian Research
- National Defense University
- Naval War College
- New America Foundation
- Nixon Center
- Pacific Council on International Policy
- RAND
- Royal Institute of International Affairs (Chatham House)
- Stiftung Wissenschaft und Politik (German Institute for International and Security Affairs)
- Stockholm International Peace Research Institute (SIPRI)
- Strategic Studies Institute, Army War College
- Washington Institute for Near East Policy
- Woodrow Wilson International Center for Scholars
- World Economic Forum
- World Policy Institute
- United States Institute of Peace

10

AUTHOR AN *AMICUS CURIAE* BRIEF

LEARN THE RULES FOR WRITING BRIEFS FOR THE U.S. SUPREME COURT

When people are parties to disputes before the U.S. Supreme Court, the attorneys representing each side prepare written documents called *briefs on the merit*, which explain the nature of the dispute and present an argument for the side the attorney represents. The justices read the briefs, hear oral arguments, hold conferences to discuss the case, and then write opinions to announce both the Court's decision and the views of justices who disagree in whole or in part with that decision. Cases that come before the Supreme Court are usually important to many people who are not actually parties to the specific case being presented because the Court's decisions contain principles and guidelines that all lower courts must follow in deciding similar cases. *Roe v. Wade*, for example, did not become famous because it allowed one person to have an abortion free from the constraints of the laws of Texas, but because it set forth the principle that state law may not restrict abortions in the first three months of pregnancy to protect the fetus.

Because Supreme Court cases are important to people other than those directly involved in the case, sometimes groups and individuals outside the proceedings of a specific case want their views on cases to be heard by the Court before it makes a decision. It is not proper, however, to go to the justices directly and try to influence them to decide a case in a particular way. Influencing government officials directly through visits, phone calls, or letters is called *lobbying*. When people want to influence the way Congress handles a law, they lobby their representatives by writing letters or talking to them personally. The lobbying of Supreme Court justices, however, is considered improper because the Court is supposed to take decisions based on the content of the Constitution and not on the political preferences of one or more groups in society.

There is a way, however, for outsiders to submit their views to the Supreme Court. The Court invites interested parties, most often organizations, to submit briefs of *amicus curiae* (*amicus curiae* means "friend of the court"). A party that submits an amicus curiae brief becomes a friend of the Court by giving it information that may be helpful in making a decision. As the Court explains, "an amicus curiae brief which brings relevant matter to the attention of the Court that has not already been brought to its attention by the parties is of considerable help to the Court. An amicus brief which does not serve this purpose simply burdens the staff and facilities of the Court and its filing is not favored."[1] In the summer of 1971, the Supreme Court began its review of *Roe v. Wade*. Roe, who was arrested for violating a Texas law forbidding abortions except to save the mother's life, argued that the Texas law was a governmental violation of the right to privacy guaranteed to her by the Constitution. Many national organizations filed amicus curiae briefs in this case. Acting as attorneys on behalf of the National Legal Program on Health Problems of the Poor, the National Welfare Rights Organization, and the American Public Health Association, Alan F. Charles and Susan Grossman Alexander filed a brief of amici curiae (*amici* is the plural of *amicus*) in support of the right to have an abortion. The Summary of Argument that Charles and Alexander included in that brief appears below as an example to assist you in writing your own amicus curiae brief:

BRIEF OF *AMICI CURIAE*

Summary of Argument

A woman who seeks an abortion is asserting certain fundamental rights which are protected by the Constitution. Among these are rights to marital and family privacy, to individual and sexual privacy; in sum, the right to choose whether to bear children or not. These rights are abridged by the state's restriction of abortions to saving the mother's life. To justify such an abridgment, the state must demonstrate a compelling interest; no such compelling interest exists to save the Texas abortion law.

The state's interest in protecting the woman's health no longer supports restrictions on abortion. Medical science now performs abortions more safely than it brings a woman through pregnancy and childbirth. Any state interest in discouraging non-marital sexual relationships must be served by laws penalizing these relationships, and not by an indirect, overly broad prohibition on abortion. There is no evidence, in any case, that abortion laws deter such relationships. The state's purported interest in expanding the population lacks any viability today; government policy in every other area is now squarely against it. And any purported interest in permitting all embryos to develop and be born is not supported anywhere in the Constitution or any other body of law.

Because of its restriction, the Texas statute denies to poor and non-white women equal access to legal abortions. It is an undeniable fact that abortion in Texas and in virtually every other state in the United States is far more readily available to the white, paying patient than to the poor and non-white. Studies by physicians, sociologists, public health experts, and lawyers all reach this same conclusion. The reasons for it are not purely economic, i.e., that because abortion

---

[1] "Rule 37: Brief for an *Amicus Curiae*." *Rules of the Supreme Court of the United States.* http://www .supremecourt.gov/ctrules/2013RulesoftheCourt.pdf (July 7, 2016).

is an expensive commodity to obtain on the medical marketplace, it is therefore to be expected that the rich will have greater access to it. It is also because in the facilities which provide health care to the poor, abortion is simply not made available to the poor and non-white on the same conditions as it is to paying patients. As a result, the poor resort to criminal abortion, with its high toll of infection and death, in vastly disproportionate numbers.

Largely to blame are restrictive abortion laws, such as the Texas statute, in which the legislature has made lay judgments about what conditions must exist before abortions can be legally performed, and has delegated the authority to make such decisions to physicians and committees of physicians with the threat of felony punishment if they err on the side of granting an abortion. Unlike more privileged women, poor and non-white women are unable to shop for physicians and hospitals sympathetic to their applications, cannot afford the necessary consultations to establish that their conditions qualify them for treatment, and must largely depend upon public hospitals and physicians with whom they have no personal relationship, and who operate under the government's eye, for the relief they seek. The resulting discrimination is easily demonstrated.

Restricting abortion only to treatment necessary to save the mother's life irrationally excludes those classes of women for whom abortion is necessary for the protection of health, or because they will bear a deformed fetus, or who are pregnant due to sexual assault, or who are financially, socially, or emotionally incapable of raising a child or whose families would be seriously disrupted by the birth of another child, and these exclusions bear most heavily on the poor and non-white.

In the absence of any compelling state interest, the harsh discriminatory effect on the poor and the non-white resulting from the operation of the Texas abortion law denies to poor and non-white women the equal protection of the laws in violation of the Equal Protection Clause of the Fourteenth Amendment.[2]

Scope and Purpose

Your task in this chapter is to write an *amicus curiae* brief for a case that is being considered by the U.S. Supreme Court. You will write your own brief, making your own argument about how the case should be decided. Of course, you do not have to be entirely original. You will examine the arguments used in others' briefs, add new arguments of your own, and write the entire brief in your own carefully chosen words. In completing this assignment, you will also be meeting five more personal learning objectives:

1. You will become familiar with the source, form, and content of legal documents.
2. You will become acquainted with the procedures of brief preparation.
3. You will become familiar with the details of a selected case currently before the Court. As you follow the news reports on this case, you will eventually learn the Court's decision.

---

[2] Charles, Alan F. 1971. *Motion for Leave to File Brief Amici Curiae in Support of Appellants and Briefs Amici Curiai. Roe v. Wade.* U.S. 70–18, 5–7.

4. You will come to understand the Supreme Court case in sufficient depth to be able to integrate the arguments of actual amicus curiae briefs into your own argument.

5. You will learn how to write a clear, logical, effective, and persuasive argument.

Remember that your goal is to *persuade* the Supreme Court to make a certain decision. Before you begin, reread Part 1 of this manual, especially the sections on how to write clearly and persuasively.

General Considerations and Format

Briefs provide the Supreme Court with the facts in a particular case and make arguments about how the case should be decided. The *Rules* of the Court state that "a brief must be compact, logically arranged with proper headings, concise, and free from burdensome, irrelevant, immaterial, and scandalous matter. A brief not complying with this paragraph may be disregarded and stricken by the Court."[3] The Court also requires those who submit an amicus curiae brief to provide a statement of permission, which may be (1) the evidence that either permission to submit the amicus curiae brief has been granted by both parties to the dispute or the permission of both parties has not been granted, and (2) the reason for the denial and the reason that the Court should consider the amicus curiae brief despite the absence of permission of the parties.

Of course, as a student writing an amicus curiae brief for a class in political science, you will not actually submit your brief to the Supreme Court, so you need not write a statement of permission. Information on such statements is provided here so that you will understand their purpose when you encounter them in your research.

Ask your instructor about the page limit for your assignment. The Supreme Court's limit for the actual text of amicus curiae briefs (exclusive of the questions-presented page, subject index, table of authorities, and appendix) is 30 pages, single-spaced. Your brief, however, will be double-spaced for the convenience of your instructor and as few as 15 pages, depending on your instructor's requirements. Because a central purpose of this assignment is for you to understand the arguments to be made in the case, your brief will be shorter than the actual amicus briefs submitted to the Court, which require much more detail than you will need to know. As you read actual amicus briefs, use your own judgment to select the material that you believe is most important for the Court to understand, and include this information, in your own words, in your brief.

The proper presentation of briefs is essential. Briefs to the Supreme Court are normally professionally printed, and the *Rules* of the Court include directions for this process. The Court does, however, also accept typed briefs, and your amicus curiae brief will conform to the Court's instructions for typed briefs in most respects, with modifications to allow your instructor sufficient space to write comments. You must therefore prepare your amicus curiae brief according to the following specifications:

- Black type on white paper, 8.5 by 11 inches, double-spaced, printed on one side only

- Text and footnotes in 12-point type

---

[3] "Rule 37: Briefs for an *Amicus Curiae*." *Rules of the Supreme Court of the United States*. http://www.supremecourt.gov/ctrules/2013RulesoftheCourt.pdf (July 7, 2016).

- A typeface as close as possible to that used in actual briefs
- Margins of 1.5 inches on the left and 1 inch on all other sides
- A binding that meets your instructor's requirements

You will submit one copy of your brief to your instructor. It is always wise, when submitting any paper, to retain a copy for yourself in case the original is lost. (The Supreme Court requires that 60 copies of a brief be submitted for a case coming to it directly under its original jurisdiction, and 40 copies for a case coming to it under appellate jurisdiction from lower courts.)

Read&Write 10.1   Write an Abridged Amicus Brief

In this assignment, after reading the materials available on the Cornell and Supreme Court websites, you will write only a relatively brief argument, and then a summary of an argument you want to make. Although you can use and elaborate on arguments others have made, you must make your own argument in your own words.

Select a Case and a Side

To find cases on the Internet that are currently before the Supreme Court, go to Cornell University's Legal Information Institute (LLI) (http://supct.law.cornell.edu/supct/). On this page, select the "Cases Pending Oral Argument" link. This link gives a list of cases in which briefs and other essential documents have been submitted to the court, documents that provide the information you need to complete this exercise. Peruse the list of cases pending oral argument and select one that generates some personal for you.

Write an Argument Outline

Read the arguments in the materials you find on the Cornell site, and then construct an outline of an argument that makes the points you believe are most important. Your outline should normally have from two to six main points. Follow the directions for constructing outlines that you find in Chapter 3 of this Manual very carefully. Submit your outline to your instructor for advice before continuing.

Write the Argument

Following the outline you have constructed, write your argument. Your writing needs to be clear and sharply focused. Follow the directions for writing in the first part of this manual. The first sentence of each paragraph should state its main point.

The *Rules* of the Court state that the argument of a brief must exhibit "clearly the points of fact and of law being presented and [cite] the authorities and statutes relied upon"; it should also be "as short as possible."[4] In addition to conforming to page limitations set by your instructor, the length of your argument should be guided by two considerations. First, content must be of adequate length to help the Court make a good decision. All the arguments necessary to making a decision must be present. Write this paper as if you were an officer of the Court. Under no circumstances should you make a false or misleading statement. Be persuasive, but be truthful. You do not need to make the opponents' argument for them, but the facts that you present must be accurate to the best of your knowledge.

---

[4] "Rule 37: Briefs for an *Amicus Curiae*." *Rules of the Supreme Court of the United States.* http://www.supremecourt .gov/ctrules/2013RulesoftheCourt.pdf (July 7, 2016).

The second guideline for determining the length of your argument is to omit extraneous material. Include only the information that will help the Court in making the decision at hand.

The *Rules* of the Court require that an amicus brief include a "conclusion, specifying with particularity the relief which the party seeks."[5] Read the conclusions of the briefs you collect, and then write your own, retaining the same format but combining the arguments for the groups you are representing, and limiting your conclusion to two pages.

Write the Summary of Argument

After you have written the argument, write the summary, which should be a clearly written series of paragraphs that include all the main points. It should be brief, not more than three double-spaced typed pages. The Summary of Argument written for *Roe* v. *Wade* that is included at the beginning of this chapter provides an example.

According to the *Rules* of the Court, briefs should contain a "summary of the argument, suitably paragraphed, which should be a succinct, but accurate and clear, condensation of the argument actually made in the body of the brief. A mere repetition of the headings under which the argument is arranged is not sufficient."[6]

The summary of your argument may be easily assembled by taking the topic sentences from each paragraph and forming them into new paragraphs. The topic sentences contain more information than your subject headings. As complete sentences arranged in logical order, they provide an excellent synopsis of the contents of your brief. Your argument summary should not exceed two double-spaced pages. Your summary should include the types of information included in the abridged version of Supreme Court's own summary in the case of *Supreme Court of the United States District of Columbia et al. v. Heller* (No. 07–290. Argued March 18, 2008—Decided June 26, 2008), printed below:

> District of Columbia law bans handgun possession by making it a crime to carry an unregistered firearm and prohibiting the registration of handguns; provides separately that no person may carry an unlicensed handgun, but authorizes the police chief to issue 1-year licenses; and requires residents to keep lawfully owned firearms unloaded and dissembled or bound by a trigger lock or similar device. Respondent Heller, a D.C. special policeman, applied to register a handgun he wished to keep at home, but the District refused. He filed this suit seeking, on Second Amendment grounds, to enjoin the city from enforcing the bar on handgun registration, the licensing requirement insofar as it prohibits carrying an unlicensed firearm in the home, and the trigger-lock requirement insofar as it prohibits the use of functional firearms in the home. The District Court dismissed the suit, but the D.C. Circuit reversed, holding that the Second Amendment protects an individual's right to possess firearms and that the city's total ban on handguns, as well as its requirement that firearms in the home be kept nonfunctional even when necessary for self-defense, violated that right.

[The Supreme Court] Held:

1. The Second Amendment protects an individual right to possess a firearm unconnected with service in a militia, and to use that arm for traditionally lawful purposes, such as self-defense within the home. pp. 2–53 . . .
2. Like most rights, the Second Amendment right is not unlimited. It is not a right to keep and carry any weapon whatsoever in any manner whatsoever and for whatever purpose . . .

---

[5] "Rule 37: Briefs for an Amicus Curiae." *Rules of the Supreme Court of the United States.* http://www.supremecourt .gov/ctrules/2013RulesoftheCourt.pdf (July 7, 2016).

[6] "Rule 37: Briefs for an *Amicus Curiae.*" *Rules of the Supreme Court of the United States.* http://www.supremecourt .gov/ctrules/2013RulesoftheCourt.pdf (July 7, 2016).

3. The handgun ban and the trigger-lock requirement (as applied to self-defense) violate the Second Amendment. The District's total ban on handgun possession in the home amounts to a prohibition on an entire class of "arms" that Americans overwhelmingly choose for the lawful purpose of self-defense. Under any of the standards of scrutiny the Court has applied to enumerated constitutional rights, this prohibition—in the place where the importance of the lawful defense of self, family, and property is most acute—would fail constitutional muster. Similarly, the requirement that any lawful firearm in the home be disassembled or bound by a trigger lock makes it impossible for citizens to use arms for the core lawful purpose of self-defense and is hence unconstitutional. Because Heller conceded at oral argument that the DC licensing law is permissible if it is not enforced arbitrarily and capriciously, the Court assumes that a license will satisfy his prayer for relief and does not address the licensing requirement. Assuming he is not disqualified from exercising Second Amendment rights, the District must permit Heller to register his handgun and must issue him a license to carry it in the home.[7]

---

[7] *District of Columbia et al. v Heller*. 2008. 07-290. *Supreme Court of the United States.* http://www.supremecourt .gov/opinions/07pdf/07-290.pdf (March 7, 2016).

POLITICAL PHILOSOPHY PAPERS

CONSIDER SOME OPTIONS FOR POLITICAL PHILOSOPHY PAPERS

The discipline of political science distinguishes between political philosophy, an examination of the writings of great political thinkers throughout human history, and political theory, which is the contemporary effort to understand political behavior. Contemporary theorists often integrate quantitative techniques, some borrowed from other disciplines (economics, psychology, sociology, neurology). Political philosophy, the subdiscipline addressed in this chapter, mines the history of the great ideas that not only provide rich insights into political behavior, but also have often shaped politics itself. John Locke's *Two Treatises of Government* (1690) helped pave the way for democratic movements leading to British Parliamentary Monarchy and for America's Declaration of Independence and Constitution. When Karl Marx and Friedrich Engels wrote *The Communist Manifesto* (1848) and a series of other works, they set the stage for the regimes that controlled more than a third of the world's population at the peak of communist influence in the twentieth century.

Reading the works of political philosophers is a deeply enriching and satisfying experience. The contrasting regimes preferred by Plato and his student Aristotle provide many observations that echo their cogency down through the century and provide grist for arguments made around the world today.

Since many instructors assign papers with page limits, but with maximum freedom given to developing content for students, this chapter contains suggestions for writing short papers (fewer than 10 pages) and long papers (more than 10 pages) in college political philosophy courses today. First, be sure to write your paper according to the highest standards of the discipline of political science as explained in previous chapters of this manual. Research thoroughly. Cite sources accurately. Make your paper plagiarism-free. Say something meaningful to yourself and others. Carefully establish and systematically support a definite thesis. Write clearly. Write well.

Suggestions for Short Papers

Short political philosophy papers are normally topical essays, book reviews, or article critiques. Book reviews provide many interesting options. Be sure to check with your instructor before you begin writing. Consider the following approaches:

Option 1: Focus on Philosophers   You can select one or more ancient, medieval, or modern political philosophers from the "canon" lists of everyone from Plato to Nietzsche. But don't forget the marvelous works of the twentieth century authors like Oakeshott, Popper, Rand, Aron, Sartre, Arendt, Berlin, Aron, Rawls, Foucault, Baudrillard, and Habermas and Wolin. Also, consider some of the important philosophers alive and writing today such as Michael Walzer (b. 1935), Giacomo Marramao (b. 1946), James Tully (b. 1946), Slavoj Žižek (b. 1947), Olavo de Carvalho (b. 1947), Judith Butler (b. 1956), and Rae Helen Langton (b. 1961).

Here are some philosopher-centered short paper options:

- Review a new book or critique a new article.
- Compare scholarly interpretations of a major work by a particular philosopher.
- Apply an author's theory to a new or different political problem or challenge.

Option 2: Focus on Ideas or Issues   Here are some topic-centered short paper options:

- Explain Plato's definition of justice.
- Explain Marx's concept of "species-being."
- Explain Foucault's notion of the political power inherent in "normal."
- Explain Rawls' concept of a "veil of ignorance."

Read&Write 11.1   Write a Political Philosophy Paper

You will find directions for writing political science papers in general, including political philosophy papers, in Parts 1 and 2 of this manual.

Consider Some Ideas for Long Political Philosophy Paper Topics:

- Explain how political and economic conditions in eighteenth century Scotland influenced the political philosophies of David Hume and Adam Smith.
- Compare the reactions of Jean-Jacques Rousseau and Edmund Burke to the French Revolution.
- Describe the influence of Epictetus on Roman political thought.
- Compare the concepts of political freedom in the works of John Stuart Mill, Isiah Berlin, and Ayn Rand.
- Identify the most important challenges that face political philosophers in the twenty-first century.
- Explain the importance of the contributions of Michel Foucault to understanding the subtle operations of social and political power in society.

- In *The End of History and the Last Man* (1992), Francis Fukuyama argued that history, in the sense of a process of evolving forms of society, has ended, because the best society (capitalist democracy) was making strong progess to dominating the entire world. Now, nearly a quarter of a century later, to what extent do world events support Fukuyama's thesis?
- In 1996, Samuel P. Huntington published *The Clash of Civilizations and the Remaking of World Order*, arguing that future world conflicts will not be based on ideology or economics, but on the conflicting ambitions of civilizations. Among the important rising and competing civilizations that the United States must deal with will be the nations with large Islamic populations. To what extent do current world events support Huntington's thesis?

APPENDIX A
POLITICAL SCIENCE JOURNALS

The American Political Science Association (APSA) publishes three major journals:

The American Political Science Review

Perspectives on Politics

PS: Political Science and Politics

Further information about these journals may be found at:

http://www.apsanet.org/PUBLICATIONS/Journals

Some of APSA's sections (see TO THE STUDENT in this Manual) publish their own journals. Find information about these journals at:

http://www.apsanet.org/PUBLICATIONS/Journals/Organized-Section-Journals

Finally, a list of scores of other political science journals can be found at:

http://www.apsanet.org/otherjournals

APPENDIX B
PROPER FORMS OF ADDRESS

This table was adapted from Appendix 6 of the *Department of Defense Manual for Written Material* (March 2, 2004, Director of Administration and Management, Office of the Secretary of Defense). It provides proper address formats for a wide variety of elected and nonelected public officials at local, state, national, and international levels of government.

Addressee	Address on Letter and Envelope	Salutation and Close
The President	The President The White House 1600 Pennsylvania Avenue, NW Washington, DC 20500	Dear Mr./Madam President: Respectfully yours,
Spouse of the President	Mr./Mrs. (full name) The White House 1600 Pennsylvania Avenue, NW Washington, DC 20500	Dear Mr./Mrs. (surname): Sincerely,
Director, Office of Management and Budget	The Honorable (full name) Director, Office of Management and Budget Washington, DC 20503	Dear Mr./Ms. (surname): Sincerely,
The Vice President	The Vice President 276 Eisenhower Executive Office Building Washington, DC 20501	Dear Mr./Madam Vice President: Sincerely,
The Chief Justice	The Chief Justice The Supreme Court Washington, DC 20543	Dear Chief Justice: Sincerely,
Associate Justice	The Honorable (full name) The Supreme Court Washington, DC 20543	Dear Justice (Surname): Sincerely,
Judge of a federal, state, or local court	The Honorable (full name) Judge of the (name of court) (address)	Dear Judge (surname): Sincerely,
Clerk of a court	Mr./Ms. (full name) Clerk of the (name of court) (address)	Dear Mr./Ms. (surname): Sincerely,
Senator (Washington office)	The Honorable (full name) United States Senate Washington, DC 20510-(+4 Code)	Dear Senator (surname): Sincerely,

Speaker of the House of Representatives	The Honorable (full name) Speaker of the House of Representatives U.S. House of Representatives Washington, DC 20515-(+4 Code)	Dear Mr./Madam Speaker: Sincerely,
Representative (Washington office)	The Honorable (full name) U.S. House of Representatives Washington, DC 20515-(+4 Code)	Dear Representative (surname): Sincerely,
Resident Commissioner	The Honorable (full name) Resident Commissioner from Puerto Rico, U.S. House of Representatives Washington, DC 20515-(+4 Code)	Dear Mr./Ms. (surname): Sincerely,
Delegate	The Honorable (full name) Delegate from (location) U.S. House of Representatives Washington, DC 20515-(+4 Code)	Dear Mr./Ms. (surname): Sincerely,
Members of the Cabinet addressed as Secretary	The Honorable (full name) Secretary of (name of Department) Washington, DC (ZIP+4 Code)	Dear Mr./Madam Secretary: Sincerely,
Attorney General	The Honorable (full name) Attorney General Washington, DC 20530	Dear Mr. Attorney General: Sincerely,
Deputy Secretary of a department	The Honorable (full name) Deputy Secretary of (name of Department) Washington, DC (ZIP+4 Code)	Dear Mr./Ms. (surname): Sincerely,
Head of a federal agency, authority, or board	The Honorable (full name) (title) (agency) Washington, DC (ZIP+4 Code)	Dear Mr./Ms. (surname): Sincerely,
President of a commission or board	The Honorable (full name) President, (name of commission) Washington, DC (ZIP+4 Code)	Dear Mr./Ms. (surname): Sincerely,
Chairman of a commission or board	The Honorable (full name) Chairman, (name of commission) Washington, DC (ZIP+4 Code)	Dear Mr./Madam Chairman: Sincerely,
Postmaster General	The Honorable (full name) Postmaster General 475 L'Enfant Plaza West, SW Washington, DC 20260	Dear Mr./Madam Postmaster General: Sincerely,
American Ambassador	The Honorable (full name) American Ambassador (city) (city), (country)	Dear Mr./Madam Ambassador: Sincerely,
Foreign ambassador in the United States	His/Her Excellency (full name) Ambassador of (country) Washington, DC (ZIP+4 Code)	Dear Mr./Madam Ambassador: Sincerely,
Secretary General of the United Nations	The Honorable (full name) Secretary General of the United Nations New York, NY 10017	Dear Mr./Madam Secretary General: Sincerely,

Addressee	Address on Letter and Envelope	Salutation and Close
United States Representative to the United Nations	The Honorable (full name) United States Representative to the United Nations New York, NY 10017	Dear Mr./Ms. (surname): Sincerely,
State Governor	The Honorable (full name) Governor of (state) (city), (state) (ZIP Code)	Dear Governor (surname): Sincerely,
State Lieutenant Governor	The Honorable (full name) Lieutenant Governor of (state) (city), (state) (ZIP Code)	Dear Mr./Ms. (surname): Sincerely,
State Secretary of State	The Honorable (full name) Secretary of State of (state) (city), (state) (ZIP Code)	Dear Mr./Madam (surname): Sincerely,
Chief Justice of a State Supreme Court	The Honorable (full name) Chief Justice Supreme Court of the State of (state) (city), (state) (ZIP Code)	Dear Mr./Madam Chief Justice: Sincerely,
State Attorney General	The Honorable (full name) Attorney General State of (state) (city), (state) (ZIP Code)	Dear Mr./Madam Attorney General: Sincerely,
State Treasurer, Comptroller, or Auditor	The Honorable (full name) State Treasurer (Comptroller) (Auditor) State of (state) (city), (state) (ZIP Code)	Dear Mr./Ms. (surname): Sincerely,
President, State Senate	The Honorable (full name) President of the Senate of the State of (state) (city), (state) (ZIP Code)	Dear Mr./Ms. (surname): Sincerely,
State Senator	The Honorable (full name)\ (state) Senate (city), (state) (ZIP Code)	Dear Mr./Ms. (surname): Sincerely,
Speaker, State House of Representatives, Assembly or House of Delegates	The Honorable (full name) Speaker of the House of Representatives (Assembly) (House of Delegates) of the State of (state) (city), (state) (ZIP Code)	Dear Mr./Ms. (surname): Sincerely,
State Representative, Assemblyman, or Delegate	The Honorable (full name) (state) House of Representatives (Assembly) (House of Delegates) (city), (state) (ZIP Code)	Dear Mr./Ms. (surname): Sincerely,
Mayor	The Honorable (full name) Mayor of (city) (city), (state) (ZIP Code)	Dear Mayor (surname) Sincerely,
President of a Board of Commissioners	The Honorable (full name) President, Board of Commissioners of (city) (city), (state) (ZIP Code)	Dear Mr./Ms. (surname): Sincerely,

APPENDIX C
GLOSSARY OF POLITICAL TERMS AND SLANG

affirmative action — The correcting of discrimination, usually racial in motivation, through government policy.

amendment — A formal action taken by the legislature to change an existing law or bill.

***amicus curiae* brief** — A "friend of the court" brief, filed by a third party to a lawsuit who is presenting additional information to the court in the hopes of influencing the court's decision; a "friend of the court" brief filed by an individual or organization not directly involved in the case.

anarchism — The belief that all political authority is inherently oppressive and that government should be reduced to a minimum.

anarchy — Political chaos; as a political movement, the belief that voluntary cooperation among members of a society is better than any form of organized government, because government generally favors one group over others.

anchor baby — A child born in the U.S. to a mother who is not a citizen.

antifederalist — One who opposed ratification of the United States Constitution in 1787.

antinomianism — A belief that faith without adherence to law is sufficient for religious practice.

appeal — The process of asking a higher court to consider a verdict rendered by a lower court.

apportionment — The system under which seats in the legislative houses are apportioned among the states.

appropriation — The act of designating funds in the legislature for particular agencies and programs.

APSA — American Political Science Association.

aristocracy — A system of government in which power is held by a small ruling class whose status is determined by such factors as wealth, social position, and military power; for Aristotle, government by the best or most capable people; in common terms, government by a privileged, hereditary ruling class.

authoritarianism — A belief that absolute power should be placed in the hands of one person or a small group; rule without popular consent, requiring obedience to law but not necessarily active support for a regime.

authority — The power to make, interpret, and enforce laws.

autocratic — Having unrestricted power.

autonomous — Self-governing; independent.

bandwagon effect	The practice of government officials' attaching themselves to a piece of legislation or a political movement because of its popularity.
beltway bandits	Consulting firms on Washington DC's highway outer loop.
bicameral legislature	A legislature that is divided into two branches or houses.
birther	Someone who thinks a politician was not born in the U.S.
blue dog democrat	A conservative southern democrat.
blue state	A state with a majority of liberal or democratic voters.
boll weevil	A southern Democrat opposed to the civil rights movement.
bourgeoisie	For Karl Marx, the capitalist middle class.
brief	A compilation of facts, arguments, and points of law concerning a specific law case, prepared by an attorney and submitted to the court.
bureaucracy	Any large, complex administrative system, but used most often to refer to government in general.
calendar	The agenda listing the business to be taken up by a legislative body.
capitalism	An economic system in which most of the means of production and distribution are privately owned and operated for profit.
case study	A detailed examination of a representative individual or group.
caucus	A closed meeting of party officials for the purpose of selecting candidates for government office.
censure	A method by which a legislative body may discipline one of its members.
census	The counting, every 10 years, of the total population of the United States, for such purposes as the apportionment of legislators and the determination of direct taxes.
centralization	The concept of focusing power in a national government instead of in state or local governments.
checks and balances	A method of government power distribution in which each major branch of the government has some control over the actions of the other major branches.
civil rights	The rights of a citizen that guarantee protection against discriminatory behavior by the government or private owners of public facilities.
civil servants	Government employees who are not in the military.
claims court	A court that hears various kinds of claims brought by citizens against the government.
class stratification	The differentiation of classes within a society for political or economic purposes.
closed primary	A primary election in which only party members may vote.
cloture (closure)	A rule allowing a three-fifths vote of the Senate to end a filibuster.
coattail effect	The tendency of a candidate or officeholder to draw votes for other candidates of his or her party.

cognitive dissonance	A perceived discrepancy between what is stated to be reality and what is reality in fact.
collectivism	An economic system in which the land and the means of production and distribution are owned by the people who operate them.
commerce clause	A clause in Article 1, section 8, of the U.S. Constitution, giving Congress the power to regulate trade among the states and with foreign nations.
communism	A collectivist social system in which all land and means of production are theoretically in the hands of the people and are shared equally by all individuals; a collectivist social system in which the means of production are owned by the state and in which the products of society are distributed according to need.
communitarian	One who advocates communal life, in which possessions are shared by commune members.
concurrent powers	Powers shared by state and national governments, including the power to tax and the power to maintain a system of courts.
confederacy	A political system characterized by a weak national government that assumes only those powers granted it by strong state governments.
conservatism	An ideology normally associated with resistance to changes in culture, and less government intervention in the social and economic life of the nation.
conservatives	Citizens who resist major changes in their culture and their society; political conservatives tend to favor less government intervention in the social and economic life of the nation.
constituent	An individual who resides in a government official electoral district.
constitutionalism	A belief in a system of government limited and controlled by a constitution, or contract, drawn up and agreed to by its citizens.
contract theory	An explanation of the relationship of the government to the governed in terms of contractual obligation by consenting parties.
corporatism	An approach to the study of politics focusing on the activities of economic interests.
court of appeals	One of 12 national courts in the United States set up to hear appeals from district courts.
cybernetics	The study of government that focuses on how information is transmitted and received.
dark horse	A candidate for political office who has little chance of winning.
deductive logic	Reasoning from a general premise to a specific conclusion.
demagogue	A political leader who obtains popularity through emotional appeals to the prejudices and fears of the voters.
democracy	A system of government in which the people govern either directly or through elected representatives; a system of government in which the majority governs and in which the rights of minorities are protected.
deregulation	The process of reducing government regulatory involvement in private business.
detente	The relaxing of tension between nations.

dialectic	A process of arriving at the truth in which succeeding propositions transform each other.
district court	The most basic federal court, where federal cases generally are first heard.
divine right	The belief that a ruler maintains power through a mandate from a Supreme Being.
due process	The right accorded to American citizens to expect fair and equitable treatment in the processes and procedures of law.
earmark	A congressional appropriation for a specific project in a specific location.
eclectic	Combining a variety of approaches or methods.
electoral college	Electors who meet in their respective state capitals to elect the president and vice president of the United States.
elite theory	The concept that, in any political system, power is always controlled by a small group of people.
empiricism	The idea that all knowledge results from sense experience; a scientific method that relies on direct observation.
epistemology	The study of what knowledge is.
ethnocentricity	A tendency to believe that one's own race is superior to other races; a focus of attention upon one race, to the exclusion of others.
faction	A group of people sharing certain beliefs who seek to act together to affect policy.
fascism	A right-wing totalitarian political system in which complete power is held by a dictator who keeps rigid control of society and promotes a belligerent nationalism.
favorite son	A presidential candidate, usually with no chance of winning the party nomination, whose name is placed in nomination at the national convention by the person's home state, usually either to honor that individual or to allow the state's delegation to delay committing their votes to a viable candidate.
federal	A type of government in which power is shared by state and national governments.
filibuster	The Senate process of interrupting meaningful debate on a bill with prolonged, irrelevant speeches aimed at "talking the bill to death."
flow model	A diagram illustrating the relationships among elements of a system.
franking privilege	The ability of a member of Congress to substitute his or her facsimile signature for a postage stamp and thereby send mail free of charge.
free stuff	Disparaging term for education, welfare, and other appropriations that benefit the poor.
gag rule	A rule limiting the amount of time that can be spent debating a bill or resolution in the legislature.
gaia hypothesis	James Lovelock's conservationist concept of the earth as a living entity needing the same sort of nurture that all organisms require.

game theory	A method of understanding and predicting socio-political attitudes and events through devising mathematical models of social behavior.
gerrymandering	Redesigning the boundaries of a legislative district so that the political party controlling the state legislature can maintain control.
grand jury	A group of 12–23 citizens selected to hear evidence against persons accused of a serious crime in order to determine whether or not a formal charge should be issued.
grants-in-aid	Funding given to state and local governments for them to achieve goals set by the national government.
grassroots	Political organizing on the local level.
green	In politics, a name for those policies, politicians, and activists who advocate environmental responsibility in policy decisions.
habeas corpus	A court order requiring that an individual in custody be presented in court with the cause of his or her detention.
hard left	In Gabriel Almond's methodological approach to the study of politics, the mode that stresses the scientific analysis of quantitative data in the interests of promoting social, economic, and political equality.
hard right	The method of studying politics, in Gabriel Almond's research, that stresses the scientific analysis of quantitative data and rational thinking and focuses on the study of power.
hockey mom or soccer mom	A woman who drives her children to their sports events.
horse race	A close electoral contest in the polls.
humanism	The concept that humanity, and not a deity, is and should be the central focus of concern in philosophy, politics, the arts, etc.
ideology	The combined beliefs and doctrines of a group of people that reveal the value system of their culture.
impeachment	The process by which the lower house of a legislature may accuse a high official, such as the president or a Supreme Court justice, of a crime, after which the official is tried by the upper house.
implied powers	Powers held by the federal government that are not specified in the U.S. Constitution but are implied by other, enumerated powers.
incumbent	A political official currently in office.
independent	A voter not registered as a member of a political party.
indictment	A formal accusation, brought by a grand jury, charging a person with a crime.
individualism	The belief in the importance of the needs and rights of the individual over those of the group.
inductive logic	Reasoning from a series of specific observations to a general principle.
inefficient game	In game theory, a game in which no player completely achieves a desired end.
inherent powers	Powers not specified in the U.S. Constitution that are claimed by the president, especially in foreign relations.

initiative	A process by which individuals or interested groups may draw up proposed legislation and bring it to the attention of the legislature through a petition signed by a certain percentage of registered voters.
interest group	An organization of like-minded individuals seeking to influence the making of government policy, often by sponsoring a political action committee (PAC).
intrasocietal	The environment existing inside the structure of a given society.
Iron Curtain	Those countries of Eastern Europe dominated by the Soviet Union.
iron law of oligarchy	The principle stating that all associations eventually become dominated by a minority of their members.
iron triangle	The interrelationship of government agencies, congressional committees, and political action groups, as they influence policy.
irrationalist	One who believes that human behavior is determined by factors other than reason.
item veto	The power of governors in most states to veto selected items from a bill and to approve others.
Joe Sixpack	A man of the working class.
Knesset	The legislative body of the Israeli government.
laissez-faire	A "hands-off" policy rejecting government's involvement in the economic system of the state.
left	Liberal.
left wing	An outlook favoring liberal political and economic programs aimed at benefiting the masses.
legitimacy	The quality of being accepted as authentic; in politics, the people's acceptance of a form of government.
libel	A written statement aimed at discrediting an individual's reputation. *See also* slander.
liberals	Citizens who favor changes in the system of government to benefit the common people.
libertarians	Advocates of freedom from government action.
literature review	In a research project, the task of canvassing publications, usually professional journals, in order to find information about a specific topic.
lobbyists	People who seek to influence legislation for the benefit of themselves or their clients—usually interest groups—by applying pressure of various kinds to members of Congress.
logrolling	A process by which two or more legislators agree to support each other's bills, which usually concern public works projects.
majority rule	The concept, common in a democracy, that the majority has the right to govern.
millenarian	Member of any of many religious movements that challenged the church after the year 1000 CE.
millennium	A time period of 1,000 years.

moderate Within reasonable limits; in politics, one who is opposed to extremely liberal or conservative views.

monarchy A political system in which power is held by a hereditary aristocracy, headed by a king or queen.

myth A story or narrative intended to explain a natural or social phenomenon beyond normal human understanding.

NASCAR dad A southern man of the working class.

natural law The concept, popularized by eighteenth-century philosophers, that human conduct is governed by immutable laws that are similar to the laws of the physical universe and can, like physical laws, be discovered.

naturalization The process by which an alien becomes an American citizen.

nazism The political movement led in Germany by Adolf Hitler, combining nationalism with anti-Semitism.

negative freedom Isaiah Berlin's phrase for the freedom from obligation or restraint on one's actions.

neoconservatism A conservative reaction to liberal and radical movements of the 1960s.

nepotism The policy of granting political favors, such as government contracts or jobs, to family members.

new left A liberal political movement begun in the 1960s, largely due to the civil rights movement and the Vietnam War, that brought about widespread reevaluation of political beliefs.

normative theory Any theory attempting to assign value judgments to its conclusions, as opposed to quantitative theory, which attempts to produce value-free results.

oligarchy A political system in which power is held by a small group whose membership is determined by wealth or social position; government of the many by and in the interests of the few.

open primary A primary election in which voters need not disclose their party affiliation to cast a ballot.

orthodox "Right belief," holding the basic beliefs of the faith. A model or example.

panopticon A model prison designed by philosopher Jeremy Bentham and used by philosopher Michel Foucault as a metaphor for freedom in society.

paradigm A member of the wealthy class or aristocracy.

patrician The study of the development of human consciousness and how it attempts to assimilate sensory data.

patronage The power of government officeholders to dole out jobs, contracts, and other favors in return for political support.

phenomenology In common use, of the common people, as opposed to the aristocracy.

pigeonhole The action of a congressional committee that, by failing to report a bill out for general consideration, assures its demise.

platform	The set of principles and goals on which a political party or group bases its appeal to the public.
plebeian	Ordering societal relations.
pluralism	The concept that cultural, ethnic, and political diversity plays a major part in the development of government policy.
plurality	The number of votes by which a candidate wins election if that number does not exceed 50 percent of the total votes cast; a plurality need not be a large number of votes, as long as it is a higher number than that claimed by any other candidate.
pocket veto	A method by which the president may kill a bill simply by failing to sign it within ten10 days following the end of a legislative session.
police power	The power, reserved to legislatures, to establish order and implement government policy.
political action committees (PACs)	Officially registered fund-raising committees that attempt to influence legislation, usually through campaign contributions to members of Congress.
political correctness	A measure of how closely speech, attitude, or policy conforms to certain affirmative action standards. The term is pejorative when used by conservatives warning of liberal attempts at controlling the public's modes of expression and thought processes.
political machine	A political party organization so well established as to wield considerable power.
political party	An organization of officeholders, political candidates, and workers, all of whom share a particular set of beliefs and work together to gain political power through the electoral process.
politics polity	For Aristotle, government by the many in the interests of all.
poll	A survey undertaken to ascertain the opinions of a section of the public.
poll sample	A selection, usually random, of the larger population of individuals polled.
populism	A political philosophy that aims at representing the needs of the rural and poor populations in America rather than the interests of the upper classes and big business.
pork barrel legislation	A congressional bill passed to benefit one specific congressional district, with the aim of promoting the reelection of representatives from that district.
positive freedom	Isaiah Berlin's phrase for the freedom to do what one wills.
pragmatism	The notion that ideas and concepts should be judged by their practical consequences instead of their correspondence to abstract or ideal criteria.
precedent	A court decision that sets a standard for handling later, similar cases.
primary election	An election, held prior to the general election, in which voters nominate party candidates for office.
progressivism	Any doctrine calling for changes within a system, to be made in the light of recent findings or achievements.

proletariat	The urban, industrial working class.
pundit	A political news commentator.
purple state or swing state	A state whose voters are virtually equally divided between Republicans and Democrats.
quantification	Determining or measuring quantity or amount.
quorum	The minimum number of members of a legislative body that must be present to conduct business.
radical	One calling for substantial change in institutions, society, political systems, etc.
ratification	The process by which state legislatures approve or reject proposed agreements between states and proposed amendments to the U.S. Constitution.
rational actor theory	In public policy analysis, the theory that people and institutions tend to act in ways which they perceive to be in their own best interests.
rationalism	The belief that reasoned observation is the proper foundation for problem solving.
reactionary	One who opposes liberal change, favoring instead a return to policies of the past.
recall	A process by which an elected official can be turned out of office through a popular vote.
recidivism	A tendency for criminal offenders to return to criminal habits.
red state	A state with a majority of conservative or Republican voters.
referendum	Method by which voters in certain states can register their approval or dissatisfaction with a bill proposed in their state legislature.
republic	A government that derives its power from the consent of the people, who control policy by electing government officeholders.
reserved powers	Powers of the U.S. Constitution reserved to the state governments.
right	Conservative.
right wing	An outlook favoring conservative or reactionary political and economic programs.
sample plan	An essential step in setting up a survey; the task of establishing which elements of the general population are to be asked to participate in the survey.
sampling frame	That specific part of a population from which a sample is drawn for a survey.
separation of powers	A method of stabilizing a government by dividing its power among different branches or levels of government.
short ballot	A ballot-listing candidates for only a few offices, as opposed to a long ballot, which lists candidates for a great number of offices.
single-issue group	A lobby group attempting to influence legislation concerning only one cause or issue, such as gun control or funding for education.

single-member district
An electoral district from which voters elect only a single representative.

slander
An oral statement intended to damage an individual's reputation. See also libel.

social contract
The agreement, either formally stated or implied, among members of a society that allows for the establishment and continuance of the social structure and the government.

socialism
A political system establishing public ownership and control of the means of production; an economic system in which the state owns the means of production.

soft left
In Gabriel Almond's terms, a methodological approach to the study of politics which favors philosophical and descriptive analysis of political in the interests of social, economic, or political equality.

soft right
The analytical mode described by Gabriel Almond that takes a philosophical or descriptive rather than a quantitative approach to the study of power and rational thinking in politics.

sovereignty
The concept that the state is self-governing and free from external control.

Soviet Bloc
Those Eastern European countries dominated by Soviet communism from 1945 to 1990.

spin
An attempt to give a political phenomenon a certain interpretation.

split ticket
A situation in which a voter casts ballots for candidates from different political parties.

spoils system
The practice of rewarding supporters and friends with government jobs.

stalking horse
A candidate whose primary function is to set up a constituency and a campaign base for another candidate, deemed stronger by the party, who will be announced later.

statute
A law passed by Congress or a state legislature.

straight ticket
The practice of voting for all candidates on a ballot solely on the basis of their party affiliation.

straw vote
An opinion poll with a small sample.

structural-functionalism
A method of studying political systems introduced by Gabriel Almond in which various elements of a political system are analyzed according to the types of tasks they perform.

subjectivism
A theory of knowledge in which truth is individually determined by each person's preferences or perceptions.

theocracy
A political system whose leaders assume that their power to govern comes from a Supreme Being who guides the actions of the government.

third party
A political party different from the two traditional parties and typically formed to protest their ineffectualness.

totalitarianism
A political system characterized by state control of cultural institutions and all forms of industry and means of production; a type of authoritarian government in which the state demands active support of its policies.

tree hugger	An environmentalist.
typology	A classification of phenomena according to differing characteristics.
unicameralism	A legislature with only one house or chamber.
unitary	Referring to a political system in which all power resides in the national government, which in turn delegates limited power to local governments.
utopia	An ideal social environment.
validity	In statistics, the characteristic that a measuring instrument, such as a survey, has when it actually measures what it purports to measure.
variables	The elements of an equation, experiment, or formula that are under study and subject to change in accordance with changes in their environment.
veil of ignorance	A hypothetical state, proposed by philosopher John Rawls, in which people, before beginning their lives, are unaware of what characteristics, advantages and disadvantages they will have in life.
veto	The process by which the president may send a bill back to Congress instead of signing it into law.
welfare state	A state in which the government is characterized by governmental redistribution of income.

"About the *Congressional Record*." Thomas. Library of Congress. Retrieved March 7, 2016 (http://thomas .loc.gov/home/abt.cong.rec.html).

"About the *Federal Register*." *Federal Register*. Retrieved March 7, 2016 (http://www.archives.gov/ federal-register/the-federal-register/about.html#whysho).

Aristotle. *Politics*. 1.1253a. Retrieved March 7, 2016 (http://data.perseus.org/citations/urn:cts: greekLit:tlg0086.tlg035.perseus-eng1:1.1253a).

Babb, Drew. 2014. "LBJ's 1964 Attack Ad 'Daisy' Leaves a Legacy for Modern Campaigns." *Washington Post*, 5 September. Retrieved February 23, 2016 (https://www.washingtonpost.com/opinions/ lbjs-1964-attack-ad-daisy-leaves-a-legacy-for-modern-campaigns/2014/09/05/d00e66b0-33b4-11e4- 9e92-0899b306bbea_story.html).

"Born in Slavery: Slave Narratives from the Federal Writers' Project, 1936–1938." Library of Congress. Retrieved March 7, 2016 (http://memory.loc.gov/ammem/snhtml/snhome.html).

Brooks, David. 2015. "The Minimum-Wage Muddle." *New York Times*, July 24. Retrieved March 7, 2016 (http://www.nytimes.com/2015/07/24/opinion/david-brooks-the-minimum-wage-muddle.html?_r=0).

Bulwer-Lytton, Edward. 1839. *Richelieu: Or, the Conspiracy, a Plan in Five Acts*. II, ii, p. 39. New York: Samuel French [186–?]. *Making of America*. Ann Arbor: University of Michigan Library, 2005. Retrieved February 23, 2016 (http://name.umdl.umich.edu/AAX3994.0001.001).

Charles, Alan F. 1971. *Motion for Leave to File Brief Amici Curiae in Support of Appellants and Briefs Amici Curiai. Roe v. Wade*. U.S. 70–18, 5–7.

"Collections with Manuscripts." Library of Congress. Retrieved March 7, 2016 (https://www.loc.gov/ manuscripts/collections/).

District of Columbia et al. v. Heller. 2008. 07-290. Supreme Court of the United States. Retrieved March 7, 2016 (http://www.supremecourt.gov/opinions/07pdf/07-290.pdf).

"Dukakis Furlough Program." YouTube.com. Retrieved March 7, 2016 (https://www.youtube.com/ watch?v= Nch860E_Df0).

Forster, E. M. [1927] 1956. *Aspects of the Novel*. New York: Harvest.

Hartwell, Patrick. 1985. "Grammar, Grammars, and the Teaching of Grammar." *College English* 47(Feb.): 105–27.

"History of the Library." Library of Congress. Retrieved March 7, 2016 (https://www.loc.gov/about/ history-of-the-library/).

"'I Do Solemnly Swear': Presidential Inaugurations." Library of Congress. Retrieved March 7, 2016 (http:// memory.loc.gov/ammem/pihtml/pihome.html).

Kaminer, Ariel. 2010. "What New York Needs: More Water Taxis." *New York Times*, June 4. Retrieved March 7, 2016 (http://www.nytimes.com/2010/06/06/nyregion/06critic.html?_r=0).

Krugman, Paul. 2015. "Liberals and Wages." *New York Times*, July 17. Retrieved March 7, 2016 (http:// www.nytimes.com/2015/07/17/opinion/paul-krugman-liberals-and-wages.html).

Moravcsik, Andrew. 2014. "Transparency: The Revolution in Qualitative Research." *PS*, January. Retrieved March 7, 2016 (https://www.princeton.edu/~amoravcs/library/transparency.pdf).

"Obama: Republicans Left Me with the Check for a Steak Dinner." 2016. *Real Clear Politics*, 12 June. Retrieved July 03, 2016 (http://www.realclearpolitics.com/video/2012/06/12/obama_republicans_left_ me_with_the_check_for_a_steak_dinner.html).

Obama, Barack. 2016. "Weekly Address: Making America Safer for Our Children." The White House, 1 January. Retrieved February 23, 2016 (https://www.whitehouse.gov/the-press-office/2016/01/01/ weekly-address-making-america-safer-our-children).

"Office of Management and Budget." N.d. The White House. Retrieved March 7, 2016 (https://www.whitehouse .gov/omb/policy_analyst/).

Partlow, Joshua. 2016. "Actor Sean Penn Secretly Interviewed Mexico's 'El Chapo' in Hideout." *Washington Post*, 10 January. Retrieved February 23, 2016 (https://www.washingtonpost.com/world/actor-sean-penn-secretly-interviewed-el-chapo-in-hideout-before-capture/2016/01/09/4cce48db-1dc5-40b2-9b21-aa412c87e7bc_story.html).

Pearce, Catherine Owens. 1958. *A Scientist of Two Worlds: Louis Agassiz*. Philadelphia: Lippincott.

"Population of Cities (1920–2005)," "Historical Statistics of Japan: Chapter 2 Populations and Households." In *Statistics Japan*. Retrieved March 8, 2016 (http://www.stat.go.jp/english/data/chouki/02.htm).

Roosevelt, Franklin D. 1941. "'Four Freedoms Speech': Annual Message to Congress on the State of the Union." Franklin D. Roosevelt Presidential Library and Museum. January 6. Retrieved March 8, 2016 (http://www.fdrlibrary.marist.edu/pdfs/fftext.pd).

"Rule 37: Brief for an Amicus Curiae." *Rules of the Supreme Court of the United States*. Retrieved July 7, 2016 (http://www.supremecourt.gov/ctrules/2013RulesoftheCourt.pdf).

Scheiber, Noam and Patricia Cohen. 2015. "For the Wealthiest, a Private Tax System That Saves Them Billions: The Very Richest Are Able to Quietly Shape Tax Policy that will Allow Them to Shield Billions in Income." *New York Times*, 29 December. Retrieved February 23, 2016 (http://www.nytimes.com/2015/12/30/business/economy/for-the-wealthiest-private-tax-system-saves-them-billions.html).

Scott, Gregory M. 1998. "Review of Political Islam: Revolution, Radicalism, or Reform?" Ed. John L. Esposito. *Southeastern Political Review* 26(2): 512–24.

"Stray Bullet That Killed Long Island Girl Was Fired in Retaliation for Hoverboard Theft, Police Say." 2016. *New York Times*, January 11. Retrieved March 7, 2016 (http://www.nytimes.com/2016/01/12/nyregion/stray-bullet-that-killedlong-island-girl-was-fired-in-retaliation-for-theft-police-say.html?_r=0).

"Why Visit the National Archives?" National Archives. Retrieved March 7, 2016 (http://www.archives.gov/locations/why-visit.html).

INDEX